D0903924

The
COMPLETE GUIDE
to
WOOD
FINISHES

The COMPLETE GUIDE to WOOD FINISHES

DERRICK CRUMP
CONSULTANT *Ronnie Rustin*

A FIRESIDE BOOK
Published by Simon & Schuster Inc.
New York London Toronto Sydney Tokyo Singapore

A QUARTO BOOK
Fireside
Simon & Schuster Building
Rockefeller Center
1230 Avenue of the Americas
New York, New York 10020

This book was designed and produced by
Quarto Publishing Inc
The Old Brewery
6 Blundell Street
London N7 9BH

SENIOR EDITOR Kate Kirby
AMERICAN EDITOR Bob Flexner
EDITOR Nick Gibbs
COPY EDITOR Peter Leek
SENIOR ART EDITOR Penny Cobb
DESIGNER Terry Jeavons
PICTURE RESEARCHER Anne Marie Ehrlich
PHOTOGRAPHER Paul Forrester
ILLUSTRATOR Rob Shone
ART DIRECTOR Moira Clinch
PUBLISHING DIRECTOR Janet Slingsby

Typeset in Great Britain by Bookworm Typesetting, Manchester
Printed in Singapore by Star Standard Industries Private Ltd
Manufactured in Hong Kong by Regent Publishing Services Ltd

10 9 8 7 6 5 4 3

Special thanks to Andy Hills, Tony Miller and Katie Preston.

Library of Congress Cataloging-in-Publication Data
Crump, Derrick.
The complete guide to wood finishes/Derrick Crump.
p. cm.
"A Fireside book."
Includes index.
ISBN 0-671-79669-0
1. Furniture finishing. I. Title.
TT199.4.C78 1993
684.1'043--dc20 92-20299
CIP

Publisher's note

Working with wood finishes demands care, as some of the chemicals you will be using are poisonous and/or corrosive. This means you must take precautions when you use them; always follow the manufacturer's instructions; always store chemicals securely in clearly marked non-food containers and keep them well out of reach of children.

As far as the composition of the finishes mentioned in this book, the techniques used to apply them and the effects they produce are concerned, all statements, information and advice given here are believed to be true and accurate. However, neither the author, copyright holder or the publisher can accept any legal liability for errors or omissions.

Acknowledgments and picture credits

QUARTO would like to thank the following for their help with this publication and for permission to reproduce copyright material.

KEY *l* = *left*, *r* = *right*, *a* = *above*, *b* = *below*.

P. 61	Lawrence Kemp/*Forgotten Finishes*/photo Loraine Freeman
P. 69	Howard Raybould
P. 79	Non-drip varnish with Teflon/Natural Wood Finishes from Dulux
P. 89	Elrose Products Ltd/Infopress
P. 99	Crown Paints
P. 101 *l*	Elrose Products Ltd/Infopress
r	Lawrence Kemp/*Forgotten Finishes*/photo Loraine Freeman
P. 110 *l*	Crown Paints
r	Elrose Products Ltd/Infopress
P. 111 *b*	Elrose Products Ltd/Infopress
P. 117 *a*	A. Holmes/Crafts Council
b	Crown Paints
P. 145	Crown Paints

Every effort has been made to trace and acknowledge all copyright holders. Quarto would like to apologize if any omissions have been made.

QUARTO would like to thank the following organizations who kindly lent equipment for photography.

The Art Veneers Co. Ltd.: *veneers.*

Axminster Power Tools Centre: *power sanders and accessories, soldering irons, ear protectors, filling knives.*

Bolloms: *Spray equipment.*

F.A. Heffer & Co. Ltd.: *badger brush, mottler brush.*

John Mylands: *safety equipment, abrasives, brushes, sanding belt, sponge.*

Stanley Tools: *hand scrapers, razor-blade knives, clamps, chisels, drill.*

CONTENTS

Decorative finishes . . 84-123

Spray finishes 124-149

Guide to woods 150-163

Troubleshooting 164-167

Health and safety . . . 168-169

FOREWORD

Wood looks dull and unattractive until it has been finished with materials that will preserve, protect and bring out the inherent beauty of the grain. For thousands of years the only treatment was to apply beeswax or oils, or to color the woods with a mixture of pigments and binders to hold the pigment on the surface. Now an extremely large range of wood finishing products is available, many for specific uses, such as on floors, and others which can be used for a variety of purposes. There are also finishes specifically made for furniture and cabinetwork where the highest standard of finish is required.

There has always been a mystique about wood finishing but, with the modern materials available, the amateur can obtain results that in most cases are far superior to the finishes seen on mass produced furniture.

Remember that however well made an article may be, it is by the final finish that it is judged. The surface must be clean, smooth and free from all blemishes, as unless the surface is being painted any imperfections will be made more apparent when a finish is applied. The main processes in finishing are filling, staining and applying the finish. Bleaching may also be necessary to remove stains in the wood or to lighten it. If you are renovating a piece and the original finish is in very bad condition then the only satisfactory treatment is to strip it completely, preferably with a solvent paint and varnish remover and to start again as if treating new wood.

Wood finishes which leave a surface film are of three main types. They can dry either by evaporation of the solvents, as

with French polish; oxidization and polymerization by absorbing oxygen from the air, as with linseed and other drying oils; or by cross-polymerization, that is the linking together of the molecules after the addition of the catalyst, as occurs with acid-catalyzed lacquers and two-part polyurethanes. The latter type of products will give the most durable surface which is also resistant to heat, solvents and abrasions. When you are considering what type of finish to apply bear in mind to what use the piece you are finishing will be put. For instance, it is not worth using an expensive two-part lacquer on wall cladding that will not be subjected to the same wear and tear as would a floor or a table top. The golden rule is always to read the manufacturer's instructions, and if using a finish of which you have had no previous experience to experiment on a spare piece of wood.

It is often possible to buy old furniture from garage sales and attic sales, as well as from auctions, and as long as the basic construction is sound, the finish can be restored to its original or better condition, usually without having to strip back to the bare wood. I once purchased a chair for a couple of dollars which turned out to be a genuine George III chair and was later valued at over $600. It only required a new upholstered seat and for the finish to be cleaned.

I hope that you too will find similar bargains, and I am sure that, whether you are working on new furniture or restoring old furniture, you will have a great sense of satisfaction when you see the results you can achieve.

Ronnie Rustin

Ronnie Rustin

1

Tools and equipment

Few specialized.tools are needed for finishing. A woodworker with a basic toolkit will only require a selection of brushes and cloths. Novices need a work surface and some scrapers, but little more

Basic tools and equipment

SEE ALSO

30–32 REPAIRING VENEERS

40–43 HOW TO USE WOOD FILLERS

94–97 MARBLED EFFECTS

Although one attraction of finishing is the limited selection of tools required, experienced finishers will have built up a sizable toolkit. Novice finishers will not necessarily need a wide range of tools, but certain items, which may not at first seem obvious, are essential aids to successful finishing.

The scalpel is perhaps one of the most underrated of tools. Often, only the point is used for cutting, but the sharp edge can also be useful for gently scraping unwanted finishes or marks from a surface. Masking tape is useful when you need to protect a particular area while finishing another. Cover the sensitive area with tape and cut very gently around the shape. A metal ruler will help for straight edges. When cutting through masking tape it is

Natural sponge
▶ *A sponge is useful for applying finishes, especially decorative ones.*

Hand drill
◀ *A drill is useful when hammering in molding and panel pins that may split the timber.*

C-clamp
▲ *Do not be tempted to buy a large and unwieldy clamp. A 4 inch clamp is fine.*

Soldering iron
▶ *For melting shellac fillers, the soldering iron does not have to be an expensive model. Remember to unplug it after use, and note that even cheap soldering irons get very hot.*

better to make multiple cuts, rather than try to cut through with one stroke of the scalpel.

Masking tape can also be used for holding small chips in place while they are being glued. Carry a small C-clamp for those circumstances when tape will not provide enough force.

Other useful tools that are worth buying are a natural sponge, a small drill and a small soldering iron. Natural sponges are better for applying finishes, especially decorative effects, than artificial ones. The drill is useful when hammering in molding and finishing nails that may split the wood. A soldering iron is useful for warming shellac filler before pushing the filler into a dent or crack.

Putty knife
▶ *Tailor-made for applying wood fillers. Do not let the wood filler dry on the knife.*

Scalpel
▶ *A scalpel is vital for cutting and can also be used for scraping unwanted finish.*

Chisel
▼ *Chisels are handy for cleaning off glue when working on old pieces.*

Masking tape
▲ *Masking tape is excellent if you need to protect a particular area while finishing another.*

CLOTHS, MOPS AND WADDING

- French polishing cloth, which is sold by weight, is a pure cotton rag that has no starch. It is used for making the skin of a polishing pad.
- Stockinet (a stretchy machine-knitted cloth) is used for polishing, when applying burnishing cream, wax or oil. It is sold by the roll.
- Burlap is a loose-woven sacking, used for applying and taking off grain fillers.
- Batting, available from fabric stores, is generally used as the core of the polishing pad. Buy it in a bundle, by length, and store on a roll. Some finishers like to remove the skin before using batting in a polishing pad. At a pinch, instead of batting, cotton can be used but it does get soggy.
- Coloring mops are like round-tipped brushes. They are more convenient than cloth for working finishes and stains into moldings.
- A lamb's wool pad is a round pad used, on a disk, for burnishing.
- An edge pad can be used for burnishing, usually powered by an angle grinder.

Brushes for finishing

SEE ALSO

50–52 BLEACHING WOOD
58–65 FRENCH POLISHING
84–123 DECORATIVE FINISHES

Brushes are an important part of any finisher's equipment, and most suppliers offer a variety of designs for specialist applications. They are made of different bristles and hairs, both synthetic and natural, and there are many names given to these brushes. Generally the higher the price, the better the quality of bristle and brush. In the long run, it is worth purchasing quality brushes. The finest hair commands the highest price, with badger, horse, sable, camel and hog providing the raw materials.

Natural-hair brushes give a fine finish and have a spring in them, which allows the material being coated to cling to the hair. Brush manufacturers use a mixture of bristles to suit requirements. Sable artists' and round brushes are the most expensive, but bring the best results.

Lining *or* quill
◀ *These are small brushes for touching up.*

Mop *or* roun brush
▶ *These are us for applying st color or polish. are available i 2 to 20 and are from hog or sa*

Mottler *or* spalter
▶ *These are used to mottle glazes and scumbles when marbling or graining. They are made from hog hair.*

Artists' brush
▼ *These are used for touching up and for graining and grain simulation. They are sold in sizes 2 to 10 and are made from camel, sable or synthetic hair.*

Wire brush
▼ *Useful for opening up the grain when applying a limed finish and for stripping moldings and carvings.*

Badger *or* softener
▲ *These are for "softening in" grain or marble effects. They are made from badger hair.*

Stencil brush
▼ *These are specifically designed for stenciling. They are shaped like shaving brushes and are used with a dabbing action.*

Flitch
▼ *These are for work on moldings and edges. They are made from hog hair.*

Shoe brush
▼ *These, made from short hog hair, are used for dulling down finishes.*

Synthetic-bristle brush
▲ *These are made from vegetable fibers, and are ideal for bleaching.*

Stippling brush
▼ *Made from coarse hog-hair bristles and used to produce a decorative stippled effect on wood and other substrates.*

Flat *or* paintbrush
◀ *These can be used to apply stains, varnish, undercoats and glazes. They are made from hog or horse hair.*

Graining brush
▶ *These are for use in the graining process and are made from hog hair.*

CARE OF BRUSHES

- Keep round and artists' brushes in a polyethylene bag.
- Suspend brushes in solvent to soak them clean.
- Think of brushes as tools. Look after them properly, and they will last for years and pay for themselves.

Scrapers

SEE ALSO

18–19 POWERED SANDERS
20–21 ABRASIVES
30–32 REPAIRING VENEERS

Scrapers are used for taking off the finest of shavings, to produce the smoothness of surface not always possible with a plane – or even, some would say, with abrasive. Skilled woodworkers use them as an alternative to a progression of increasingly fine sandpapers, which tend to clog the surface with dust (see pages 20–21). Scrapers are particularly useful for smoothing areas of wild interlocking grain, which a plane might tear; and on veneer, which is vulnerable because of its thinness. They are easier to control than a plane, and can be shaped to work moldings or corners.

Although there are a variety of scrapers, they are in essence little more than a thin sheet of steel and they cut with a burr – rather than the edge, as a plane blade does. Creating that burr is achieved with a file and burnisher, but care is needed to maintain a scraper in good working order, as it will only cut well if the edge is kept straight and square.

Using a scraper

To use a scraper, hold it in both hands, with your thumbs at the back, and push it across the surface. Alternatively, some people prefer to use a pulling action, with their fingers behind the scraper creating the pressure.

The angle at which the scraper is

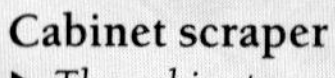

Cabinet scraper
▶ *The cabinet scraper is the most common version. In its simplest form it is a rectangle of steel, usually about 4 × 2 inches.*

Molding or gooseneck scraper
▶ *A development of the cabinet scraper is the molding or gooseneck scraper, found in a variety of shapes, combining profiles and radii.*

Paint scraper
▶ *Other types of scrapers with a handle are available and are popular in the decorating trades – including, of course, paint scrapers.*

held is determined by the angle of the burr. Experiment until thin shavings are produced. By pushing with your thumbs or fingers the scraper can be bent to aid the cut, with a tighter curve producing a narrower cutting area. However, take care not to remove too much material, as it is easy to produce furrows in the surface.

HINTS AND TIPS

- A drop of oil or saliva on the burnisher helps during sharpening and gives extra bite.
- Try different angles for sharpening and using the scraper.
- Broken glass makes an effective scraper, but the edge is short-lived and care is needed when breaking it.

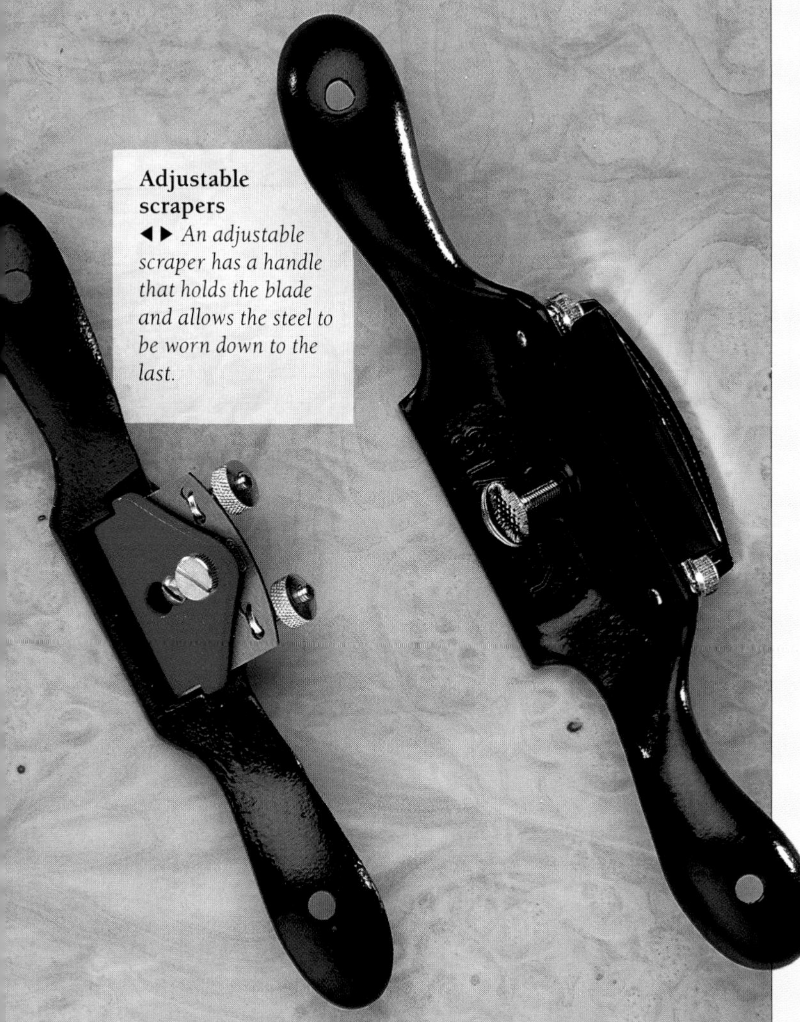

Adjustable scrapers
◀ ▶ *An adjustable scraper has a handle that holds the blade and allows the steel to be worn down to the last.*

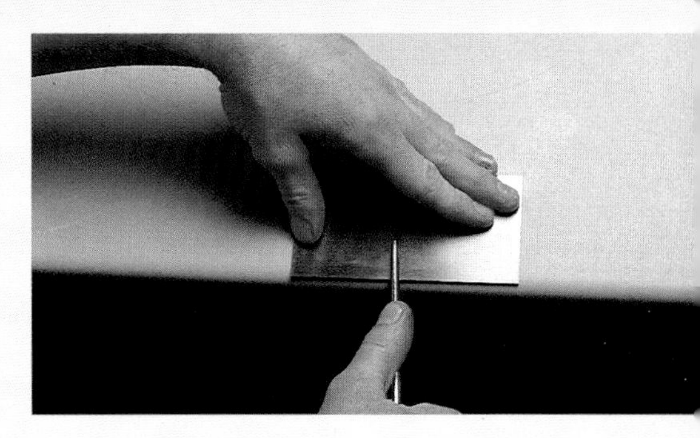

Sharpening a scraper
▲ 1 *File the edge of the scraper flat, then run a burnisher along its face to remove any burrs. The edge is now ready to be sharpened.*

▲ 2 *Hold the scraper securely, either in a vice or against the worktop, and rub the burnisher along the edge. As the burr is produced, roll the burnisher over to give the burr a hook of about 5 degrees.*

Using the scraper
▲ *Hold the scraper with your fingers to the back and thumbs to the front. Angle it away from your body, using your thumbs to curve the blade of the scraper, as you push to cut.*

Powered sanders

SEE ALSO

20-22
ABRASIVES

168-169
HEALTH AND SAFETY

Sanders provide the potential for fast stock removal and a fine finish. They come in a variety of shapes and sizes, and there is a range of hand-held and static machines. The former are powered by electricity, battery or compressed air. Of the static machines, belt or pad sanders are the most common. The belts are available in a range of lengths and widths. Lathes can often be fitted with abrasive disks, but by the time a piece has reached the finishing stage it should only need smoothing with a sander.

Portable belt sanders are powerful tools that can easily destroy veneer. They leave obvious marks when used across the grain. Orbital sanders can sand with and across the grain simultaneously, though when sanding with them you should be follow the grain whenever possible.

An important feature of any sander is some form of suction device to remove the dust into a bag. Wearing a mask when using a sander is recommended in any circumstance, especially when no extraction facility is present.

Disk sanders

▼ *In their crudest form (on angle grinders, for example), sanding disks scratch too deeply for finishing purposes and leave obvious rings. But they are very useful for smoothing curved surfaces on carvings and sculpture – with a rubber backing, they can follow the shape of the piece as no other powered sander can.*

There are also various drumlike sanding accessories that can be attached to a drill. These are particularly popular among turners for working on revolving pieces at the lathe.

Sanding accessories to accompany power drills
◀ *Accessories such as these are useful for sanding turnings and moldings.*

Belt sanders
▼ *From a finishing point of view, the only advantage of a belt sander is its ability to remove material quickly from large workpieces. If you use one for abrasive stripping, you will find that it removes paint fast and effectively.*

Never start a belt sander when it is in contact with a workpiece, and always lift it from the workpiece before stopping. Be prepared for a sudden jerk when applying the sander to the surface. The belts, which are supplied in all grades, revolve very fast between two rollers.

Orbital sanders
◀ *Although there are smaller palm and cordless versions, the most common orbital sanders are designed to take a third of an abrasive sheet. The motion drives the sanding plate in an elliptical or random orbit – but, though their light action makes them suitable for finishing work, they tend to leave fine curly scratches. The more sophisticated versions incorporate dust-extraction systems that suck the dust away from the surface and so reduce scratching.*

Abrasives

SEE ALSO

26-27
BRUISES, DENTS AND SCRATCHES

18-19
POWERED SANDERS

30-31
REPAIRING VENEERS

Sandpaper comes in a number of grits and types. Even the backing varies greatly, ranging from paper to cloth to Velcro. Each is designed to suit a different type of work. It is therefore worth investigating the various options, as the cheapest and most commonly supplied sandpaper previously found in local hardware stores (brown flint paper) has almost entirely disappeared. At any rate, flint paper clogged easily and wore out quickly.

Sandpaper is graded by grit size on the back of each sheet – the lower the number, the coarser the grit. You will rarely need sandpaper coarser than 80 grit, while at the other end of the scale 240 grit is very fine and is sufficient for preparing surfaces for finishing. You may want to use a finer grit between coats, but note that when machine-sanding the speed of the sandpaper over the surface makes each grit more powerful than when sanding by hand.

Woodworkers and finishers often talk about "working through the grits," referring to the technique of using a series of grits, progressing from coarse to fine, when preparing a piece. Three steps are normally enough – starting with 100 grit, then changing to 180 grit and finishing with 240 grit. These descriptions of grits are not always standard, so look out for alternative methods of grading when selecting sandpaper.

Types of paper
1 *For rubbing curves and shaped areas, use a flexible sandpaper.*
2 *Self-lubricating silicon-carbide paper can be used for denibbing (rubbing down between coats).*
3 *Self-lubricating silicon-carbide paper (as above).*
4 *Flint paper for sanding raw timber.*
5 *Fine garnet paper is used for working on wood, and between coats of finish.*

2

5

6

3

1

7

4

Garnet

Garnet remains the most common general-purpose sandpaper. By nature it is self-sharpening, with new cutting edges appearing as it breaks down. Although it retains an even cut, it is sometimes worth rubbing garnet paper on a scrap piece of oak or metal before using it on a surface for finishing, as the grit is sharp and can carve out deep scratches. Garnet paper is best used by hand, as the bond is not strong enough to survive machine sanding. It can be employed for work on either raw or polished wood.

Pumice powder
◄ *Use pumice powder for dulling and as a fine abrasive between applications of French polish. Rub the powder in with a shoe brush or a clean cloth.*

Grades of steel wool
1 *Use No. 0 steel wool for dulling with wax.*
2 *No. 00 steel wool produces a satin finish.*
3 *No. 000 steel wool is used to obtain a very fine flat effect.*
4 *No. 0000 steel wool is so fine that, in some circumstances, it glosses the surface.*

1

2

3

4

Cork block
▲ *Use a cork block for sanding flat surfaces by hand. Fold the abrasive around the block and work with the grain. This ensures even preparation and reduces the chance of producing furrows.*

6 *Coarse garnet paper is used for preparation.*
7 *Coarse aluminum-oxide paper is used for preparation. Fine aluminum oxide can be used between coats of finish.*

HINTS AND TIPS

- You can cut up sandpaper sheets with scissors or by folding and tearing. One recommended technique is to cut sheets into quarters.
- Maintain an even pressure when sanding by hand.
- Use a block, made of cork, wood or rubber when sanding flat surfaces.
- Convex or concave blocks (as appropriate) make sanding curved surfaces easier and more efficient.
- If sandpaper is too sharp, take off the first edge by rubbing it on scrap wood or metal.
- Do not simply fold sheets in four, as abrasive coats will then be facing each other and are likely to wear more quickly.
- Tap sandpaper on the back when it becomes clogged with dust.
- If you need to raise the grain, wet the wood and allow it to dry before sanding.
- Check the surface of the wood frequently, using an oblique light source to show up imperfections.
- Use your fingers to check finish – they are often better than eyes.

Aluminum oxide

Aluminum oxide is the manmade alternative to garnet as a general-purpose sandpaper. It is supplied on a variety of backings and can be used for machine sanding as readily as by hand.

Use aluminum oxide with a medium paper backing for hard sanding and with orbital sanders. Its open coat allows rapid stock removal with little clogging. Surface scratches when sanding are generally caused by dust particles collecting among the grit, so a sandpaper that reduces clogging is best for a fine finish.

Cloth-backed aluminum oxide has a longer life and is more flexible than many paper-backed grades. Use the cloth-backed versions when sanding with a disk sander or angle grinder. They should also be used when sanding with abrasive flaps, soft drums or pneumatic drums, all of which are excellent for contour sanding.

Silicon carbide

Never is it more important to reduce scratching than when sanding between coats of finish. The traditional method is to use soap and water or mineral spirits. As a modern alternative manufacturers have developed a silicon-carbide paper with a powder substance filling the gaps between the abrasive grains, thus reducing the likelihood of clogging and scratching. It works well for hand and machine sanding.

Steel wool

An alternative to sandpaper, steel wool has the advantage of being non-clogging. It is available in a range of grades, each suited to a different purpose.

Sanding by hand
▲ **1** *Wipe the surface with a damp cloth to raise the grain.*

▲ **2** *Cut the sandpaper sheet into quarters and wrap around a cork block, folding edges sharply.*

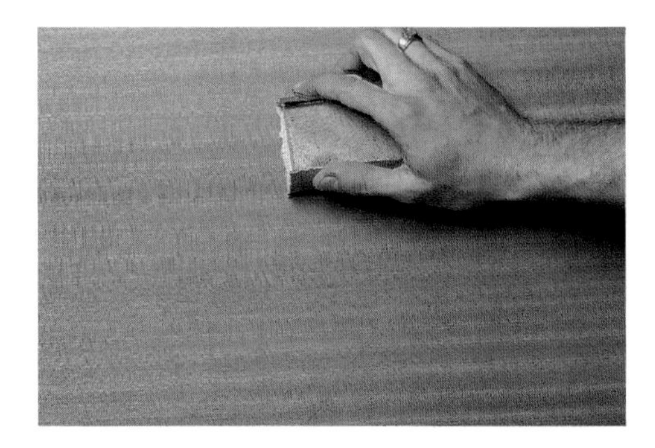

▲ **3** *Do not press the block too hard, but follow the grain with even pressure.*

The finishing shop

SEE ALSO

168-169
HEALTH AND SAFETY

STORING TOOLS AND MATERIALS

- Fit out the workshop with ample storage space for holding tools, materials, brushes, rags, batting and abrasives. Flammable finishes and materials must be kept separate in a lockable cupboard out of the way.
- Collect airtight containers for storing French polishing pads for future use. Do not use old food containers (in case the contents are mistaken for food), or glass food jars. Containers should be labeled carefully and dated. Always have a sealable container at hand for waste materials, which must be disposed of safely (see pages 168-169).

The layout, lighting and heating of the workshop play a vital role in achieving a quality finish. Your workshop must be dry and warm, and have plenty of natural light. There are also a number of jigs, fittings, and ideas for benches and storage that make finishing that much easier.

In all probability, your finishing workshop is also used for operations such as sawing and sanding. In this case, you will have to ensure that dust is kept under control. A good exhaust fan or industrial vacuum cleaner helps, but make sure the workshop is free from drafts and that nooks and crannies, which serve as dust traps, are kept to a minimum.

Heating and ventilation

Manufacturers of most finishing materials advise that the minimum temperature at which their products will dry is about 60°F. If drying does not take place at the proper rate, defects such as chilling and blushing appear in the surface.

Make sure materials are stored in the workshop for at least an hour before work commences. If it is very cold and you are not able to heat the workshop, use a powerful electric light or a hair dryer to bring the surface temperature nearer to the optimum (the wood will hold the heat for a surprisingly long time).

Finishing materials are designed to flow and are sensitive to heat. If they do not flow, brush marks are likely to create an uneven coat. Make sure there are no cold drafts, but keep the workshop ventilated to reduce condensation.

Lighting

When finishing, you will be continually judging color and degree of gloss. To be able to do this successfully, it is essential to have a good light source. The best source is, of course, natural light, which defines subtle differences of color and shade most clearly. This is particularly important when color matching.

If possible, arrange the workshop with northern light, which is constant and natural. Direct sunlight is not advisable, as judging color can be tricky in fierce sunlight. Otherwise, the best alternative to the real thing is to fit fluorescent tubes or light bulbs that give a "natural light."

Drying racks

An important feature of any finishing shop is a drying rack. This can either be fixed or portable, but make sure there is plenty of room for air to circulate between the pieces while they are drying. Dowels jointed into uprights works well for racking, with at least 4 inches between each level. The configuration depends on the type of work you expect to be finishing. For example, chairs need a different set-up than panels – but the principle always remains the same.

The workbench

The workbench can simply be a board on sawhorses. This helps bring small items and panels up to a convenient height, but can be dismantled when there are large or freestanding pieces in the workshop. Cut up some thin strips of wood on which flat panels can rest while being finished.

2

Preparation

No finish is better than its preparation. A smooth and clean surface is essential, as any blemish will be exaggerated by the finish. Use fingers and eyes to check for faults assiduously – but you will soon be able to judge instinctively whether a surface has been adequately prepared

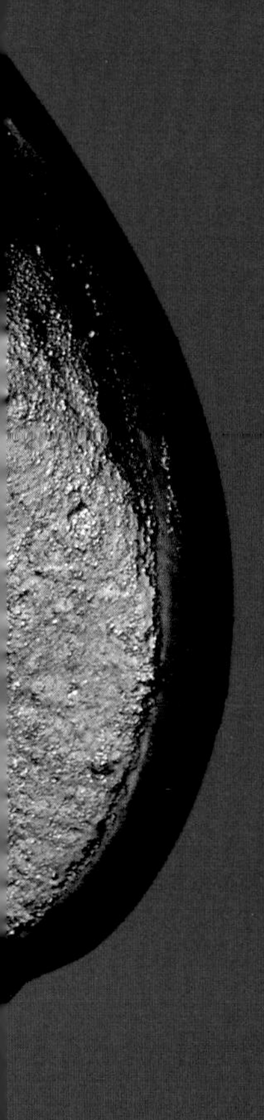

Bruises, dents and scratches

SEE ALSO

18–19 POWERED SANDERS

30–31 REPAIRING VENEERS

40–43 HOW TO USE WOOD FILLERS

80–83 RESTORING OLD FINISHES

Indentations in the surface are caused either by the compression of fibers (in the case of bruises and dents) or by the fibers being broken by scratches. These faults must be removed before sanding. If the bruises or scratches are deep, it is best to raise them rather than try to sand them out. Heavy sanding is likely to result in an uneven surface, and on a veneered piece it may even break through the veneer.

The principle of raising bruises is to swell the fibers of the wood with heat and steam. The expansion of the fibers levels the surface. This may not work fully when the fibers are badly broken, especially with deep scratches across the grain, but swelling will at least reduce the amount of filling or sanding needed to produce a surface fit for finishing.

Practice

Place a dampened cloth over the fault and push down gently with a hot iron. This produces steam. If the bruise does not come out at the first attempt, repeat the procedure until it does, rewetting the cloth each time. Take care when working on edges and moldings: these are easier to damage or burn than flat surfaces, and are often the most badly affected by faults.

Ironing out a bruise

▲ **1** *The picture frame before ironing out the bruises. The moldings and corners are most likely to be affected by bruising, because they are prominent and their rounded shape makes them vulnerable. You cannot expect scratches to be repaired by steaming, but most bruises respond to this treatment. Make sure that any old finish is thoroughly cleaned off the piece.*

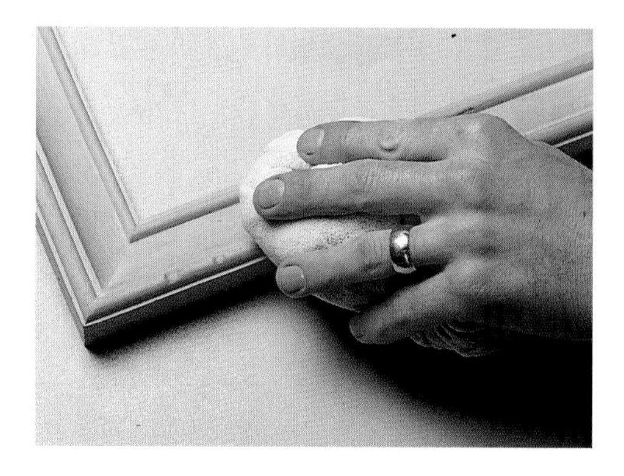

▲ **2** *Dampen the surface around the bruise with a cloth soaked in water. Always check that the water and cloth are clean – it is easy to discolor the wood. Use a clean white cloth, and certainly not one that has been used for staining. Press the cloth against the bruise so that the water soaks into the fibers of the wood, and does not simply run off. Try not to wet too much of the piece. This could lift veneer and weaken joints.*

The bruise removed
◀ *Having steamed out the bruise, leave the surface to dry, and sand with fine sandpaper.*

◀ **3** *Lay a damp piece of white cloth over the bruise. Experiment by folding the cloth once to start. You may find that it dries out too quickly. In this case, fold the cloth again or adjust the heat control on the iron. Do not use cloth that is too thin, otherwise there is a risk of burning or bruising the piece further.*

◀ **4** *Press the iron on the damp cloth. Make sure the iron is very hot – the steam should not be allowed to disperse before it has entered the wood. Press down with the iron until the steam ceases. Remove the iron and cloth to inspect the bruise. If the bruise is still there, repeat the operation, soaking the cloth with water each time. Leave the surface to dry before further finishing.*

HINTS AND TIPS

- Excess water can be removed by using the hot iron, but keep plenty of dry cloths available.
- Avoid direct contact between the iron and the workpiece, as there is always a risk of burning or further bruising.

MEMO

Safety precautions
You will be using a very hot iron – so arrange your working area carefully, ensuring it is not cluttered and that the iron can be placed out of harm's way when on.

Tools and materials
Electric iron

White or color-fast cloths

Water

Appropriate surfaces
Softwoods react faster than hardwoods to steaming. However, the differences in grain density are more prominent in softer woods, so check that bruises have been raised thoroughly.

Steaming deep bruises works better on solid wood than on a veneered surface. With veneer, the glue film can act as a barrier to the steam, and the fibers of the substrate may not expand as effectively as with solid wood.

Common problem
Where the fibers have been broken, filling and sanding will be necessary.

Drying time
Bruises can be raised within seconds – but leave the surface to dry before further work.

Dealing with blisters

SEE ALSO

16-17
SCRAPERS

18-19
POWERED SANDERS

30-31
REPAIRING VENEERS

Blisters in veneer are caused by the veneer lifting, either because air has been trapped beneath it or because the glue spread is faulty. To correct this fault the blister must be burst, which expels the air, then the veneer can be stuck down again with glue.

A similar fault, often found in old furniture, is called tenting. It tends to occur along joins between veneers or on the edges of panels when water or moisture has worked its way under the veneer. Tenting is dealt with in much the same way as a blister, but make sure the groundwork is dry before attempting to glue the veneer down.

Practice

Use a hypodermic syringe to inject glue into the blister. Do not use too much glue, as it is difficult to expel and may be forced beneath the existing bond. You may find it helpful to drill a tiny hole in the blister as a pilot for the syringe.

Another way to deal with a blister is to cut through the veneer, using a veneer saw, razor-blade knife or craft knife. Work glue under the blister, then flatten it with a hot iron. To protect the face of the veneer, put paper between the iron and the workpiece. Take care not to loosen other areas of the veneer with the heat and steam.

Once the repaired blister has dried, sand lightly or use a scraper to remove any glue marks (see pages 16-17). If you cut open the blister with a knife, a slight overlap may need to be sanded flat. Syringe holes sometimes have to be filled (see pages 40-43).

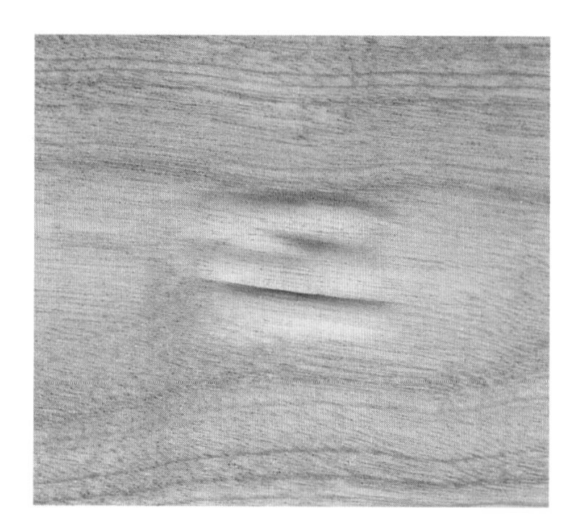

Repairing blisters in veneer

▲ **1** *Blisters occur when a veneer has not been pressed down correctly, or because an air bubble has developed. Run your hand over the piece to check for blisters and tap the surface with a finger nail, listening for a hollow sound. Blisters cannot be sanded away – the sandpaper would break through the thin skin. The veneer must be glued back in place.*

▲ **2** *Cut open the blister with a sharp craft knife or veneer saw to let out the air and allow access for new glue. Cut in the direction of the grain, following the pattern where possible. Try to cut through the veneer in one stroke, and avoid cutting into the groundwork.*

HINTS AND TIPS

- Cut along the grain.
- Use a sharp knife.
- To avoid pulling up the grain, protect veneer with waxed paper or polyethylene when clamping.
- If clamps are used, bridge unsupported areas such as drawer cavities.

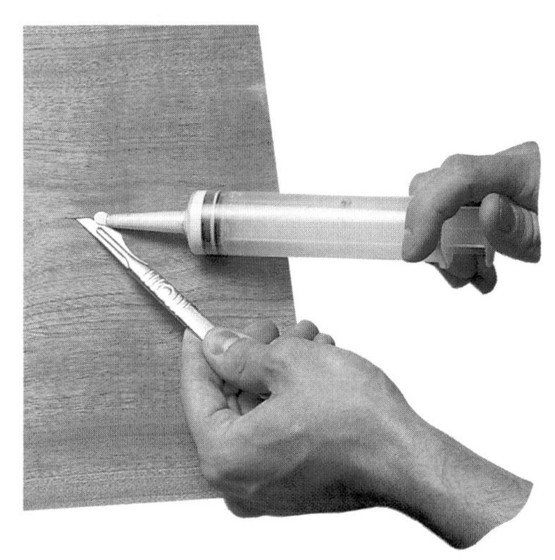

▲ 3 *Lift one side of the open blister with the point of the craft knife or veneer saw, and squeeze in the glue using a syringe. Use as little glue as possible to avoid marking the wood and overfilling the blister. Antique veneer was normally glued down with animal-hide glue, but white or yellow glue is easy to use and readily available.*

▲ 4 *If a syringe is not available, insert the glue using the point of a knife. Spread the glue under the veneer, making sure that the blistered area is completely covered. Keep a knife especially for this purpose – glue is difficult to remove from the blade and will make it blunt.*

▲ 5 *Wipe off any excess glue from the surface of the piece with a damp rag. Glue that has dried on the surface often shows up, even after careful sanding, so it is worth cleaning it off while it is still wet.*

▲ 6 *Use a clamp (a C-clamp, if possible) to ensure that the veneer remains flat while the glue is drying. Place a piece of paper over the repaired blister to stop the glue from sticking to the clamp. Thin pieces of wood between the paper and the clamp heads protect the surface from bruising. If the blister is in the center of a panel, and cannot be clamped, press it with a hot iron until the surface is completely flat. Again, a piece of paper between the iron and the blister keeps the iron free of glue. Use the tips of your fingers to check for any further bumps.*

MEMO

Tools and materials

Craft knife, razor-blade knife or veneer saw

White or yellow glue

Electric iron

Hypodermic syringe

Weights or clamps

Paper

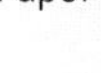

Precautions

Keep glue off veneered surface whenever possible.

Check that glue does not react adversely with veneer by testing on an inconspicuous part.

Common problems

Too much heat will loosen undamaged veneer.

Appropriate surfaces

Cutting with a knife is best on straight-grained veneers. The cut line is less likely to be seen afterward on figured veneers and on veneers with interlocking grain.

Drying time

Only use the iron for about 30 seconds.

Repairing veneers

SEE ALSO

28–29
DEALING WITH BLISTERS

40–43
HOW TO USE WOOD FILLERS

There are times when veneers need to be repaired, which probably means gluing in a piece of matching veneer, unless the damaged section can be used again. The important thing is to choose a good match and cut it correctly, so that the grain runs easily from old to new, with no joint showing.

Remember when choosing a veneer patch that grain is as important as color for a good match. Also remember that, if the workpiece has not been stripped, the patch must start lighter in color than the surrounding veneer, as the finish you intend to apply will darken it.

The most common veneer faults are along the edges of drawers or table tops, often where the cross-banding has been detached. For these repairs it is sometimes best to remove whole strips of veneer and replace them completely, rather than attempt a match. Specialist veneer and marquetry outlets sell a wide selection of cross-bandings and inlays and stock small quantities of veneer for repair work. If you know what veneer you need, these outlets will mail you the relevant items.

How to repair veneer

The most essential tool for repairing veneers is a sharp knife. When cutting out faults, try to follow the grain or cut at a tangent to it. Where possible, cut a wavy line – as the eye is less likely to be drawn toward such a repair, especially on the more figured veneers. As a result, repairs are generally easiest to disguise on those complex woods.

If you have a number of repairs to make, veneer punches are especially useful. They are designed to cut out the fault from the damaged veneer and a matching patch from the new material. Veneer punches are made in a variety of sizes and have irregular cutters to help disguise the repair.

Once a cut has been made around the fault, remove the offending piece, taking care not to damage the surrounding veneer. Also take great care choosing the orientation of the patch, marking it to ensure the fit is correct when you glue it down with white or yellow glue. Use an iron to flatten the repair in much the same way as a blister (see pages 28–29).

Repairing damaged veneer
▶ **1** *The corner of this panel has been damaged and the veneer needs to be repaired. The usual remedies for surface faults – wood fillers – are unlikely to hold on a corner like this, and color matching would be difficult. The best solution is to put in a new piece of matching veneer.*

◀ **2** *Trim off the rough edge of damaged veneer using a craft knife and a straightedge. This ensures a neat joint. Cut cleanly and firmly, with the straightedge covering the undamaged veneer, so that if there is a slip, the knife will score only the piece to be removed. Use one very light cut to mark the line, and then slice through the veneer in a single stroke. Try not to cut into the groundwork.*

◀ **3** *Remove all loose pieces of veneer. It is possible that the groundwork has also been damaged, and that pieces have come loose. If this has happened, glue any chips back in place and fill any cavities, ensuring that the surface is flat.*

MEMO

Tools and materials

Veneer to suit

White or yellow glue

Veneer saw

Electric iron

Veneer or masking tape

Veneer punch

Common problems

Cutting straight across the grain makes a more obvious repair.

Novice repairers tend not to cut close enough to the shape.

▲ **4** *Apply glue liberally to the area to be repaired. Use white or yellow glue for this. Spread the glue over the area, making sure that there is enough to be squeezed out by the new piece of veneer.*

▼ **5** *Select a piece of veneer for the repair. Try to find a piece that matches the original both in color and in grain pattern. Cut it so that the grain follows that of the panel. It is best to cut a slightly larger piece than necessary, and trim it down after the glue has dried. Try to put in the new piece of veneer at an angle of about 30 degrees to the grain.*

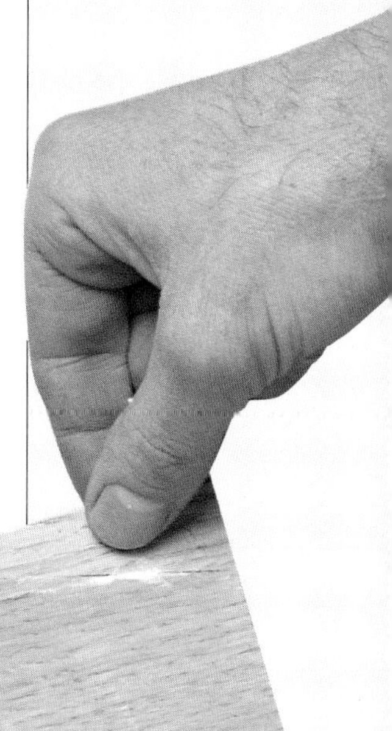

HINTS AND TIPS

- When using delicate veneers, tape the face with veneer or masking tape before cutting out the new patch. Mark the tape so you can position the patch.
- Try to hit a veneer punch with only one hammer blow in order to achieve a clean cut. Similarly, cut through the veneer as cleanly as possible when using a knife.
- Sharpen the outside of veneer punches to keep them very sharp.

◀ **6** *Use a hot iron to speed up the bonding of the glue. Place a piece of paper between the veneer and the iron to avoid marking. Press down hard with the iron for about a minute, and then check to see if the glue has dried.*

◀ **7** *Once the glue has dried, trim off any excess veneer. Take off the bulk of the surplus with a sharp knife, and then use a rasp or file, drawing it downward only.*

Types of veneer
▼ *Keep a store of veneers in a variety of colors and grain patterns. You may have to play around with your veneers to find a piece that matches, but do try to use a matching wood species – different woods all change color with time. Shown here is a range of exotic and more commonplace veneers:*
1 *Bird's-eye maple*
2 *Plane tree*
3 *Castello*
4 *Rosewood, santos*
5 *European walnut*
6 *Ash*
7 *Padauk*

▶ **8** *Sand down the inserted veneer, using 100 grit garnet paper folded around a cork block. Keep the block flat and sand along the direction of the grain.*

▶ **9** *The panel is now flat and smooth, and the repair is indiscernible from the rest. The color will change once a finish has been applied to the repair, and colors can be used later to improve the color match.*

Stains in the wood

SEE ALSO

18–19 POWERED SANDERS

50–52 BLEACHING WOOD

168–169 HEALTH AND SAFETY

Blue and iron stains are faults within the wood that occur during the kiln drying done by the sawmill. Blue stain is caused by a mold, which grows on lumber and leaves blue marks that look like ink stains.

Iron stain is caused by particles of iron from nails, screws, saw blades, corrugated-iron roofs and even shrapnel, which react with tannic acid present in the wood. Oak is renowned for reacting in this way. The stains, which appear as black flecks in the grain, usually show up after sanding.

Removing stains
▲ **1** *Iron stains are particularly common in oak. They are caused by tannic acid in the wood reacting with iron filings implanted in the grain.*

This dark stain must be bleached using oxalic acid before the piece can be finished.

▼ **2** *Oxalic acid is supplied as a white powder in dry crystal form. Remember that it is poisonous. Always wear protective gloves, and ensure that your hands are washed after working. Use glass, plastic or earthenware containers for mixing and storing the crystals.*

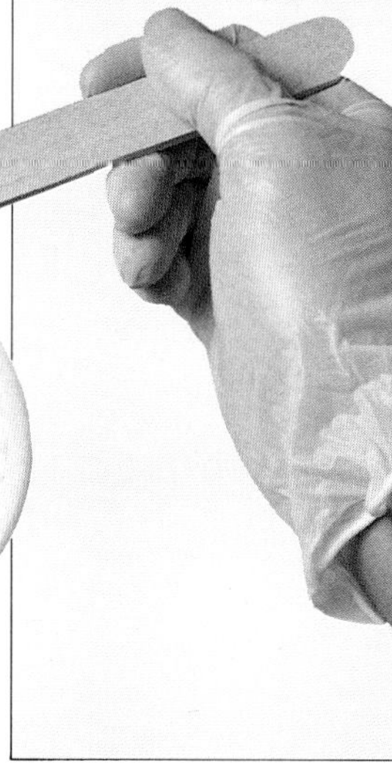

MEMO

Safety precautions

Always wear protective gloves, goggles and protection over clothing when using bleach. Only use bleach in a well-ventilated room or outdoors.

Follow manufacturer's instructions carefully and thoroughly.

Always have plenty of water available in case of spillage.

Wear a mask when sanding surfaces after bleaching.

Always pour oxalic crystals into water – never pour the water onto the crystals.

Tools and materials

Protective gloves and goggles

Oxalic acid crystals (or two-part bleach for large or deep stains)

Water and hose

Synthetic-bristle brush

Mask

Glass, plastic, enamel or earthenware container

Cleaning stains

To remove stains, use a bleach (preferably oxalic acid crystals) that is neither too strong nor too weak. A two-part bleach (see pages 50–52) may be too powerful for small isolated patches. Instead, unless the stains are large or stubborn, slowly add oxalic crystals to warm water, making up to a saturated solution (see pages 50–52). About a cupful of solution is needed to bleach a table top.

Apply the bleach solution with a brush (see pages 14–15). It is best not to saturate the wood with bleach, as adhesives may be affected. Leave the workpiece to dry, and repeat the process if the stain is persistent. Once the stain has disappeared, you must neutralize the surface with plenty of clean water. Finally, leave the piece to dry.

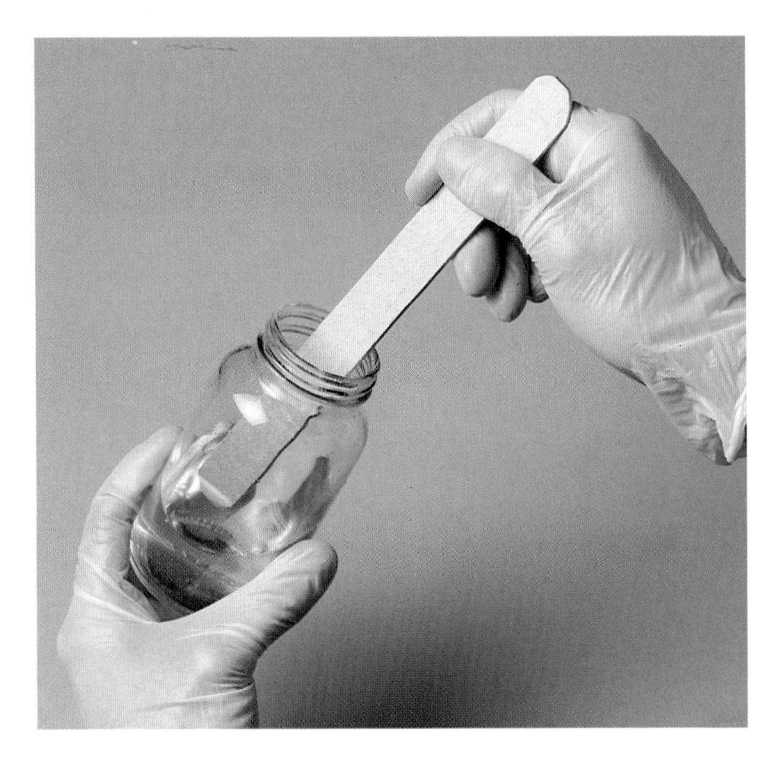

▲ **3** *Make a saturated acid solution by adding the crystals to warm water and stirring. Keep adding crystals until no more will dissolve. Always add the crystals to the water, and not the other way around. Leave to stand for about 10 minutes before use.*

▶ **4** *Apply the oxalic acid with a synthetic-bristle brush. Lay on the bleach evenly over the stain. Do not splash it around, and always wear goggles. Try not to let droplets fall on the surface where they will mark the piece.*

◀ **5** *After applying the bleach, leave it to soak into the wood for about half an hour, until dry. More stubborn stains may need further applications of bleach before they are completely removed. Avoid saturating veneered surfaces – the glue bond may be weakened by the water-based solution.*

HINTS AND TIPS

- Work outside.
- Keep a hose ready.
- When working on a large area, such as a table top, use a cleat under the board to prohibit any tendency to bow when dampened.

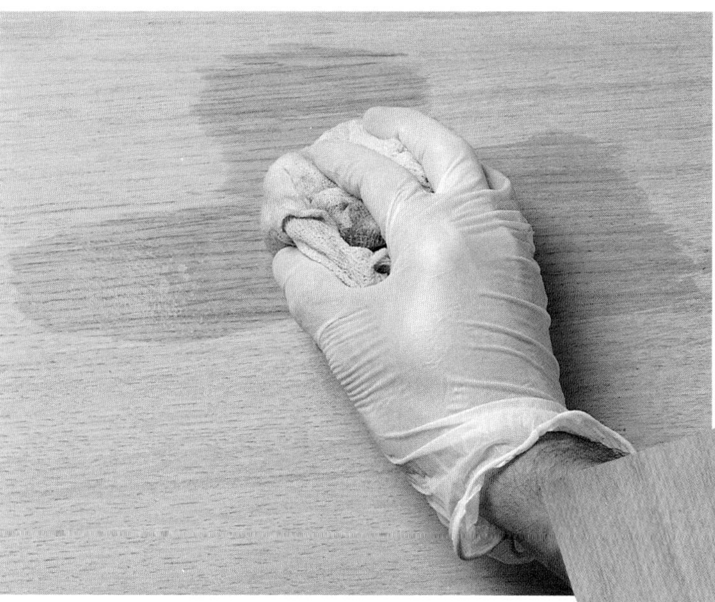

◀ **6** *Wash the surface with plenty of clean water.*

▶ **7** *Once the wood has dried there should be no evidence of stain or bleaching. Sand the surface lightly with fine 240 grit garnet.*

Chemical stripping

SEE ALSO

16–17 SCRAPERS
18–19 POWERED SANDERS
58–65 FRENCH POLISHING
80–83 RESTORING OLD FINISHES

WORKING WITH CHEMICAL STRIPPERS

- When using strippers that make the finish bubble, dab on a second coat of stripper to flatten and burst the blisters in order to bring the stripper into contact with the surface again.
- Leave stripper on the surface for at least 15 minutes before removing it.
- It does not help to "paint" the stripper onto the surface – it is better to lay down the first coat, and dab on subsequent coats.

The removal of old finishes can be a laborious task, but must be carried out properly if subsequent finishing is to be a success. It is essential to clean any evidence of previous decoration or protection from the grain. Otherwise, it will show up later – and all the effort of stripping and finishing will have been wasted.

Using cabinet scrapers or sanders is an alternative to chemical stripping, but is much more time-consuming and unlikely to produce a better result. In addition, sanding or scraping removes the patina that certain woods such as mahogany acquire on ageing. Sanding will also not remove the residue of finish from open-grained woods. It is often better to use a solvent paint remover (see below).

Abrasives may also be used for stripping, but they can cut through the fibers of the wood and there is always a chance of an uneven finish, with some areas sanded back more deeply than others.

A further alternative is to take the piece to a stripping shop that has a caustic dipping tank. Unfortunately, caustic strippers often loosen joints in furniture and doors.

When doing the work oneself, the choice of stripper is determined by the workpiece and the original finish. It is of course easy to distinguish paint from wax, but other finishes are more difficult to identify. The best way to test a finish is to try a solvent on a less prominent part of the work, for example, inside rails on a chair.

Mineral spirits

To clean wax or grime from a workpiece without harming other finishes, use mineral spirits on a rag. If nothing seems to happen, rub with

Stripping old finishes

◀ **1** *Decant the stripper carefully into a coffee can. Apply it to the piece with a flat brush. Always wear protective gloves, goggles and protective clothing when working with chemical strippers. Take care when opening cans of stripper – pressure can build up and force the liquid to spurt out into your eyes.*

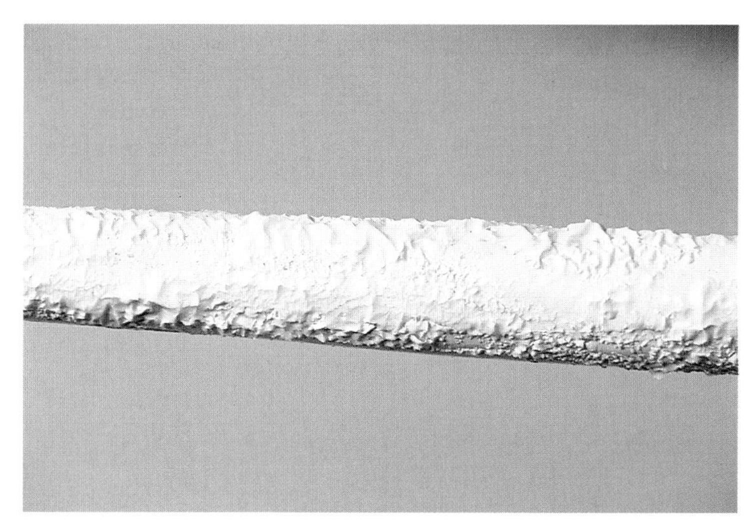

◀ 2 *Allow the stripper to soak into the old finish. Make sure that enough is applied to keep the surface wet. Do not spread the stripper – this will cause it to evaporate too quickly.*

▶ 3 *Test with a scraper to see if the finish has dissolved and is ready for scraping. Do not try to scrape the surface too soon – the job will be easier if you wait for the stripper to take effect fully. Use a paint scraper to remove the waste, working along the grain. The old finish is soaked in stripper, so roll it up in newspaper and make sure it is discarded out of harm's way.*

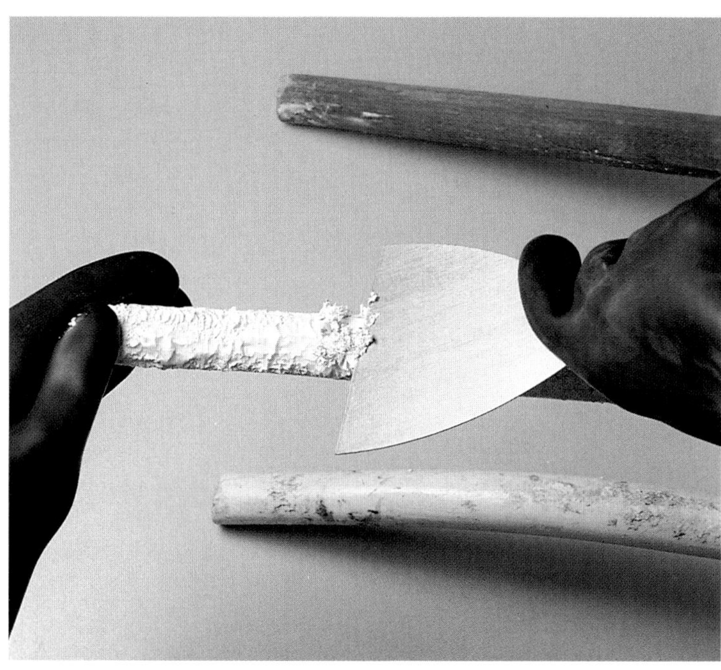

◀ 4 *Having cleaned the surface with a scraper, apply a further coat of stripper, wait for a few minutes and then rub off using coarse steel wool (3 or 4 grade). Steel wool is very sharp. Use a pair of old scissors to cut it, and always wear protective gloves. Rub the remaining finish away, working into every nook and cranny, leaving the surface clean.*

MEMO

Safety precautions

Wear butyl or neoprene gloves and goggles at all times when using strippers.

Wash strippers off skin immediately with water.

Only use strippers outdoors or in well-ventilated areas. Do not use them in a confined space.

Solvents can cause dizziness.

Scrape off residue onto an old newspaper for disposal.

Some strippers are flammable, so do not smoke or light a flame near them.

Make sure all stripper is removed before handling the workpiece.

Make sure the stripper is removed from all corners, nooks and crannies. Otherwise, it will react with stains and finishes.

Tools and materials

Gloves and goggles

Chemical stripper

Steel wool

Brush

Mineral spirits

Cabinet scraper or paint scraper

◀ **5** *Once the piece has been cleaned, check on the label to see if the product needs neutralizing. It is often sufficient to wipe the surface with a rag and mineral spirits. To neutralize an acid-based stripper make up a solution of washing soda and water. Mix 2 cups of soda with 5 quarts of hot water.*

▲ **6** *Swab the surface with the soda solution on a rag, washing away any residue, and making sure all the corners and less accessible parts are treated. Any stripper that is left in or on the wood will react with later finishes.*

USING STEEL WOOL

- There is a range of steel wool grades, the finest usually being referred to as 0000 and the coarsest as number 3.
- Do not try to pull pieces of coarse steel wool from a roll, as the strands of metal are sharp and can easily cut your hands and fingers.
- Cut steel wool with old or cheap scissors.
- Use steel wool in wads about fist-size.
- When clogged with wax or dirt, turn steel wool inside out to make full use of it. Large wads are very wasteful.
- The finest steel wool burnishes the surface when used with some modern finishes, instead of dulling it.

fine steel wool instead of a rag, using small wads about the size of a golf ball. Replace the wad of steel wool when it becomes clogged with wax and dirt.

Solvent strippers

Solvent strippers are supplied ready mixed. They contain methylene chloride, with some wax to stop them from evaporating, and are used to remove French polish, lacquer, oil and wax. To apply, simply lay the stripper on the surface, using a flat brush. Do not move the stripper around once it is positioned on the workpiece, as that is likely to hasten evaporation.

Leave the stripper to soak into the finish keeping the surface wet. You will then be able to remove the finish with a paint or cabinet scraper. Always scrape in the direction of the grain. (If the direction isn't obvious, remove a small area of finish from an inconspicuous part to check which way the grain runs.) It may be necessary to apply several coats of stripper before the bulk of the old coating is removed.

Once most of the original coating has been cut back, use steel wool to pick up the last flecks of finish. This is particularly useful for moldings, nooks and crannies, and wood with a deep and open grain structure. Before further work on the surface, some solvent strippers need to be neutralized. Always check on the product's label. To neutralize an acid-based stripper apply a wash of water and soda and leave to dry. The water will raise the grain and the wood will then need to be sanded down before refinishing takes place. To neutralize an alkaline stripper use denatured alcohol.

Unless a manufacturer specifically states that a product needs neutralizing, it is usually sufficient to wipe the surface with a rag dipped in

◀ **7** *If the piece is very badly scratched or dented, sand with progressively finer sandpaper, starting with 100 grit and working up to 240. However, bear in mind that certain woods acquire a beautiful patina on ageing that sanding would remove. Check the surface thoroughly for any remnants of finish, or any bruises and dents, before starting the next stages of restoration.*

mineral spirits. This does not raise the grain.

Be warned that solvent strippers in paste form sometimes contain caustic soda and will cause many woods to darken.

▶ **8** *Stripping can reveal many problems formerly concealed under years of paint. Some of the joints may be loose, and the piece may need some filling, but otherwise it is ready for finishing.*

How to use wood fillers

SEE ALSO

16–17 SCRAPERS

18–19 POWERED SANDERS

44–49 STAINING WOOD

53–55 GRAIN FILLERS

Fillers are used for filling larger indentations in wood, in much the same way as plaster fillers are used for making good dents and cracks in plasterwork. The main difference is that fillers have to match the color of the piece, and require an elastic nature to cope with the movement of wood. It is best to avoid using fillers, if at all possible, because a good match is always difficult. However, for cracks, knots and deep scratches there is often no alternative.

Select the best filler for the situation. When choosing a filler, it is important to bear in mind the type of finish you intend to use on the piece. While shellac sticks are suitable for any finish, plastic wood (in either two-part or one-part form) is a difficult material to match. If you intend to use a stain to do so, make sure it is compatible. The instructions will say whether it is oil or water based.

As a general rule use shellac sticks under traditional finishes, and two-part fillers under modern spray finishes. Only use wax fillers for small chips, and then only while polishing, or with a wax or oil finish. Plastic wood is most commonly used under varnishes.

Although some fillers will take a stain once dry, a more successful technique is to mix pigment with the filler before applying.

Shellac sticks

Shellac sticks are sold in a variety of colors to suit a range of woods, and are a concentrated form of the shellac used for French polishing. They are available from only a few specialist paint stores and by mail order (see "Useful Addresses" in the back of this book).

Select a good color match and hold the shellac stick over the affected area. Using a soldering iron or hot knife, melt the shellac into the fault, melting enough to leave the filler protruding a little after pushing it well into the hole.

Shellac filling should not be used under catalyzed lacquers.

Plastic wood

This is a common filler, available from most hardware and paint stores. It comes in a can or tube and is made in a range of colors. Plastic wood dries out quickly, so remember to replace the lid immediately after use.

Plastic wood does not always adhere effectively, so make sure any faults are clean and free from dust. Apply with a knife or chisel, pressing the filler well into the cavity. Plastic wood has a tendency to shrink, so leave it a little thick to dry. It may even be necessary to use more than one application; for large holes, fill gradually.

Filling with wood filler
▲ **1** *Wood filler is used as a filling when pieces of a finish have chipped away. For this picture frame, shellac stick filler has been used. Shellac sticks are available from mail-order suppliers.*

◀ **2** *Mask the area around the fault with masking tape to protect the original finish.*

▲ **3** *Hold a soldering iron just above the surface of the piece, and press the shellac stick against it so that it melts and drops into the fault like sealing wax. Build up the filler gradually.*

▲ **5** *Leave the filler to set for about 5 minutes. Once it is set it may be necessary to level it with a small chisel. Do not try to take too much filler off at a time – it is brittle and likely to break up if too much pressure is used.*

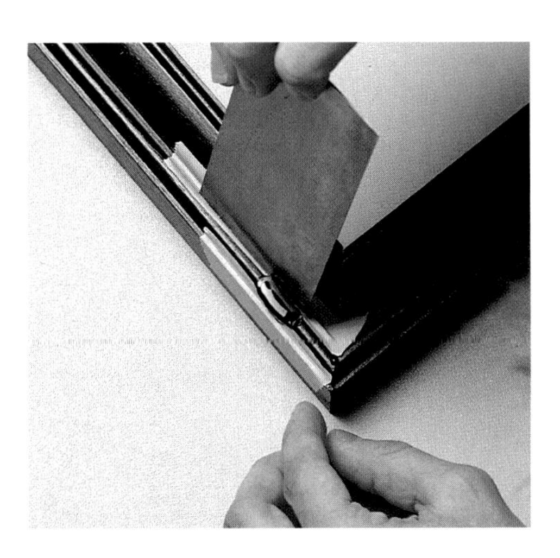

▲ **4** *Level the filler with a steel scraper or other tool before it sets. It is important to manipulate the filler to follow the contours of the surface as closely as possible. Do not overfill the hole, but do leave the filler slightly protruding.*

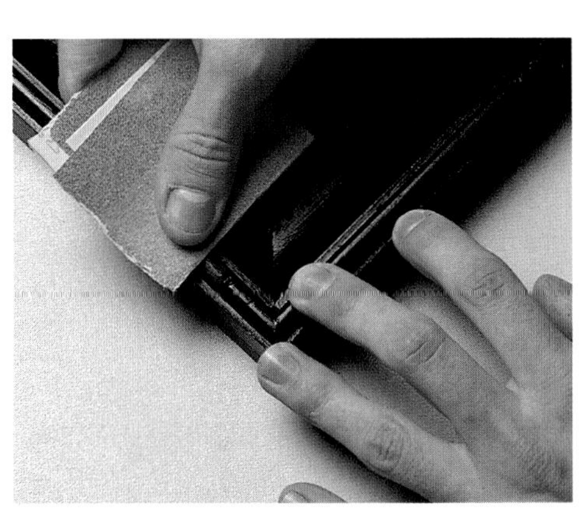

▲ **6** *Use coarse sandpaper for final leveling. On flat surfaces sand with a sanding block, but on moldings just fold the 100 garnet paper and delicately work with the corners. Do not over-sand, creating a hollow. When it is smooth, finish with fine sandpaper.*

MEMO

Safety precautions
Wear a mask when sanding two-part fillers.

Tools and materials
Filler or sawdust to suit

White, yellow or urea-formaldehyde glue

Soldering iron

Chisel

Putty knife

Thin sticks for mixing

Common problems
The color description on the can or bottle may not give an accurate indication of how the filler or stain will dry.

Sprayed lacquers can dry unevenly on fillers.

Plastic wood tends to fall out of large cavities and does not adhere well.

Appropriate surfaces
Use plastic wood for pinholes and tiny dents.

Glue and sawdust mix are best for joint lines.

Drying time
Shellac sticks dry instantly.

Plastic wood needs about 15 minutes to dry.

Two-part fillers dry in about 30 minutes.

Glue and sawdust takes at least 3 hours.

Wax sticks do not need any drying time.

Mixing glue and sawdust
▲ **1** *A quick and cheap filler can be made by mixing glue with sawdust to match the workpiece. Mix white or yellow glue with the appropriate sawdust on a piece of cardboard. Add the sawdust to the glue until it has a thick but workable consistency, for large holes. Make sure the glue is thoroughly mixed in for a good bond.*

▲ **2** *Use dry or paste pigments to achieve the desired color, mixing them gradually into the glue and sawdust filler. Always mix enough to fill the hole – the exact color may be difficult to repeat.*

▶ **3** *Apply the filler with a plastic or cardboard spatula. Spread it over the fault, building up to the surface until it is smooth but a little protruding.*

▶ **4** *Glue and sawdust filler must be left for at least two or three hours to dry. It will then be stuck firmly into the hole, and hard enough to be shaped and smoothed with files and sandpaper.*

Two-part fillers

Two-part fillers are harder versions of plastic wood. A catalyst or hardener reacts with the filler to create a very strong repair. They can be matched using stains and pigments (see pages 44–49). But achieving an exact match can be difficult, so they are better used for structural repairs (especially on particle board) than for filling conspicuous faults.

Follow the instructions carefully, applying the filler with a knife or chisel and leaving it slightly protruding. These two-part fillers do shrink, but not to the extent of plastic wood, and they set very hard – so beware of over-filling, which will necessitate time-consuming chiseling and sanding later.

Water-based wood fillers

As their name suggests, water-based wood fillers can be thinned with water. They have the advantage of being quick-drying and suffer very little shrinkage. They are available in a wide range of colors and are cheaper than two-part fillers.

Glue and sawdust mix

A quick and cheap filler can be made by mixing glue with sawdust to match the workpiece. It is not a good filler for large areas, and not all finishes take to it, but it works well for gaps along joint lines.

When using white or yellow glue, mix with sawdust produced by sanding either the piece to be repaired or a cut-off of the original wood. As white and yellow glue will not fill gaps, plenty of wood dust is needed to act as a filler. Alternatively, for larger holes, use a urea-formaldehyde adhesive mixed with sawdust.

Leave all these mixtures slightly protruding, then chisel and sand them flat when dry. These homemade fillers are all water-based and take stain fairly well once dry – but it's best to mix in the stain and experiment with color before application.

Wax sticks

Manufacturers of wax finishes also make sticks for small repairs. These are colored and designed for use either on surfaces to be waxed or on pieces already polished. Clear beeswax may be sufficient in many circumstances, especially when the hole is small. However, wax must not be used under modern finishes. Use wax sticks like shellac sticks, warming the wax with a soldering iron. Push the wax into the holes or chips with a small filling knife, then scrape off any excess with a chisel or scraper once hard.

Using pigments to color fillers

▲ **1** *Having sanded the filler smooth and level, use pigments to match the repair with the rest of the surface of the piece. Pigments are opaque colors, held in suspension. They do not dissolve.*

▶ **2** *Use the pigments to mask out the defect. A selection of nine colors is sufficient, stored in a tray. Experiment with combinations of pigments to judge the color matches they produce.*

▶ **3** *Mix the pigments with shellac polish and apply with an artists' brush. Dip the brush into pale polish, and then into the required pigment, and mix. Here titanium white and yellow ocher are being mixed to produce a light color.*

▶ **4** *Apply the mixture of pigment and polish with a No. 6 artists' brush, stroking on the color and imitating the grain pattern. Blend in the color gradually.*

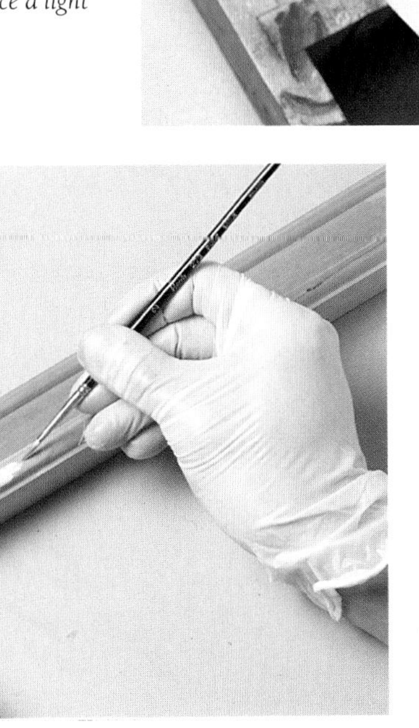

▲ **5** *Leave to dry for 2–3 minutes. Gradually apply polish over the filler to bring out the color. Too much polish at a time will rub off the color.*

Staining wood

SEE ALSO

73-75
WAXED FINISHES

124-149
SPRAY FINISHES

Stains consist of dyes dissolved in a medium and are used for coloring wood. They do so by soaking into the grain of the wood, giving it a tint – unlike pigments used for coloring paint, which lie on top of the surface as solid matter.

The medium carrying the dye determines the characteristics of the stain, such as drying time, compatibility and spread. A stain should enhance the grain and improve the appearance of the wood; it needs to be easy to apply, has to be compatible with the finish, and should dry within a reasonable time. It should also maintain its color, without fading. Stains are particularly good at upgrading wood and making unattractive surfaces more interesting.

Although most wood stains are designed to soak into the wood, for exterior work the stain forms a film on the surface, creating an effect similar to paint. Nevertheless, most stains do not offer protection and so need further finishing.

When choosing a stain, select the one that has the most suitable characteristics. The same color can be produced using different types of stains. Color is therefore not the only criterion for selection. Rather, your choice should be determined by a number of important considerations, which you need to keep in mind when investigating the various options. For example: how fast do you want the stain to dry? What finish and wood do you want to use the stain with? Will the stained piece be affected by wear and tear? Does the stain have to match an original antique color?

A selection of different stains to show color range
◀ *Substrate: Red oak.*
1 *Yellow.*
2 *Blue-black.*
3 *Golden oak.*
4 *Light oak.*
5 *Olive.*
6 *Rosewood.*

What are water stains?

Water stains are supplied in a dry powder or crystal form and then dissolved in water. They have been used for hundreds of years, originally being made with vegetable dyes obtained from trees and plants. They are now the cheapest of all stains and can be bought by mail order from finishing suppliers. Although the original dyes are no longer available, the manmade alternatives are useful to have around the workshop.

The most useful dyes are Vandyke crystals (brown), mahogany crystals (warm brown), and nigrosine (black). You can mix these dyes in order to produce different colors. By changing the ratio of water to powder, you can adjust the depth of color. Always test water stains on a cutoff before applying them. Also check the effect of adding a finish.

Working with water stains

Apply the stain with a cloth or brush. You can use any of these methods – but you will find that a brush is best for moldings, corners and carvings, and that a cloth holds the most stain. Wet the wood before applying the first coat of stain, to aid an even spread. Rub the stain into the grain, keeping a wet edge all the time.

For a table top you will need about a cupful of stain, but make sure you have enough for the whole piece. Use plenty of stain, only stopping short of pouring it onto the surface. Water stains dry slowly, so you will have time to wipe off the excess with a cloth or paper towel. Once the stain has dried, go over any light areas with another coat.

MEMO

WATER STAINS

Tools and materials

Powder

Water

Cloth or brush

Cloth or paper towels for wiping off

Common problems

Water stains expand the fibers of the wood and raise the grain. As a result, the stain is likely to be sanded off the higher areas. To prevent this, dampen the surface of the wood and let it dry, then sand back before staining.

Drying time

Water stains take about 40 minutes to dry – but allow them to dry for 12 hours, or overnight, before applying further coats or other finishes.

Using water stains

▶ **1** *Water stains are supplied in powder form. Make up the stain by adding the powder to water in different proportions depending on the color required. Add more stain to make it darker, and more water to make it lighter.*

HINTS FOR STAINING

- Although stains dry lighter, they are darkened by subsequent finishes – so test the effect on a offcut or hidden area first.
- You can always make a surface darker with more stain, but it is impossible to lighten the color without resorting to bleach.
- A dark stain has a stronger effect on a light wood than on a dark one.
- Always keep a wet edge when applying stain, to avoid patchy color.
- Plan your staining pattern before starting, so you maintain a uniform color.
- If the workpiece is dampened very slightly with water, that will give some idea of the color effects of applying a clear finish before or after staining.
- When trying to match colors, do so gradually. Don't attempt to mix the perfect combination of dyes straight off – rather, use progressive coats of individual dyes.

▼ **2** *Stir the solution thoroughly to ensure the powder has dissolved. Keep one spatula for stirring and another for picking up powder. Hot water and a few drops of ammonia added to the solution can improve the stain's penetration. Leave for 10 minutes before use.*

What are oil dyes?

These dyes are supplied ready-mixed, and in powder form. They are mineral spirits, dissolved in naphtha or a similar hydrocarbon solvent. They are classified by wood color, with names such as "dark mahogany" or "light oak." However, all these dyes can be used on any wood, and the names are no more than general guides. Oil dyes are seldom used anymore, but they can be purchased through mail-order suppliers.

Select the wood dye closest to the color required, and build it up to produce the desired shade. If the color is too dark, it can be thinned with the appropriate solvent.

▼ **3** *Apply the stain with a rag. Use plenty of stain, keeping it wet on the surface all the time, to produce an even spread. Rub it in with a circular motion. Use a brush for staining moldings, but as with a flat surface always keep a wet edge.*

Working with oil dyes

Oil dyes do not raise the grain, but they do bite into deep and uneven grain (as occurs in beech), which may show up as dark patches. It is therefore important to prepare rough areas especially carefully. Wood dyes are convenient to use and penetrate deeply into the wood. They are useful for working outdoors, since water stains take a long time to dry and alcohol stains dry too quickly for large areas to be stained.

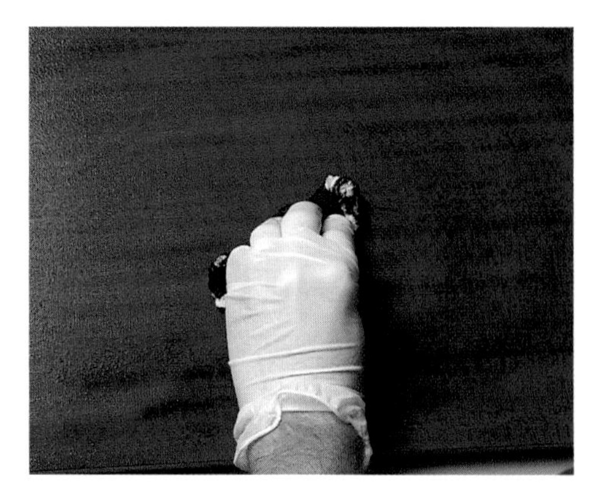

▲ **4** *Water stain dries slowly so you will have plenty of time to wipe off any excess. Do this with a cloth, following the grain. Leave to dry for about an hour before continuing the finishing process.*

▼ **5** *The stain may well dry lighter, as is the case with most finishes. It will also feel rough where the water has raised the grain, so use 240 grade fine sandpaper to lightly sand the surface. Work with the grain, sanding very gently so as not to sand through the color, especially on the corners.*

PROBLEMS WHEN STAINING

- Faults and end grain often absorb great quantities of stain, which makes them look darker. You may therefore need to seal them with a shellac sealer before staining.
- Avoid stain runs by working on the underside of a piece first.
- It is not possible to create a "rosewood" effect with a single stain. The only way is to apply a mahogany stain – then, when dry, add black streaks with ebony stain, using an artists' brush.
- Because of the absorption differences with the grain, it is sometimes better to use a varnish stain (see pages 76-79) for pine.

What are alcohol stains?

These stains are aniline dyes dissolved in denatured alcohol. Professional woodworkers like using them because of the wide range of colors available.

Dyes are named by their color (for example, yellow and green), except for Bismarck brown which, confusingly, is nearer red. They can be applied by brush, cloth or spray gun and are also used for dipping work. Because of the alcohol base, they can be mixed with shellac polish for color matching and touching up during the polishing process.

Alcohol stains dry very fast. As a result, they are ideal for spraying. Also, the wood is ready for coating almost immediately. However, the fact that they dry so quickly makes them difficult to apply successfully and can result in a patchy finish. Use alcohol stains for items such as toys that are small enough to be dipped in a small dipping tank or container.

One disadvantage of an alcohol base is that if coats of shellac are applied later, they are likely to lift the stain and affect the color.

Working with alcohol stains

Alcohol stains are sold in powder form, as aniline dyes, and mixed to the desired color – more powder being used to provide a darker shade. The dyes can be mixed together for a wider range of colors. Apply the stain sparingly, or the dye will be removed by the polish. When dipping, leave the item in the tank for about 5 minutes.

It is a good idea to add a small quantity of transparent French polish to the formulation to "fix" the alcohol stain on the wood.

What are chemical stains?

Chemical stains have been used for hundreds of years and can produce many different effects – some attractive, some less so. Strictly speaking, they are not stains in the true sense. Most of them are colorless, and they do not stain the wood but change its color when they are applied. This color change is brought about by the "stains" reacting with chemicals present in the wood. As the chemicals in wood differ from one piece to another, the color can vary (the chemical structure of the wood depends on the climate and location of the tree during growth). The best-known of these chemicals is probably tannic acid, which occurs in oak. These chemicals are difficult to get hold of in paint stores. However they are available direct from suppliers by mail order (see the list of "Useful Addresses" in the back of the book).

The main chemicals used for staining are listed below:

- Ammonia (as a 10 percent solution in water to darken wood)
- Bichromate of potash
- Sulfate of iron (green copperas)
- Permanganate of potash

Working with chemical stains

Dissolve the chemical powder in water, creating a saturated solution, as with water stains. Warm water helps to dissolve the chemicals faster. About 2 teaspoons of bichromate of potash to 2½ cups of water is a standard solution for mahogany. Apply with a brush, wiping off the surplus, then leave the "stain" to work. Once the desired color has been achieved, neutralize the chemicals with denatured alcohol. Don't use bichromate of potash under a catalyzed

MEMO

OIL DYES

Tools and materials

Brush

Cloth

Stain

Cloth or paper towels for wiping off

Container

Common problems

Do not use oil dyes with spray finishes, as they can cause discoloration and poor adhesion.

Oil dyes penetrate very fast, so you may find that when you use a brush the first touches remain darker even when dry. It is therefore better to use a cloth for application whenever possible.

Drying time

About 30 to 40 minutes.

ALCOHOL STAINS

Tools and materials

Stain powders

Denatured alcohol

Cloth

Brush or spray gun

Common problems

If the alcohol stain is drying too fast, mix with a little shellac to make application easier.

Drying time

Alcohol stains take only 5 minutes to dry.

lacquer, as this can result in a fault known as pinholing, in which the surface of the wood is pitted with tiny holes.

What are pigment stains?

This range of finishes is made from finely ground pigments, suspended in a medium. The pigments do not dissolve, as dyes do.

Pigment stains give a semi-opaque color to wood. They are useful for improving low-grade wood, producing greater tone and making the piece more attractive.

Working with pigment stains

Pigment stains are available in a ready-mixed range of colors. Apply pigment stains generously with a brush or cloth. Be sure to remove surplus stain, otherwise the color may look patchy and opaque.

What are wax stains?

Wax stains are supplied in soft wax form, ready-made in various colors, and are used directly on the wood or over existing stain. Wax stains cannot be used under finishes such as polyurethane or lacquers.

Sealing inlay before staining

▼ **1** *The contrast in color between different inlays may be lost when a piece is stained. To prevent this, apply white or blonde polish to seal an inlay before staining.*

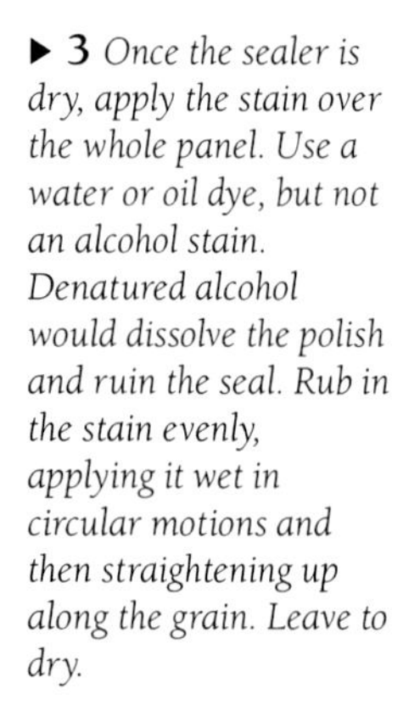

▶ **2** *On this rosewood panel with boxwood stringing, the outer inlay is to be sealed, but the thinner, inner one is not. Pick out the inlay carefully so that no part of it is missed, using a No. 6 artists' brush, and be sure to keep to the line. Leave to dry for 15 minutes.*

▶ **3** *Once the sealer is dry, apply the stain over the whole panel. Use a water or oil dye, but not an alcohol stain. Denatured alcohol would dissolve the polish and ruin the seal. Rub in the stain evenly, applying it wet in circular motions and then straightening up along the grain. Leave to dry.*

▼ **4** *After the stain has dried, the outer, sealed inlay has retained its natural pale yellow color. However, the inner string has absorbed the stain, and has turned a light brown.*

Working with wax stains

Apply wax stains with a cloth, like a wax polish, rubbing the wax into the wood. Leave the surface to dry, preferably overnight, before buffing.

What are non-grainraising stains?

Non-grainraising stains (NGR) are made from synthetic dyes dissolved in ethanol solvent mixes. The mixture can be varied to suit brushing, spraying or dipping. They do not fade, are supplied ready-mixed, and are available in regular colors.

Working with NGR stains

For hand applications, use a brush, keeping an even wet coat, then wipe off surplus. You can also spray NGR stains with a gravity-feed gun .

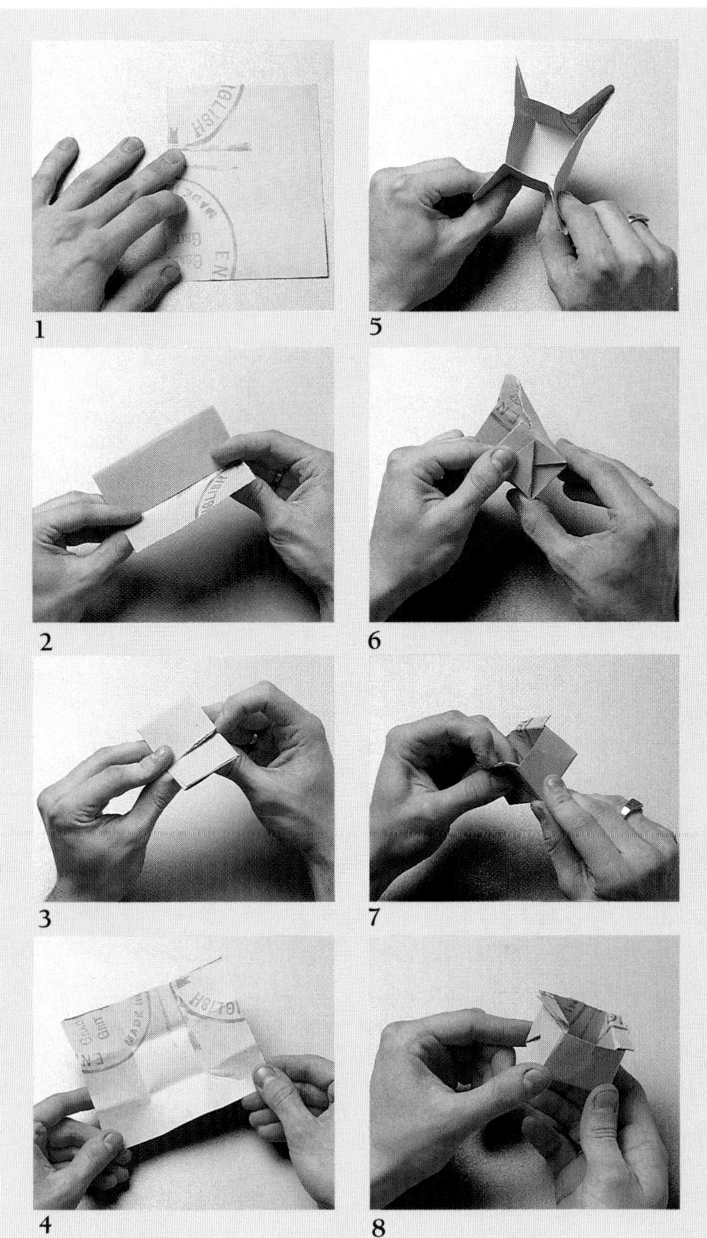

Making a paper boat
Boats are traditionally used for mixing and holding small quantities of finish. They are a useful way of using up old sandpaper, and can be disposed of after use.

1 *Take a piece of sandpaper (3 × 5 inches).*

2 *Fold in the two long ends.*

3 *Fold in the two short ends.*

4 *Open out to show folds.*

5 *Fold corners together.*

6 *Fold long ends over to hold in shape.*

7 *Fold over ends to form rim.*

8 *Both ends folded over holding the container square.*

MEMO

CHEMICAL STAINS
Tools and materials
Chemical powder

Water

Brush

Glass, plastic or earthenware container

Safety precautions
Always wear gloves and goggles.

Drying time
Allow to work until the effect is achieved.

PIGMENT STAINS
Tools and materials
Brush or cloth

Powder or ready-mixed stain

Drying time
About 1 hour.

WAX STAINS
Tools and materials
Soft cloth

Fine steel wool

Wax stain

Drying time
Leave overnight.

NGR STAINS
Tools and materials
Brush, spray gun or dipping tank

Stain

Drying time
About 20 minutes.

Bleaching wood

SEE ALSO

14-15
BRUSHES FOR FINISHING

23
THE FINISHING SHOP

44-49
STAINING WOOD

168-169
HEALTH AND SAFETY

Bleaches are used to lighten the color of wood. This may be desirable for purely aesthetic reasons, as a matter of taste, on new materials or older darkened wood; or to remove blemishes and stains; or to make darker components compatible with other parts of a piece. Bleaching may be needed to tone down the color of stripped wood, and is also used to remove ink marks and water marks (see pages 33-35).

There are many different types of bleaches, and the household variety can be used on wood; but the best approach is either to mix your own, using oxalic acid with water, or to buy a special bleach for wood (sold in a two-part pack) that generates a stronger reaction with the surface. For the latter product a neutralizer is essential, in order to halt the chemical reaction and ensure that any residue of bleach does not further harm finishes. A 50 percent solution of white vinegar in water is the traditional way to neutralize two-part bleach, with plenty of water to clean the surface.

Since bleaches are likely to react with metal (they are used to reverse the effects of iron filings on wood), always use glass, plastic or earthenware containers when working with these chemicals. They are dangerous substances, so read the manufacturer's instructions carefully and follow the safety advice given. Always keep bleaches away from children; and never store or use in food containers, in case they are mistakenly eaten or drunk.

HINTS AND TIPS

- Decant bleach into a glass, plastic or earthenware container.
- Use a synthetic-bristle brush, as normal bristles tend to fall out.
- If you want to stop the bleaching action, wash with clean water.

Using two-part bleaches

▲ **1** *Bleaching will tone down the color of this piece and remove the marks.*

▲ **2** *Apply the contents of pack A or 1 with a brush, keeping both the container and brush clearly marked to avoid confusion between this and pack B or 2. Always wear heavy protective gloves, and apply the chemical thoroughly so that the piece has an even coat.*

▶ 3 *Five minutes after coating the surface with the first application, apply the contents of pack B or 2, also with a brush, and also wearing gloves. The surface will look darker at this stage. The reaction of the two chemicals lightens the wood, and sometimes this will produce a foam. Leave the piece until the desired effect is achieved.*

MEMO

Tools and materials

Bleach

White vinegar for neutralizing two-part bleaches

Synthetic-bristle brushes

Plastic, glass or earthenware container

Water

Bucket and sponges

Common problems

Watch out for wide pieces bowing from being damped. Attach a cleat underneath as a precaution.

If scum forms on surface, remove with a scrubbing brush and water.

Bleaching veneers can cause them to shrink, so when restoring furniture bleach and neutralize the new veneer before gluing it in place.

Drying time

Oxalic acid takes 30 minutes to work.

Two-part bleaches need several hours.

Leave household bleach to dry as required (usually about half an hour at room temperature).

◀ 4 *Once the required color has been achieved, the reaction must be neutralized. Use a 50 per cent solution of vinegar and water, applied with a brush.*

▼ 5 *Rub the vinegar solution into the grain to neutralize all the bleach, otherwise the result will be patchy. Leave to dry.*

◀ 6 *The bleached item.*

USING BLEACH SAFELY

- Preferably work outside, with easy access to a hose or buckets of water.
- Wear goggles, protective gloves and overalls.
- Work with a drain or waste pipe within easy reach.
- If working inside, keep a bucket of water and a sponge handy.
- Make sure the workshop is well ventilated.
- If bleach comes into contact with skin, wash with water immediately.
- Store chemicals away from sunlight, in a cool, dark place.
- When sanding bleached surfaces, always wear a mask.
- Always pour oxalic acid crystals slowly into water – never pour water onto acid.
- Oxalic acid is a poison, and needs to be kept well out of reach of children.

Oxalic-acid bleach

Oxalic-acid crystals, available at pharmacies and some paint stores, are mixed with water to a saturated solution to produce a weak bleach. They are adequate for removing stains and marks on most woods, but not really strong enough for changing the color of large surfaces. Oxalic acid is cheap and the crystals are easy to mix, using 1lb of crystals to 5 quarts water. The water does not have to be warm, but warm water does help to dissolve oxalic acid. Always measure the water into the container (which must not be metal) first, and then pour in the crystals.

Apply evenly and wet using a synthetic-bristle brush (see pages 14-15), following the grain, then leave to dry. If the color has not lightened sufficiently, apply the bleach again and leave. Once the desired effect is achieved, wash thoroughly with plenty of clean water. The bleach will have done most of its work within half an hour. More will be needed for further change.

Oxalic acid can also be used for cleaning off dirt from old wood, especially oak, and for degreasing oily surfaces such as teak.

Two-part bleaches

These bleaches are powerful lightening agents and can change wood to a much lighter shade. They are also dangerous, so take care with both storage and use. The bleaches are supplied in two plastic bottles, normally labeled A and B or 1 and 2. The first bottle contains a solution, which may darken the wood; by adding the peroxide solution in the second bottle the bleaching action is sparked off. It is important to check which bottle is which and they must be kept separate, as mixing them causes a violent reaction and they can even explode.

Apply the contents of the first bottle (A or 1), using a brush, and leave for 5 minutes before applying the contents of the second bottle. Use equal quantities of each part, without drenching the wood. They will foam on the surface, and bleach the wood by oxidizing. Leave until dry, or until the required effect is achieved. Then the bleach must be neutralized with water and vinegar.

Household bleach

Household bleach is applied like an oxalic-acid solution, but it only has a limited effect and is most useful for removing marks. Leave it to dry and then wash down with water.

BLEACHING GUIDE

EASY TO BLEACH	TWO APPLICATIONS NECESSARY	HARD TO BLEACH
Ash	Mahogany	Cherry
Elm	Oak	Rosewood
Beech	Walnut	Satinwood
Sycamore	Western red cedar	Padauk
Birch	Eucalyptus	Ebony
Pear	Chestnut	Wenge
Apple	Yew	Black walnut
Hemlock	Douglas fir	Jacaranda

Grain fillers

SEE ALSO

20-22
ABRASIVES

44-49
STAINING WOOD

Some woods, such as oak, have an open grain structure that makes the perfectly smooth finish characteristic of French polishing hard to achieve. With these woods, the open pores need to be filled with a fine powder applied as a paste or liquid. This choking of the grain also makes polishing quicker, as the grain does not have to be filled with polish – which is the alternative time-consuming solution.

Originally grain fillers were made of plaster of Paris mixed with water and a pigment, but these plaster fillers tended to turn white and show up in the grain. Modern grain fillers are therefore made from a mixture of filling powder, binder, pigment and solvent. There are many variations on this theme, each recommended for specific tasks, the distinguishing feature being the type of binder used.

Fillers are sold in quarts and gallons and in a variety of colors. A selection of mahogany, walnut and light oak is sufficient to start with. Oil dyes or pigment colors can be mixed with neutral filler to make any color you want.

Use burlap or a coarse cloth to apply grain fillers, rubbing them into the grain in a circular motion. Don't work the filler in the direction of the grain, or the filler may not hold in the pores. Wipe off excess filler across the grain with a piece of burlap. If a mineral-spirits-based filler has been used, then wipe off across the grain with a piece of rag dampened with mineral spirits to remove any filler sitting on the surface. Leave other fillers to dry, then lightly rub with fine sandpaper to remove any small particles of filler that may remain on the surface.

WHICH FILLER TO USE

Oil-bound fillers
Oil-bound fillers are often called paste wood fillers. They are not recommended for use with nitrocellulose finishes, but can be applied before a polyurethane or shellac polish. They are easy to use and are supplied ready-mixed.

Plaster of Paris
Although it is a traditional filler, plaster of Paris has a tendency to go white with age. However, it remains a useful means of flattening rough surfaces (such as particle board) before applying special paint effects that hide the grain. Wipe plaster of Paris dry with linseed oil. This makes the filler transparent.

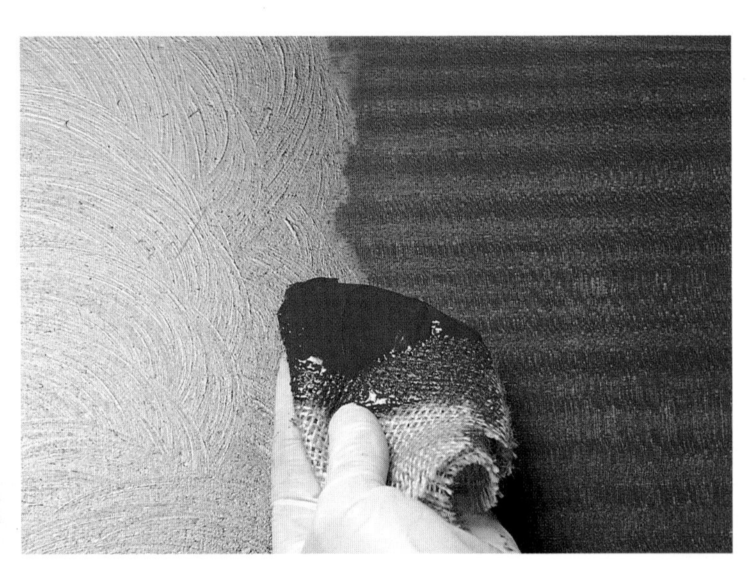

Applying grain filler
▲ 1 *Grain fillers are supplied in quart or gallon cans, in a range of colors. This one is medium mahogany. They are used to fill the open pores in the grain to produce a mirror finish and to save later coats of polish. They often settle in storage, and will need stirring to a thick consistency before use.*

▲ 3 *Use burlap to apply the thick grain filler. Take a piece of burlap, bunch it up in your hand, and dip it into the filler. The burlap must be wet with filler. The swab must be well filled with filler.*

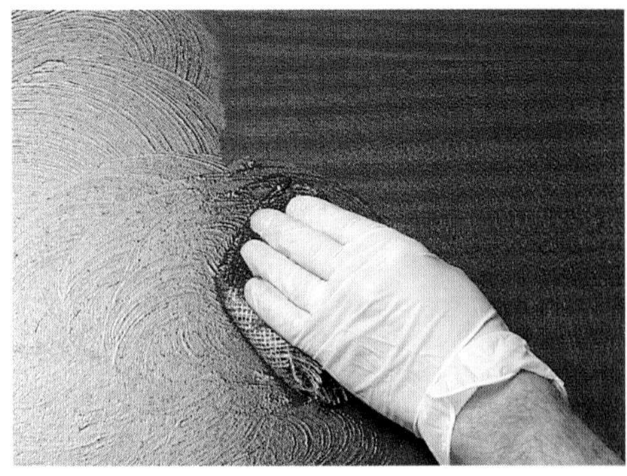

▲ 4 *Rub the burlap over the surface using a circular motion, keeping it wet at all times and sliding across the surface, to push the filler gently into the pores. Apply more grain filler as required and keep rubbing until the whole surface has been covered.*

▲ 2 *Prepare the surface to be filled by sanding, and staining if required. Make sure the surface is clean of dust and dirt so that the grain filler clings effectively to the timber.*

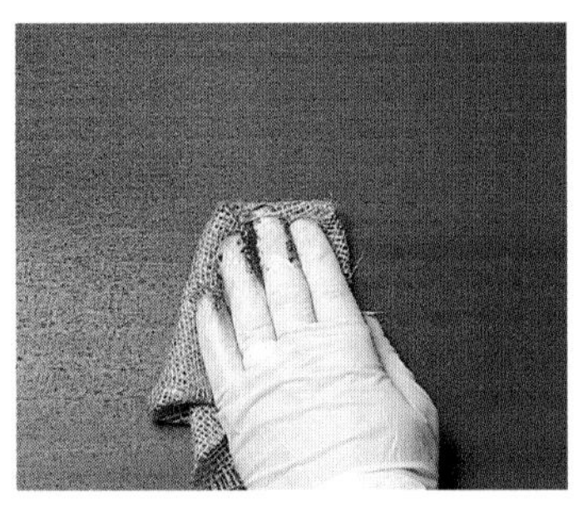

▲ 5 *Wipe off surplus filler with a clean piece of burlap, working across the grain. (For fillers that can be thinned with mineral spirits, wipe off across the grain with a rag damped with mineral spirits.)*

▲ 6 *Once filled, the surface loses some of its grain pattern. This surface will have to be very lightly sanded to remove surplus filler.*

Mixing plaster of Paris filler

▶ **1** *Plaster of Paris is a traditional grain filler which can be mixed with pigments. It is good for deep pores but it does tend to turn white with time. Traditionally, the surface was rubbed with linseed oil to "kill" the whiteness. However, plaster of Paris can cause problems if used under lacquer.*

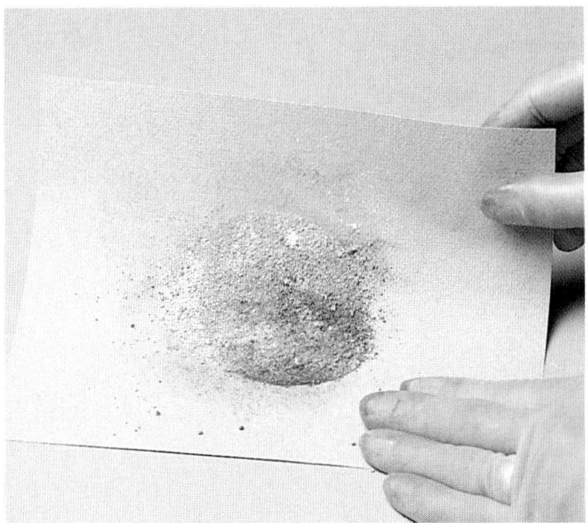

◀ **2** *Mix the pigments and plaster of Paris on a piece of thick paper or cardboard. The color of the mixed plaster and pigments is roughly the same as it will be once dry in the pores of the wood.*

► **3 (inset)** *Dip a clean piece of burlap into a shallow container of water and then mix with the plaster to create a creamy mixture that is ready to apply.*

▲ **4** *Apply with circular motions, and then along the grain. The filler will dry quickly.*

HINTS AND TIPS

- Do not overthin fillers.
- Test filler on a piece of scrap wood.
- Always wipe off filler across the grain.
- Fillers dry light, so always start with a color darker than the workpiece.
- Fill after staining, and seal with a thin coat of shellac sanding sealer.
- Mineral-spirits-based fillers can be mixed with oil dye.

MEMO

Tools and materials

Burlap or coarse cloth

Grain filler

Soft cloth

Mineral spirits

Sandpaper

Common problems

Fillers can turn white if not allowed to dry thoroughly.

Clarity of finish can be lost with the use of fillers.

Fillers not wiped off completely can result in a patchy finish.

Wood stain may be partly removed when sanding back surplus filler if the stain is applied before filling.

Appropriate surfaces

Grain fillers are popular for open-grained woods, such as oak and ash. They can also be used on close-grained woods, such as mahogany and walnut.

Drying time

Plaster of Paris dries in about 15 minutes.

Oil-bound fillers take up to 24 hours to dry.

Allow 1 to 1½ hours for other fillers to dry.

3

Basic finishing techniques

Most woodworkers are introduced to finishing by the varnishing of their own projects. Varnish can be the perfect finish for specific tasks, but there are times when French polishing, oiling and waxing are more suitable – and they are surprisingly easy to accomplish

French polishing

SEE ALSO

12-13
BASIC TOOLS AND EQUIPMENT

23
THE FINISHING SHOP

40-43
HOW TO USE WOOD FILLERS

44-49
STAINING WOOD

53-55
GRAIN FILLERS

66-69
WORKING WITH COLORS

73-75
WAXED FINISHES

The simple principle of French polishing is to build up a lustrous finish with thin coats of transparent or colored polish. The joy of this finish is that it is worked into the surface, rather than laid on top like a paint, varnish or sprayed lacquer.

Few tools are needed, and the small stock of materials can be bought either ready-mixed or in a raw state for home mixing. Start by buying ready-mixed shellac – then, as confidence grows, you can try mixing your own to suit the needs of particular jobs. As a general description the term French polishing is now something of a misnomer, as French polish is only one of the many shellac-based products sold by finishing suppliers. However, "French polisher" remains the time-honored title of the skilled craftsman who undertakes this style of finishing.

French polish in its many guises is perhaps most highly regarded on mahogany, as the close grain of the wood is admirably suited to the finish and its attractive figure is enhanced by the "depth" of the polish. Woods such as walnut, rosewood, sycamore and stained pine are equally suitable. Oak is less so, and is given a wax finish more often than not.

Practice

The essential components of a polishing kit (shellac, denatured alcohol and linseed oil, with a "polishing pad" for application) have hardly changed over hundreds of years, though the original formula for French polish died with its Parisian inventors in the eighteenth century.

When applying French polish, the

(Continued on page 62.)

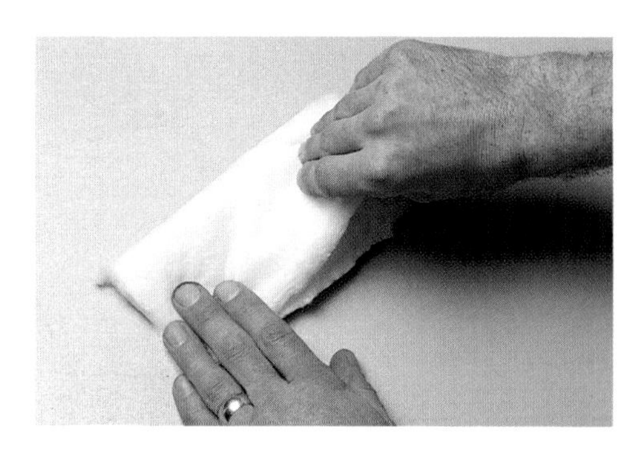

Making a French polishing pad
▲ **1** *The polishing pad is used to apply French polish. Start by folding a 6-inch-square piece of batting in half. (Cotton can be used but the result will not be as good.)*

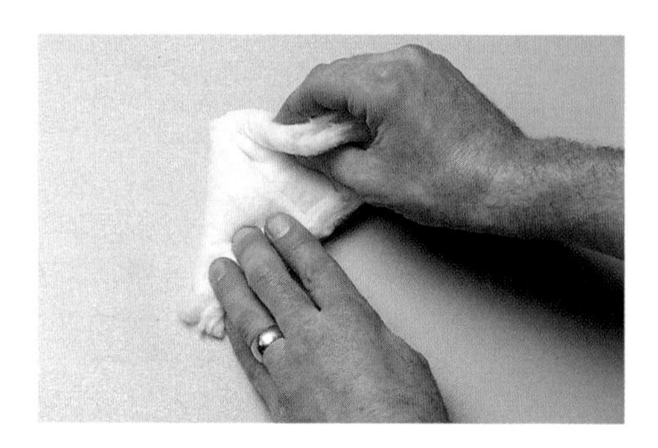

▲ **2** *Fold over the ends of the batting to make a point. At this stage it will look a little like a pointed hat.*

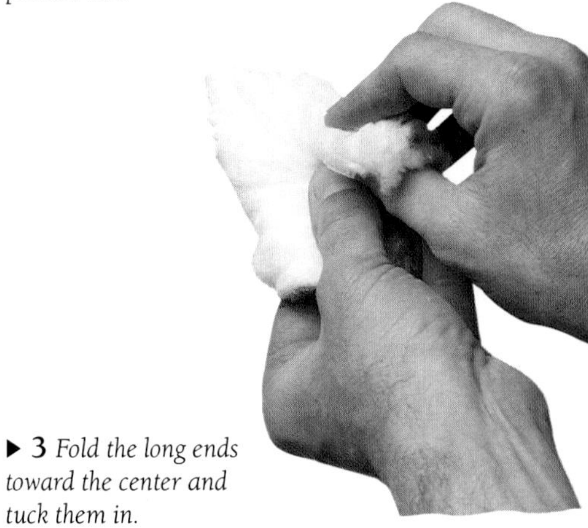

▶ **3** *Fold the long ends toward the center and tuck them in.*

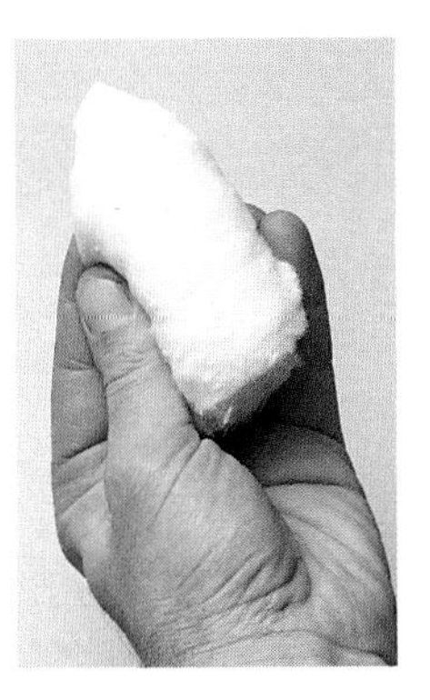

◀ 4 *Work the batting into a pear shape. It is important the sole is flat when held between the fingers. The idea is to produce a firm core to the polishing pad.*

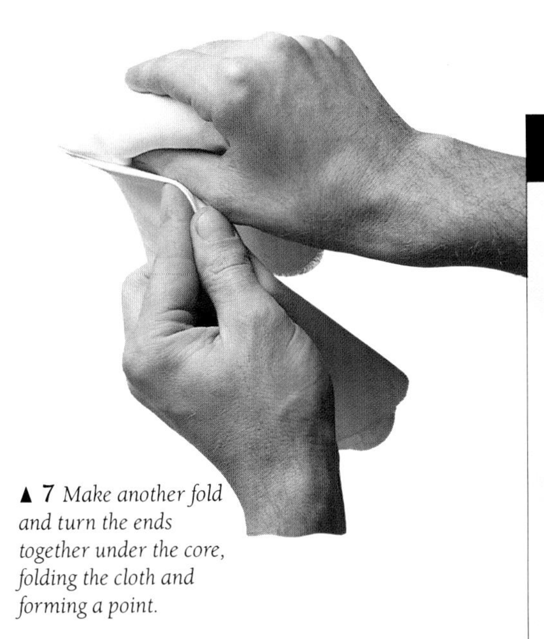

▲ 7 *Make another fold and turn the ends together under the core, folding the cloth and forming a point.*

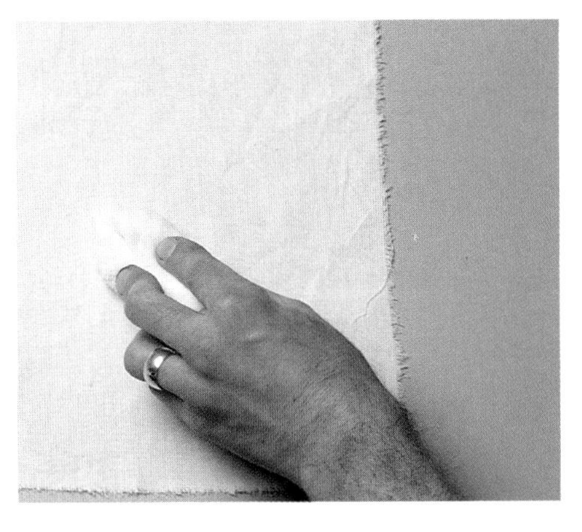

▲ 5 *Place the batting core diagonally on the corner of a piece of 9-inch-square white cotton cloth with the sole of the batting facing downward. The cloth must not be starched or colored.*

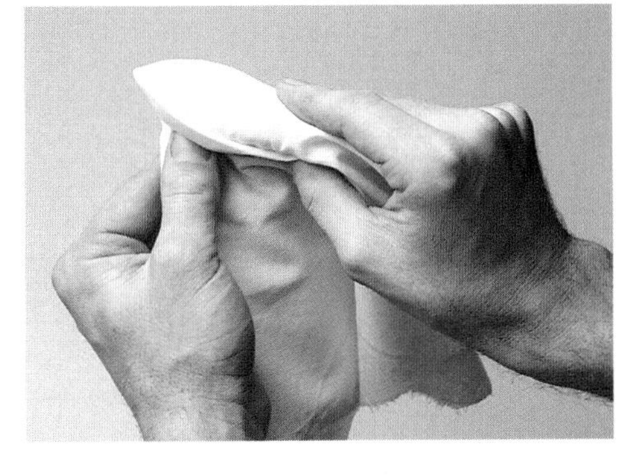

▲ 8 *Pull the excess cloth across and start to twist together to tighten.*

▼ 9 *Make a final twist, bringing all the loose ends together, and leaving nothing hanging.*

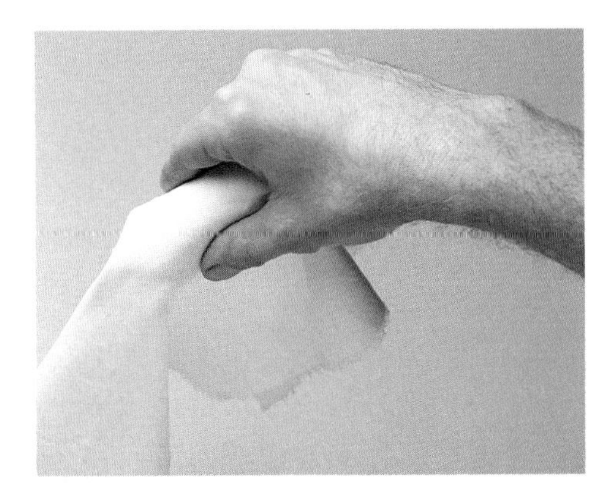

▲ 6 *Turn the cloth over and hold the core between index finger and thumb to let the folds of the cotton cloth drop down to the sides. Make a fold to form the point.*

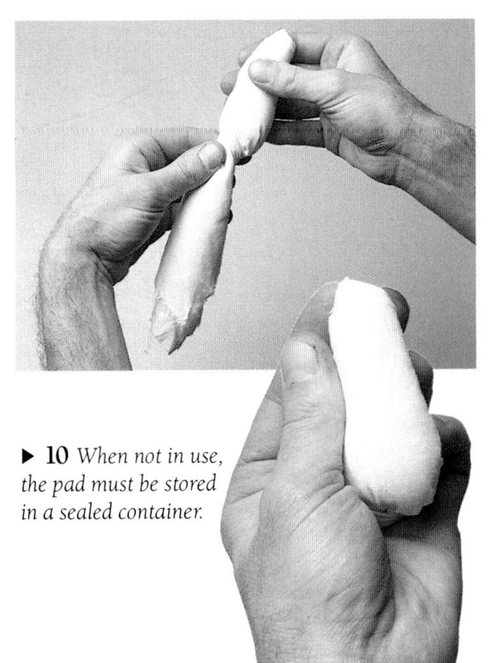

▶ 10 *When not in use, the pad must be stored in a sealed container.*

MEMO

Tools and materials

Polish to suit

White cotton cloth

Wadding or cotton

Linseed oil

Fine silicon-carbide paper

Denatured alcohol

Airtight container

Common problems

Uneven pressure while bodying up can create ridges.

Concentrating only on the center of the piece will create a sheen there – but not in the corners and along the edges.

A cold or humid environment can cause "chilling" in the finish, similar to the white rings produced by hot water or alcohol.

Appropriate surfaces

French polishing can be used on most timbers.

Drying time

The first coat of polish dries in an hour. Keep building up until the surface is too sticky to continue (because it has started to dry) – then leave overnight before embarking on the next building up session. It is also best to leave the results of the second building up to dry overnight, as it tends to sink.

WHAT IS SHELLAC?

- It is likely to remain a mystery how anyone discovered that the excretion of the female *Lacifo lacea* beetle is an ideal substance for polishing furniture. In fact, shellac has been used for finishing for thousands of years. Traces of it have been found in Egyptian tombs and on artifacts from ancient China and Rome. Nowadays it is an ingredient of hair spray, paints and sealers, and it is even employed as a coating for electrical components.
- The history of French polishing is sketchy, but it is known that the process was first practiced by the brothers Etienne and Simon Martin in Paris around 1730. They combined shellac with alcohol, in an attempt to emulate the Japan lacquer finish that was popular on imported furniture.
- Today, although alcohol has been replaced by denatured alcohol, shellac is still produced by traditional techniques. It is sold in a variety of forms, ranging from raw flake to bleached polish, and there is even a version resistant to hot water.
- Flake shellac is the most common raw product, and is ready for dissolving in denatured alcohol. The proportion of shellac to alcohol is known as the "cut." When 2lb of shellac is mixed with 5 quarts of denatured alcohol, the polish is referred to as a 2lb cut. This terminology continues today, even though the polish is sold by the quart and gallon. Most finishers buy 4lb or 3lb cut polish and then thin it to their own requirements. Start by using this with some white polish and some garnet polish.

Sealing the surface

▶ **1** *Sealing the surface with an initial coat of shellac is known as sealing. Use a piece of batting that has previously been used in a pad (a new piece will leave fluff on the surface). Load it with polish from an unbreakable container of polish, with a small hole or slot in the lid to let the finish out slowly. Add about 2 teaspoons of polish into the batting.*

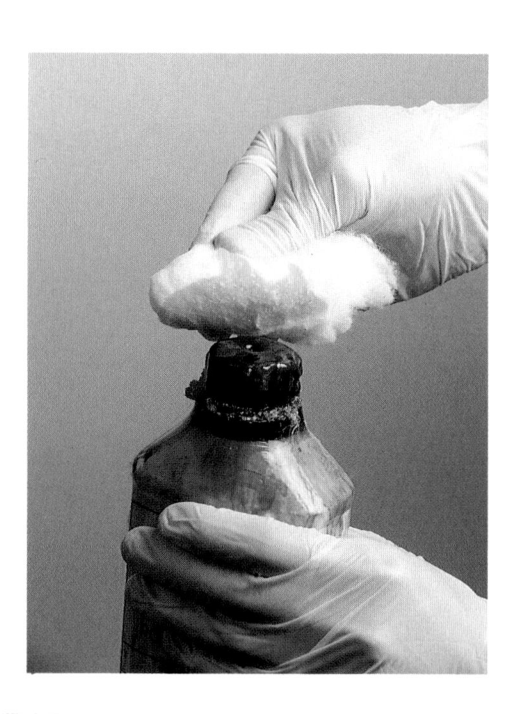

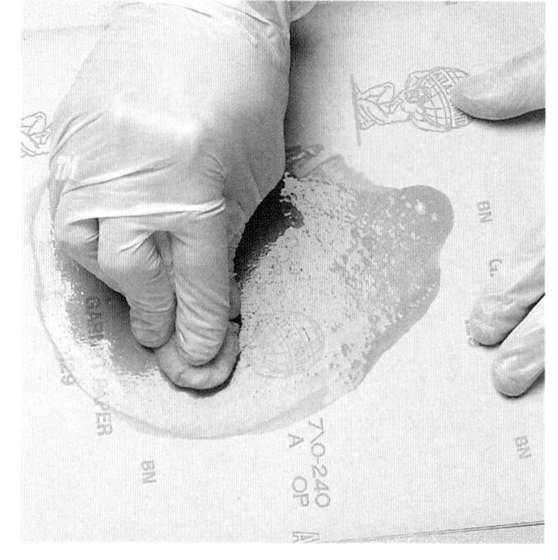

◀ **2** *Squeeze the batting to remove any excess polish. The batting must feel damp, but not soaking wet. Squeeze the polish onto a clean piece of paper, making sure no dirt or dust is picked up by the batting. The workbench is not a good surface for this operation.*

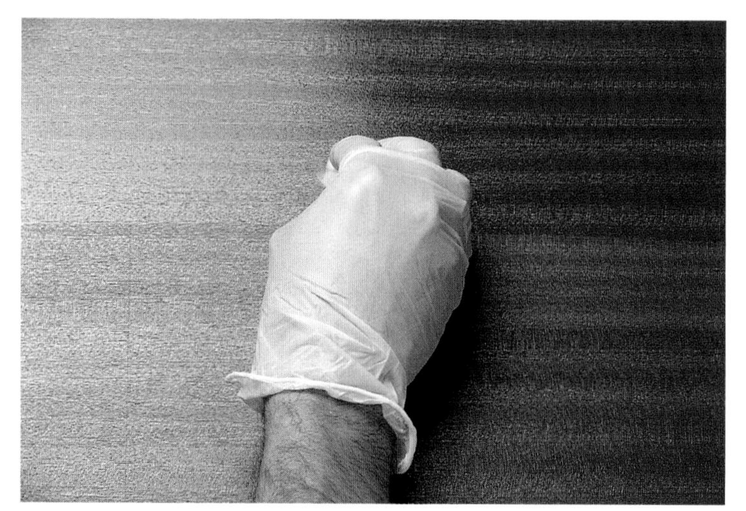

◀ **3** *Wipe the batting across the surface following the grain. Use no pressure at all to start with, for two or three passes. Continue to apply the polish in tight circles, and as the batting dries out increase the pressure, reloading when it dries out completely. Continue to work the surface until it becomes too sticky. Leave to dry.*

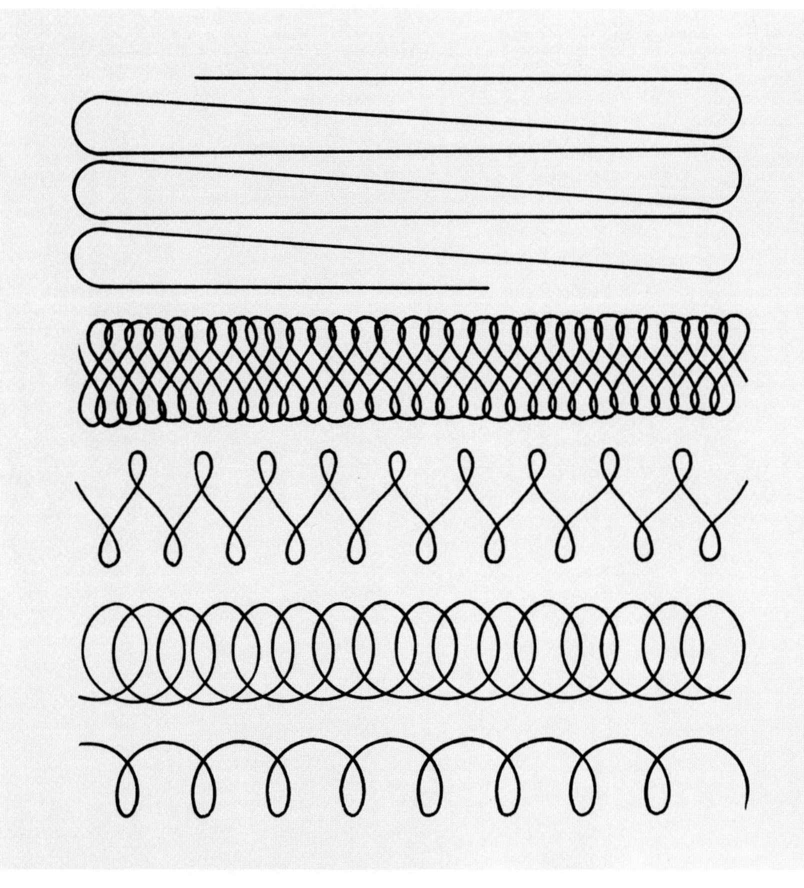

Motions for applying polish with a pad

Straight strokes must follow the grain.

Interlocking figure-eight for building up.

Wide figure-eight motions.

Interlocking circles to produce an even coat.

Wide circles for initially spreading the polish.

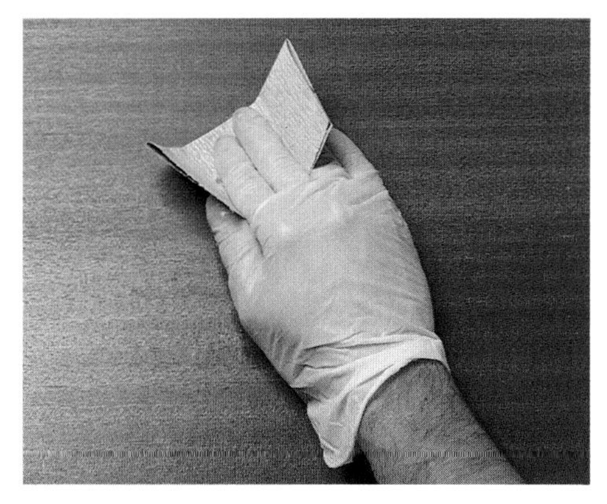

▲ **4** *When the shellac coat has dried, the surface will feel rough. Lightly sand (a process known as denibbing) using fine 320 silicon-carbide self-lubricating sandpaper. Press down flat. Make sure that all the surface is sanded, working gently across the grain and in circular motions. Always keep the paper flat on the surface.*

French-polished oak table

▲ *This round dining table has been French-polished to give a subtle, natural-looking finish.*

aim is to avoid creating marks – so the polishing pad is designed to work the mixture of shellac and denatured alcohol evenly across the surface, lubricated by linseed oil. Try at all times to use a flowing action, keeping the pad continually on the move.

To achieve the smoothness of a grand piano (the ultimate aspiration of French polishers, though pianos are now often sprayed), the preparation has to be faultless. If you want a full grain effect, fill the open pores with grain filler (see pages 53-55) and then sand through the grits (see pages 18-22), making sure that the grain has been raised and that you sand it flat.

French polish is particularly sensitive to water and alcohol – as any dining table will testify – so check there is no moisture on the surface, or you will find that it shows up later. If necessary, heat out any dampness with an iron over sheets of brown paper. When staining the piece, remember that the denatured alcohol in the polish is likely to soften alcohol stains and affect the color.

Building up

Once a sealing coat has been applied and the surface has been lightly sanded (to remove dust nibs) and dusted, you can start applying the polish to build up the finish. Start with straight strokes following the grain, then across the grain. Maintain a slight pressure. The pressure is like that needed to plaster walls or spread butter on toast. Having covered the surface two or three times, continue with circular movements, which help to smooth out the polish. Try to maintain even pressure throughout each circle; there is a tendency to press harder as your hand moves toward your body on the inward stroke. Use 5- to 6-inch circles, making sure the pad covers the circle. Larger pieces, such as table tops, need larger polishing pads; the opposite is true of smaller items.

Maintain the flow of polish with increased pressure whenever the pad seems to stick or drag. The surface is likely to soak up polish fast at this stage, so you will have to add polish to the pad frequently as the flow dries up. Continue to work the polish in with a combination of circular and figure-eight movements, keeping the pad constantly on the move.

Try to keep the pad away from soft areas of polish. Test to see if the finish is tacky – and if it is, leave it to harden for a few minutes.

When the finish develops an overall sheen, finish off with straight strokes, following the grain, and leave to dry.

Color matching

Any discrepancies in the color will show up once the polish has dried. Wooden pins in chair joints may be too light, and there may be shading around joints in veneer. Stand back and take a good look at the piece to get an overview of the finish. Color

ADDING POLISH TO THE PAD

- The polish must soak through the core, but must not then drip through the outer cloth. You need to be able to produce a small trickle by cupping the pad in your hand (with your forefinger running along the point) and gently squeezing.
- If you do accidentally get too much polish in the pad, squeeze out the excess until the steady flow stops, then wipe on a piece of clean scrap to dry off the surface.
- Use a bottle of polish for adding polish to the pad. For better control of the flow, punch holes or cut a slit in the lid of the bottle.
- Store the pad in an airtight jar after use (never store in a metal container). You do not want to throw away a polishing pad, as they take time to break in and a new one is not as easy to use. However, you will have no option but to throw away the pad if it becomes hard.

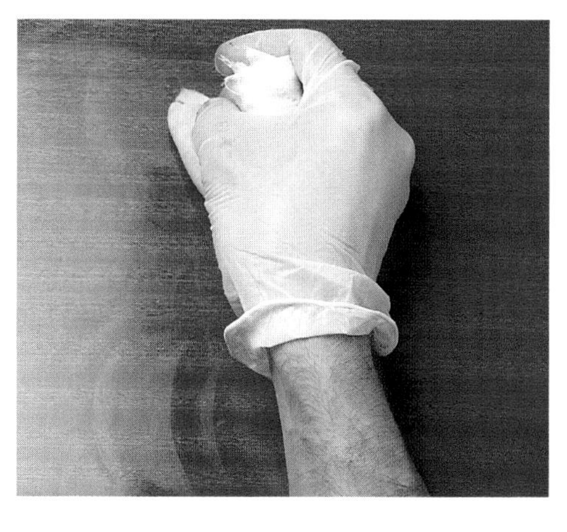

Building up

▲ 1 *Once the surface has been sealed and lightly sanded it is time to start applying polish using a polishing pad; this is known as building up. First, load the pad with polish by opening up the outer layer of cloth and pouring polish into the core until it is saturated. Squeeze out the excess by pressing on to paper or a spare piece of wood.*

▲ 2 *Build up the polish with straight strokes along the grain, making 4 or 5 passes. Then move the pad in circles. Increase the pressure as the pad dries out, and then load again. Use figure-eight patterns as well as circles.*

▶ 3 *After working the surface with 4 or 5 applications it will become sticky, and the pad will need to be lubricated with linseed oil. Dip your finger in the oil, and rub it onto the sole. Do not use too much oil. Continue working the pad in circular motions.*

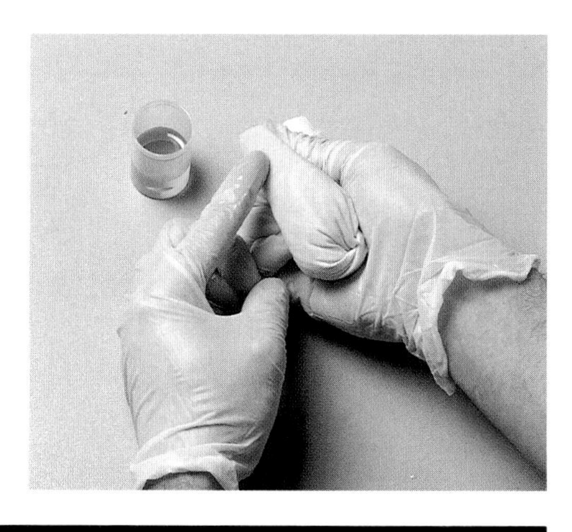

▼ 4 *The building up will have built up a finish by now, but continue to work the pad around the piece, in circles, figure-eight movements and straight up and down. Load the pad when it dries out, doing so little but often.*

WHICH POLISH IS WHICH?

The technique is called French polishing but the polishes used have different names and different applications.

French polish
French polish is orange and is used mainly on mahogany.

Button polish
A golden brown color.

Garnet polish
This is dark brown, and is recommended for renovation of old surfaces.

White polish
White polish is made from shellac that has been bleached and is milky white. It is used for light woods, such as sycamore and ash.

Super blonde polish
Super blonde polish is made from shellac that has been bleached and dewaxed.

HINTS AND TIPS

- Always keep plenty of polish on the pad – but never too much.
- Use linseed oil sparingly – little and often is best.
- Try to maintain an even pressure when using the pad.
- Work in a dust-free environment.
- To clear excess polish from a pad, simply press it down onto a clean surface.
- Keep your fingernails short, as they can scratch the surface and collect dirt, which then falls on the piece during polishing.
- Try to keep the workshop at about 65°F for polishing.

irregularities will need to be touched up and disguised. Look carefully at the surface to judge which colors are visible, or lacking, in the wood.

Use alcohol stains for matching colors, and mix them in with the polish. Go easy with these stains, as the colors are strong and are only required in a much diluted form to produce a tint (see pages 44-49 and 66-69). Remember it is easier to make a surface darker than lighter, so mix colors gradually. Apply the color with a cloth or brush.

Defects such as knots, glue marks and wood filler must be touched up and hidden, using pigments (see pages 66-69). Take care that the pigment does not show up as a blob of solid color, and if necessary use an artists' brush to add flecks of color to imitate the grain.

Wax crayon

Bruises and dents can be dealt with at this stage. Fill the indentations with wax crayon, using a small knife to press the wax in. Smooth off with the back of a piece of sandpaper. Wax crayons are available in wood tones at paint and hardware stores.

Finishing off

You are now ready to finish off the surface, using the pad, which should be ready for use in its airtight container. Apply polish, and start working on the surface. If the pad starts to drag, put a touch of boiled linseed oil on the sole for lubrication. This will leave a smear on the surface. As an even coat of polish appears, start working the pad "dry," adding only denatured alcohol, to level the surface.

Finally, add polish to the pad and, using straight strokes, work along the grain from end to end. Leave to dry once a gloss finish has been achieved.

Matching colors for touching up

◀ **1** *The scratch on this piece has removed the color and revealed the raw wood. The damage can be touched up, using alcohol colors.*

◀ **2** *Mix the alcohol colors together by adding a small amount of stain to a 50:50 solution of French polish and denatured alcohol. Use a No. 6 artists' brush. Compare the color against the workpiece by dabbing it onto a scrap of wood or a piece of cardboard.*

◀ **3** *Use the tip of the brush only to touch up the scratch, and keep your hand as steady as possible. Build up the repair gradually, with only a small amount of color at a time, until it matches the surrounding area. Try to imitate the grain pattern as you brush.*

◀ **4** *Do not touch up in one application, but build up gradually. Once the scratch has been repaired it must be polished to match the rest of the surface.*

Removing the oil

For a really high-gloss finish, add only denatured alcohol to the pad and work over the surface with circular and straight movements. The polishing pad must feel cold to the touch, and not moist. The alcohol will take off the last of the remaining oil and give the surface a high-gloss finish.

Dulling

A satin or flat finish is popular, as it provides a more natural-looking finish. Instead of polishing with a pad and denatured alcohol, dull the piece, when dry, with pumice powder or fine steel wool and wax. The pumice powder can be applied straight onto the surface and worked with a shoe brush. Follow the grain, using a mop or brush for dulling moldings and corners.

When dulling with steel wool and wax (see pages 73-75), do not use too much wax. Once the surface is dry, wipe off the excess with a clean soft cloth to produce a satin finish. The steel wool needs to be fine – either 000 or 0000. However, test the steel wool on a practice piece before dulling, to find out which is suitable. Sometimes 0000 steel wool is so fine that it actually glosses the surface.

Before and after dulling
▲ *Dulling with pumice powder reduces a high gloss to a more natural satin finish. This finish is useful for restoration, and can be lightly waxed. There are many grades of pumice. It is essential that a very fine grade is used. 3 F would be satisfactory.*

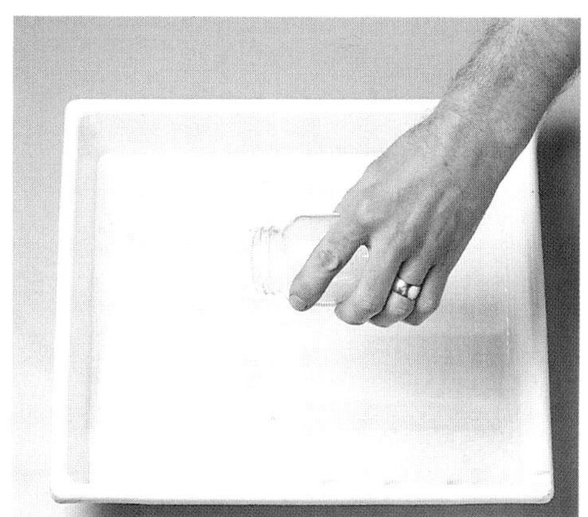

Dulling with pumice powder
▲ **1** *Pour the pumice powder into a shallow tray. Pour carefully, making sure the powder does not spill around the work.*

▲ **2** *Use a shoe brush to apply the powder. This is a specialized short-hair brush. Dip the brush into the powder, taking up only a small amount at a time. Do not use too much – it makes no difference to the finish and will only have to be cleared up to avoid contaminating other finishes.*

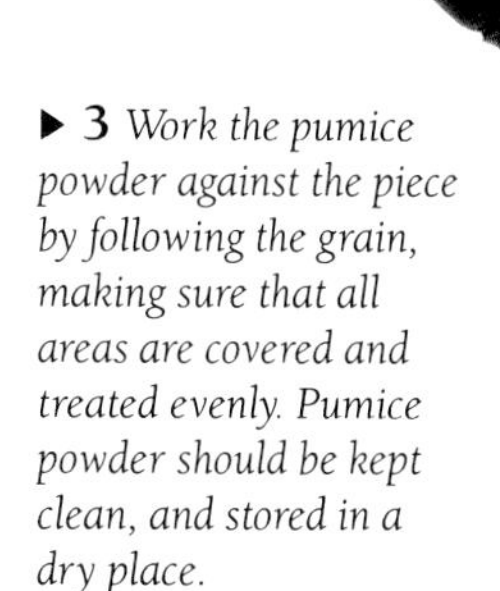

▶ **3** *Work the pumice powder against the piece by following the grain, making sure that all areas are covered and treated evenly. Pumice powder should be kept clean, and stored in a dry place.*

Working with colors

SEE ALSO

44-49
STAINING WOOD

53-55
GRAIN FILLERS

58-65
FRENCH POLISHING

76-79
VARNISHING

86-89
STIPPLING

90-93
GRAINING

94-97
MARBLED EFFECTS

98-101
RAG ROLLING

102-105
EBONIZING

106-111
STENCILING

124-149
SPRAY FINISHES

Wood can be colored with either pigments or dyes. The difference between the two is that dyes are dissolved in a solvent and penetrate into the grain of the wood, whereas pigments are used in suspension and lie on top of the grain. This is why pigments fall to the bottom of a can, having been mixed with a liquid. They are used for disguising or hiding a defect or knot, or for touching up a polished surface. Dyes are the coloring agents of stains and can be dissolved in alcohol (in the case of aniline dyes) or other solvents, such as water or oil.

Dyes and stains

Dyes become part of the wood and are used for matching woods. Their translucence allows the grain to show through. The idea is to use colors to bring out the color inherent in the wood. This might mean adding warmth with a red dye, or even cutting back red hues by using green. The whole piece may need coloring, or just small parts, especially during restoration or when components do not match within a new piece. It is quite common for the legs or rails of a table to have been milled from a different batch of lumber from that of the top. As a result the colors may vary slightly, but this can be rectified using dyes.

Study the wood to determine what colors are needed to match it exactly. The best way to learn is by trial and error, so always test color on a variety of surfaces to see what effect it has. With practice you will understand better the consequences of color, and should be able to judge the match by testing colors on scraps of wood.

Mixing colors for matching
▲ **1** *To camouflage new or restored sections of a piece with matched colors, mix alcohol stains with French polish and denatured alcohol to produce a translucent color that does not mask the grain. A traditional paper "boat" is being used to mix the colors but any non-food container can be used.*

▲ **2** *Mix a shade by adding a small quantity of color at a time. Use a No. 6 artists' brush to mix the colors with a 50:50 combination of denatured alcohol and French polish. Make sure the color is thoroughly blended into the polish and denatured alcohol.*

Do not try to obtain a perfect match in one step, but gradually blend the color in with a progression of dyes. Try to copy the subtle differences in color and shade of the grain pattern, and apply the color with brushes for small areas, and cloth for larger ones. Look for distinctive color or what is known as "natural flash." This refers to the fact that the color is seen from varying angles because of the honeycomb structure of the wood. Wenge has little natural flash, and has a flat constant color. If possible, color a piece with it standing at the appropriate level. For example, stand a chair on the floor and place a clock at chest height.

Most woods are shades of brown, ranging from the beige of light oak to the black color of ebony, with countless shades in between. Many woods can be matched using Bismarck brown (which is a reddish color) and black, with green, blue and yellow for adjustment. Remember that black and red make brown. Look for the colors in the wood.

▲**2** *Mask the mirror glass with paper, stuck down with a few small tabs of double-sided cellophane tape. Use a cloth to apply the color. Dip the cloth into the container of color, taking up only a little of the liquid. Do not try to use too much color at a time.*

MEMO

♦

Tools and materials
Brushes and cloth

Pigments and dyes

Polish

Denatured alcohol

Common problems
The most likely mistake is to make the color too dark. Work slowly and gradually. Do not try to achieve a perfect color match in one step.

Colour matching

▶ **1** *The frame of this mirror unit is slightly lighter in color than the rest of the unit. It needs to be color matched before the piece can be finished.*

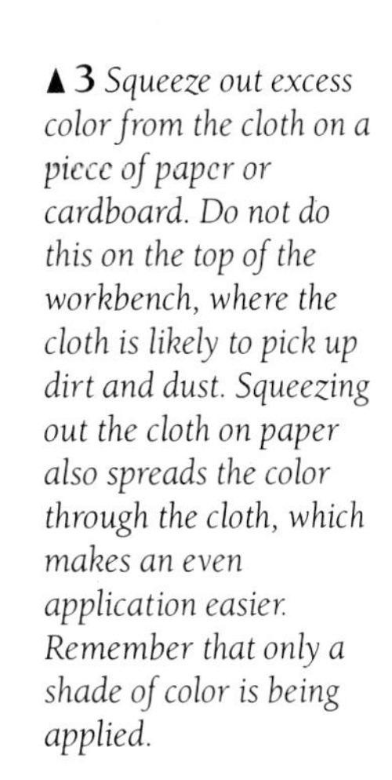

▲**3** *Squeeze out excess color from the cloth on a piece of paper or cardboard. Do not do this on the top of the workbench, where the cloth is likely to pick up dirt and dust. Squeezing out the cloth on paper also spreads the color through the cloth, which makes an even application easier. Remember that only a shade of color is being applied.*

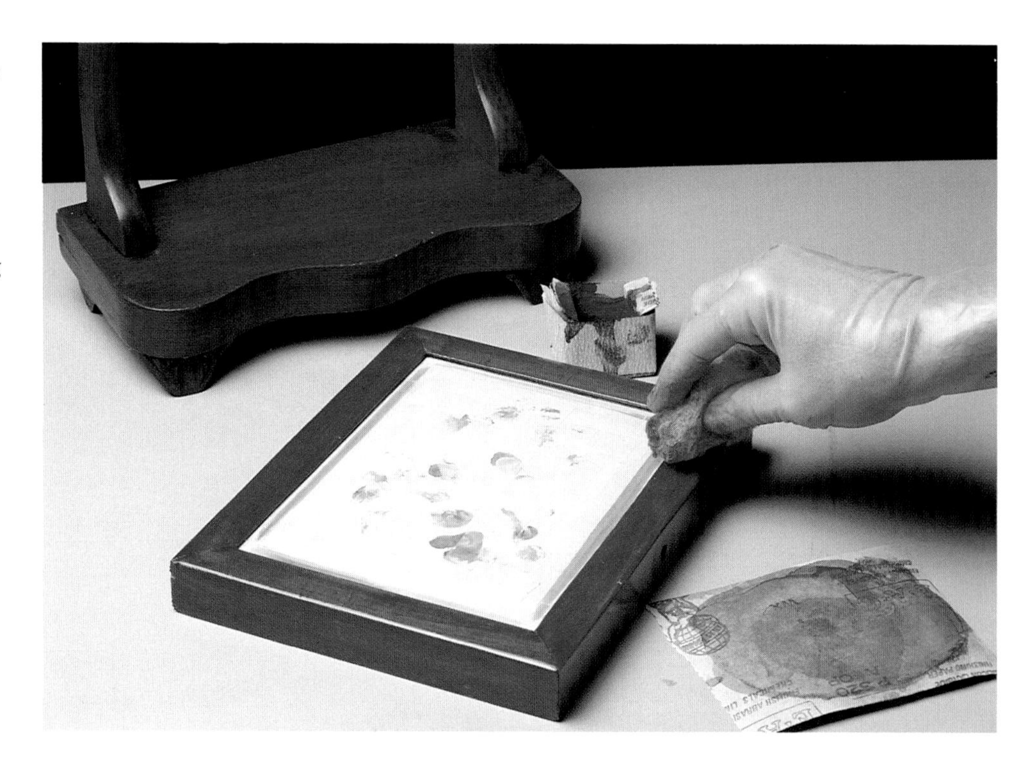

▶ **4** *Wipe the color onto the surface using straight strokes. Follow the grain and keep an even pressure. Do not start applying a second stroke of color until the first has dried. Applying more color to wet color is likely to produce a patchy finish. Build up the colour gradually until the required shade is achieved.*

▶ **5** *When the color work is done, the frame should match the rest of the piece. The color must be constant. This technique can also be used for matching new veneer that has been put in as a repair.*

HINTS AND TIPS

- Color piece with it standing at the appropriate height, for example stand a chair on the floor and place a clock at chest height.
- Mix pigments on a piece of paper for quick coloring.
- Use dyes to obtain the right color match.
- Use pigments to disguise defects.
- Mix colors gradually.
- Work in natural light.
- Study color of wood and grain pattern.

Pigments

Pigments have to be mixed together before being applied, in order to produce the correct color. Unlike dyes, they are not translucent, so one layer has little influence upon the next. They have colorful names, but a finisher only really needs about eight different pigments, which can be mixed with denatured alcohol and/or French polish to create the desired result. When using pigments in conjunction with polish, add the colored polish to the polishing pad, or use a brush. Pigments are strong and only need to be mixed in very small quantities.

Use an artists' brush to apply pigments on defects. It is important to keep a steady hand. Signwriters use a stick with a pad to rest the hand on, but an extended finger against the surface will often do.

MIXING COLORS

- Yellow ocher and white make light oak.
- Yellow ocher, titanium white and Bismarck brown make mahogany.
- Brown umber and black make dark oak.
- Brown umber and yellow ocher make brown oak.
- Brown umber, white and yellow ocher make walnut.
- Orange chrome and yellow chrome color out black marks.

Oil colors

◀ *Howard Raybould has used contrasting oil colors on this column. He applies artists' oils with a brush and then rubs the color into the grain with a soft cloth or his fingers.*

Using masks

▲ *Howard Raybould colored the top and legs of this occasional table with oils, and sprayed the side pieces, masking out specific areas with odd pieces of plywood.*

Oil finishes

SEE ALSO

18-19 POWERED SANDERS

20-21 ABRASIVES

44-49 STAINING WOOD

73-75 WAXED FINISHES

Oiling is one of the oldest treatments for preserving and finishing wood. Originally linseed oil was used, which is derived from flax and dries by oxidation. Today, oil finishes are becoming increasingly popular, as they can be restored and maintained easily – and, unlike varnishes and sprayed finishes, do not conceal the wood's tactile qualities.

It is true that oils do not have the resistance of more modern finishes, and oiled surfaces are likely to become marked. However, they are not as vulnerable as French-polished surfaces.

Teak and Danish oils dry faster than linseed, and they represent the easiest method of finishing wood.

If you want to stain the wood, do so before oiling. Use a water stain or NGR (see pages 44-49) – avoid oil dyes, as they react with the finish, resulting in patchy coloring.

Linseed oil

A linseed-oil finish is simple to produce. However, it takes time to dry and new wood will need a number of coats, especially if it is porous. During

Oiling

▼ **1** *Oil finishes can be used on most woods, to bring out the natural qualities of the wood. Apply the oil – be it linseed, tung or Danish – with a soft cloth. Load the cloth with enough oil to apply a wet, even coat to the surface.*

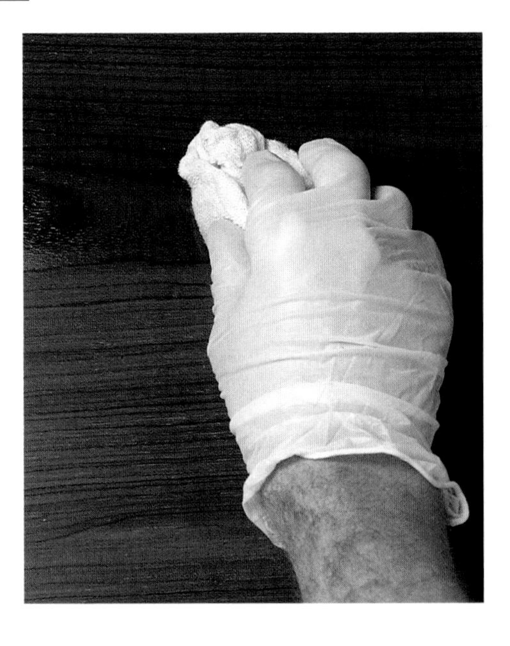

▲ **2** *Rub the oil evenly into the whole surface. It is important to check that the grain is completely wetted, otherwise the finish will turn out patchy. Use circular strokes at first, then straighten up and follow the grain to finish.*

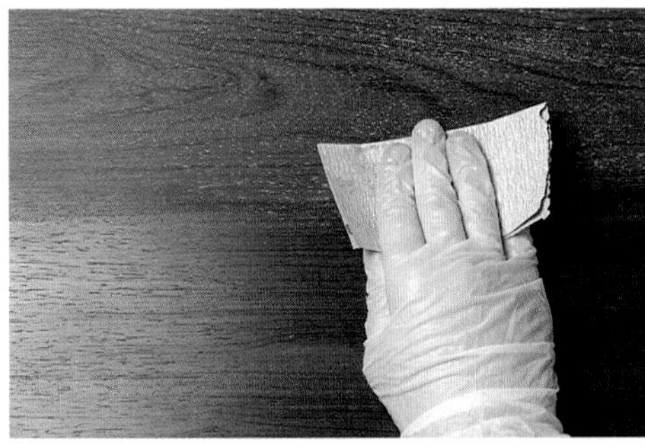

▲ **3** *Leave the oil to dry overnight. Some deep grained woods will have soaked up most of the oil, leaving little on the surface. Lightly sand the rough surface with fine 320 self-lubricating sandpaper. Apply further coats until the required finish is achieved, leaving each coat overnight to dry and lightly sanding between applications. Three or four coats of oil are usually enough.*

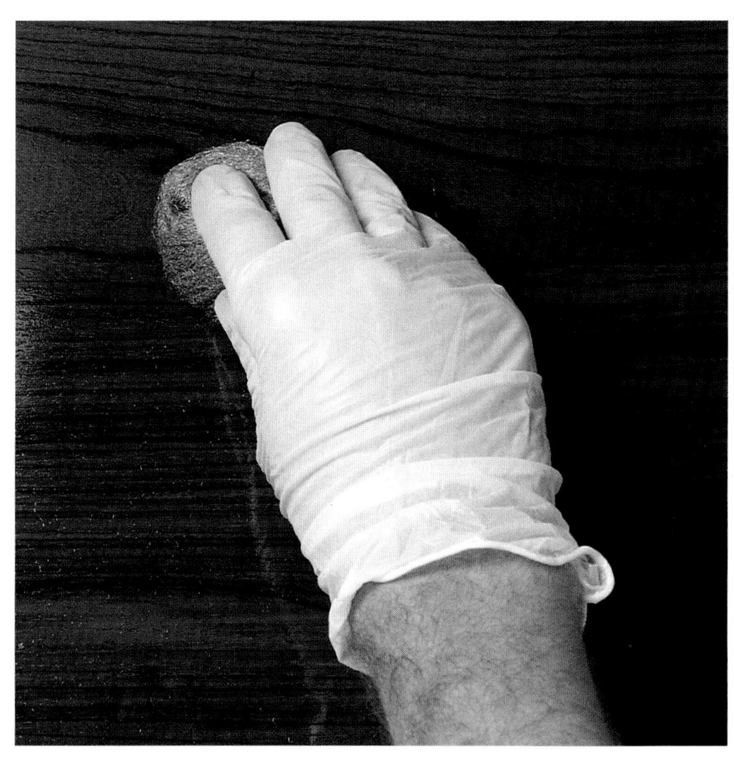

◀ **4** *Drying time varies between hours and days, depending on the type of oil (see "Memo" box, right). When dry, take a palm-sized piece of fine 0000 steel wool to give the surface a final sheen. Rub in the direction of the grain, keeping an even pressure and stroke over the whole piece to produce a satin finish.*

▶ **5** *Burnish the surface with a clean soft cloth to remove any dust that might have been left after rubbing with steel wool.*

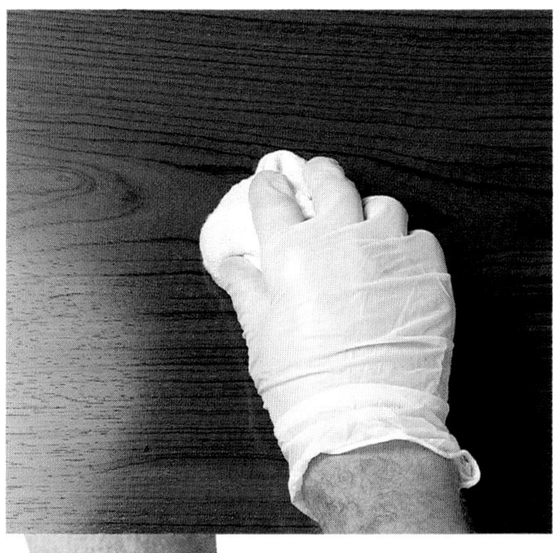

◀ **6** *Oils heat up as they dry – by oxidation – and this can be a fire hazard if they are left wadded up on the bench or in a bin. Dispose of used rags by dousing them in a bucket of water. If left overnight the rag will be safe to throw away.*

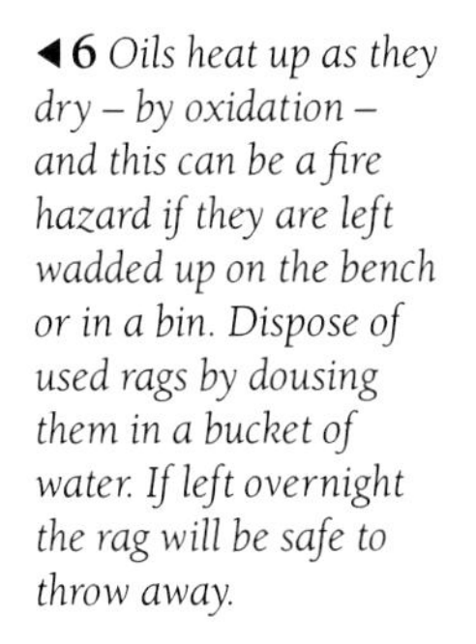

MEMO

Safety precautions

Never leave an oily rag rolled up. As the oil oxidizes, it generates heat and can combust spontaneously.

Allow oily rags to dry outdoors, unrolled, if you need to keep them for further use. Do the same before you throw them away.

Tools and materials

Flat brush

Soft, lint-free cloth

Silicon-carbide sandpaper

0000 steel wool or a plastic scouring pad

Common problems

When finishing thin pieces, there is a chance that they will warp as the oil dries.

Appropriate surfaces

Any wood can be oiled. Teaks, rosewood, afrormosia and oak are often treated with an oil finish.

Drying time

Raw linseed oil takes 3 days to dry.

Boiled linseed oil takes 24 hours to dry.

Teak and Danish oils take 12 hours to dry.

Leave polyurethane oil overnight to dry.

HINTS AND TIPS

- To thin linseed oil, so it is easier to apply, pour the oil into a container and stand it in a pot of very hot water.
- Use mineral spirits for washing excess oil from the surface.
- Enough oil has been applied when patches appear.
- Oil will darken the surface of the wood.
- Use fine silicon-carbide paper for sanding between coats.
- Non-toxic or edible oils, such as olive oil, must be used for salad bowls and other items that come into contact with food.

the complex process of oxidation raw linseed oil actually gains weight as it dries, but it does not dry as fast as the boiled variety. Boiled linseed is partially oxidized and takes a day to dry – compared with three days for pure linseed, which is more resistant to external conditions. However, neither linseed oil nor boiled linseed oil is suitable for oiling exterior woodwork.

Apply the oil by cloth and rub it into the wood. Leave it to dry for at least 24 hours. You can try mixing linseed oil equally with mineral spirits for the first few coats, to encourage the finish to penetrate the wood and dry faster. After that, apply coats of oil until a surface film is achieved. Warming linseed oil lowers its viscosity and aids penetration. However, it combusts easily, so the safest way to warm it is to pour the oil into a container and stand it in a pot of very hot water. Check whether the oil has dried, by wiping your hand across the surface and looking for oil marks, before applying the next coat. Once you are satisfied with the finish, buff with a soft cloth.

Teak and Danish oils

Teak and Danish oils dry faster than linseed, and provide a more resistant film on the surface. Teak oil produces a slight sheen; Danish oil leaves a more natural, low luster. They are better for new pieces; use linseed on older ones. Some of these oils are tinted with color. They all include driers, and sometimes tung oil to enhance their protective nature. You can buy pure tung oil, which comes from the seeds of the Chinese tung tree. It is used in a similar manner to Danish or teak oils.

Apply these oils with a cloth or flat brush. Do not use too much oil at a time, as it will not all sink in. Leave to dry for about 24 hours before applying the next coat, sanding down with fine silicon-carbide paper between applications. Most surfaces will take about three or four coats, but the number of coats is largely a matter of choice and judgment. If the finish is too thin and starts to get dirty, apply more oil.

Oil varnish

An even stronger oiled finish can be achieved by mixing linseed oil with varnish. This produces a thicker coating than oil on its own and also burnishes better.

Oil varnish is available ready-mixed, but one recipe is to mix about 2 parts mineral spirits (or turpentine) and oil to 1 part varnish. Experiment with the proportions to arrive at the desired finish. Turpentine and mineral spirits are generally interchangeable for thinning (natural turpentine has a distinctive pine smell).

Apply with a cloth or flat brush, then leave to dry. For a gloss finish, burnish with a soft cloth once the surface is dry; for a satin or matt sheen, rub with 000 steel wool and wax (see pages 73-75).

Bringing out wood's natural beauty
▶ *The use of an oiled finish on this box has brought out the natural, rich patina of the wood, making it look extremely attractive and providing excellent surface protection. All oil finishes are relatively easy to apply, but the process takes time, especially if porous new wood is involved.*

Waxed finishes

SEE ALSO

18-19 POWERED SANDERS
20-21 ABRASIVES
44-49 STAINING WOOD
58-65 FRENCH POLISHING
66-69 WORKING WITH COLORS

Waxing is a traditional way of protecting and enhancing wood. Wax finishes have been found on Jacobean furniture, beeswax was used by the ancient Egyptians, and to this day wax remains the most popular finish for oak in England. Indeed, only the introduction of French polishing diminished the popularity and general use of wax. Waxing produces a natural finish; like an oiled surface, it is never complete and the constant rubbing by hands continues to improve the finish, deepening its patina, over the years.

Beeswax and carnauba wax have been the most consistent ingredients of furniture wax. The two are often mixed together with turpentine, by warming, to produce hard but compliant waxes. Carnauba adds strength and is often an ingredient of floor polishes. Woodturners use carnauba in stick form to produce a friction finish, holding the stick against the turning piece then buffing it with a soft cloth. Care has to be taken not to press the cloth too hard, in case that melts the wax and tears it.

Tinted wax polishes can be used on dark or light woods. The dark waxes are particularly useful for restoration work and for creating antique effects. Some of the darker woods benefit from treatment with a dark water stain, to deepen their color further, before waxing.

As with any finish, it is important to prepare the workpiece carefully. Apply two thin coats of shellac sanding sealer before waxing, to protect the wood and fill the pores. Sand with fine silicon carbide (see pages 20-22) between and after the coats of sealer.

Today there are many mixed waxes available in cream, paste or stick form. Some are colored, with the dark antique variety especially good for working old oak. Waxes work well on a stained surface – but do not use over oil dye (see pages 44-49). It is also possible to mix in pigments to achieve special effects.

Waxing
▶ **1** *Waxing will give this old oak tray more life and bring out the grain.*

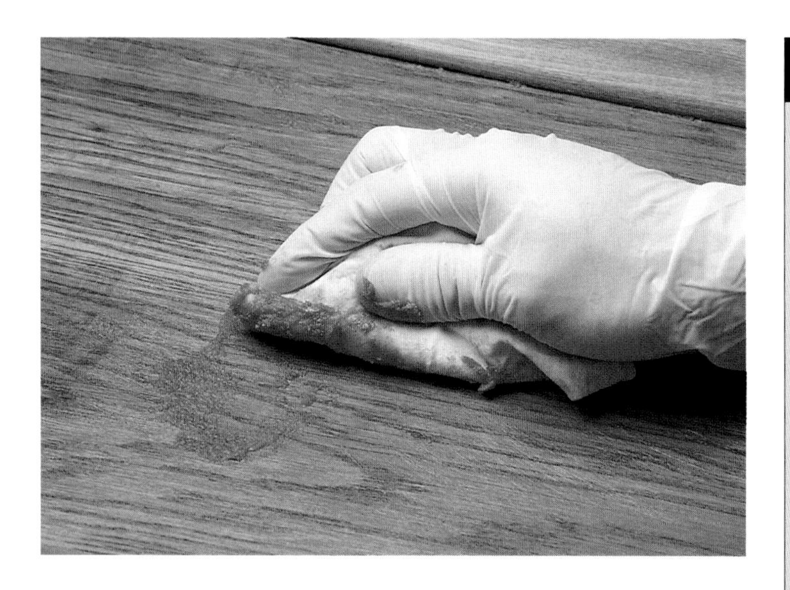

▲ 2 *Apply the wax with a soft cloth folded into layers. Pick up the wax on the cloth, and rub it liberally into the grain using a circular motion. Level off following the grain. Make sure the surface is covered evenly and thoroughly.*

◀ 3 *Leave the piece to dry for 15 minutes and then apply further coats of wax with fine 000 steel wool, rubbing with the grain. Build up the finish gradually, leaving each coat overnight to dry. Four or five coats should be enough.*

◀ 4 *For a more lustrous finish, buff the waxed surface with a soft cloth. Do not press too hard – it is possible to break up the even coat of wax.*

USING BEESWAX

Beeswax is sold commercially, refined and ready for use, as cake or block. It also provides the basis for many manufactured wax finishes.

It is, of course, possible to obtain beeswax in a more natural form, as a honeycomb, from a beekeeper. The honey will have been removed, usually by centrifuging. In order to use the wax for finishing, melt the honeycomb in a water heater or glue pot until liquid. Be careful when heating it, as wax is highly flammable. When the waste rises to the top, skim it off and throw it away. Let the wax cool and resolidify, then add 5 per cent linseed oil to keep it soft.

Although the color is normally yellow, beeswax can be bleached to produce a white wax, which is harder and more brittle. The melting point of beeswax is about 150°F. If you want to harden it, mix it with carnauba wax, which comes from the Brazilian wax palm and has a melting point of 185°F. You can also add paraffin wax or candle wax to make the finish easier to apply.

If you buy beeswax in block or cake form, use a cheese grater to grate it into a glass container, then cover with turpentine and leave overnight. This produces a paste that can be applied liberally with a brush and left to dry for 12 hours. It works well for intricate carvings and turned wood. When the first application is dry, apply more paste until a coating is built up and the surface can be burnished with a soft lint-free cloth.

▼ 5 *After waxing, the oak tray's real beauty is apparent.*

The finished wax polish
▲ *The polish is ready for use when it has cooled thoroughly.*

Making wax polish from beeswax
▲ **1** *Grate beeswax and carnauba wax into flakes onto clean paper, with 10 parts beeswax to 1 part carnauba.*

◀ **2** *Melt the wax in a double boiler over gas or electric heat or use a specialized water heater, as here. Do not boil the melted wax because this can cause discoloration. Melting takes about 10 minutes.*

◀ **3** *Remove the saucepan from the heat, then pour 10 parts turpentine to 1 part melted wax into the heater. Stir as you pour, until the mixture is creamy.*

▲ **4** *When the mixture has reached the right consistency and all the flakes are dissolved, pour it into a shallow container. Leave to cool for some time to produce an even consistency.*

HINTS AND TIPS

- Seal with shellac sanding sealer before waxing.
- Make sure the wax is dry before further applications.
- Use small quantities of wax.
- Apply the wax evenly.
- The final finish depends on the burnishing, rather than the build-up of wax.

MEMO

Tools and materials
Flat brush

Glue pot or double boiler

Lint-free, soft cloth

Fine steel wool

Beeswax and carnauba wax

Turpentine

Common problems
Waxing a surface that has been colored with an oil stain is likely to affect the stain.

If you try to rub a wax finish too soon, it may break up.

Appropriate surfaces
Oak (especially Jacobean oak furniture) is particularly suitable for a wax finish.

Finishing with polish and carnauba wax works well for turned wood.

Wax on shellac sanding sealer is appropriate for contemporary pieces made from almost any wood.

Drying time
Leave for at least 12 hours between coats.

Burnish beeswax after about 15 minutes.

Burnish carnauba immediately.

Varnishing

SEE ALSO

18-19 POWERED SANDERS
14-15 BRUSHES FOR FINISHING
44-49 STAINING WOOD
168-169 HEALTH AND SAFETY

Varnishes come in a variety of forms, with different properties and a range of applications. Unlike polishes, they sit on the surface of the wood as a coat. Some have good waterproofing qualities, others are fast-drying. Today they are known by their resin ingredients, polyurethane being the most common. They are applied by brush, and are available in gloss, flat and satin finishes. The flat and satin varnishes contain a flatting agent to produce an irregular surface that doesn't reflect light with the same directness as gloss. A flat finish shows the nature of the wood better than gloss, on which reflections tend to hide the figure.

It is certainly well worthwhile investing in a good-quality varnish brush. They can be expensive but they can make the difference between a good job and a bad one. See what's available at your local paint store.

Varnish stains

These varnishes, which are ready-mixed with stain, are supplied in a variety of colors. Some clarity of grain is lost with this type of varnish, but they are useful for covering less attractive woods. Make sure they are applied evenly, in order to maintain a constant color.

Polyurethane varnish

Polyurethane has become the symbol for do-it-yourself varnishing, since most varnishes in hardware stores are based on this resin. They are available for outdoor use; or with a thixotropic agent to form a gel, which helps on vertical surfaces. Supplied in flat, satin and gloss, they flow well and are

HINTS AND TIPS

- Decant varnish into a coffee can and attach a wire across the top of the can so you can wipe off excess varnish from the brush.
- Make sure there is no dust in the workshop. Sprinkle the floor with water, and make sure your clothes are free from hairs and dust.
- Use a good-quality brush for varnishing. A cheap paintbrush would produce a very poor varnished finish.
- Press with a thumbnail to test varnish for hardness.

A gloss finish
▲ *See how the rose reflects deeply in the gloss varnish. However, these reflections can sometimes mask the beauty of the wood.*

A satin finish
▲ *The reflection is becoming a blur. The details of the rose are less of a distraction to the view of the grain.*

A flat finish
▲ *A flat varnish produces the most natural finish, bringing out the color and pattern of the wood and producing little reflection.*

Applying varnish

▼ *Special varnish brushes are made which are worth the extra cost. Apply the varnish across the grain first to spread it evenly over the surface. Then, applying very little pressure, draw the brush diagonally across the surface; finish off with the grain, exerting a very light pressure. This method will leave the fewest brushmarks.*

Producing a flat finish

▼ **1** *A better flat finish is obtained by working with gloss varnish than by applying proprietary flat varnishes. First, apply gloss varnish as usual. Then abrade the dry surface with fine 000 steel wool. This creates very fine scratches on the surface of the piece, cutting down its ability to reflect light. Always work with the grain, rubbing gently.*

▼ **2** *Having rubbed the piece with steel wool, apply wax with a soft cloth following the grain. Do not use too much wax, otherwise it will be difficult to buff later.*

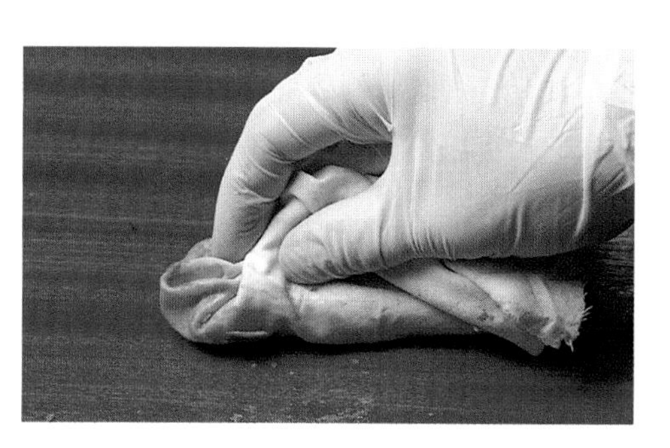

▲ **3** *Leave the waxed piece to dry for an hour or so. Then burnish the waxed surface with a clean, soft cloth. Rub along the grain. This will produce a lustrous flat finish, full of color.*

Producing a satin finish

▲ **1** *Use pumice powder and a dulling brush or shoe brush on dry gloss varnish to produce a satin finish. Put a small quantity of pumice powder into a shallow tray.*

MEMO

Safety precautions

Varnishes can cause drowsiness, so always work in a well-ventilated workshop.

Wear a mask when sanding.

Take great care when using two-part varnishes, keeping special thinners at hand and ensuring there is constant air movement.

Tools and materials

Coffee can

Flat brush

Stain, if required

Fine silicon-carbide sandpaper

Mineral spirits

Linseed oil and pumice powder, or 000 steel wool and wax

Common problems

Applying varnish before the previous coat has hardened, or even when it is starting to get tacky, is likely to mark the finish.

Do not stir thixotropic varnishes – stirring breaks the gel formation.

Drying time

Varnish takes about 6 or 7 hours to dry, but leave overnight between each coat.

Appropriate surfaces

Any wood surface can be varnished.

◀ **2** *A dulling brush has short soft bristles, rather like a shoe brush. Load the dulling brush with pumice powder by dipping it into the tray and picking up the powder.*

◀ **3** *Once loaded, work the dulling brush in straight strokes along the grain over the whole surface. For curved pieces, use a soft cloth, and pumice powder. Apply evenly, and do not miss any parts. Keep rubbing until the desired satin finish is produced.*

PREPARING A BRUSH

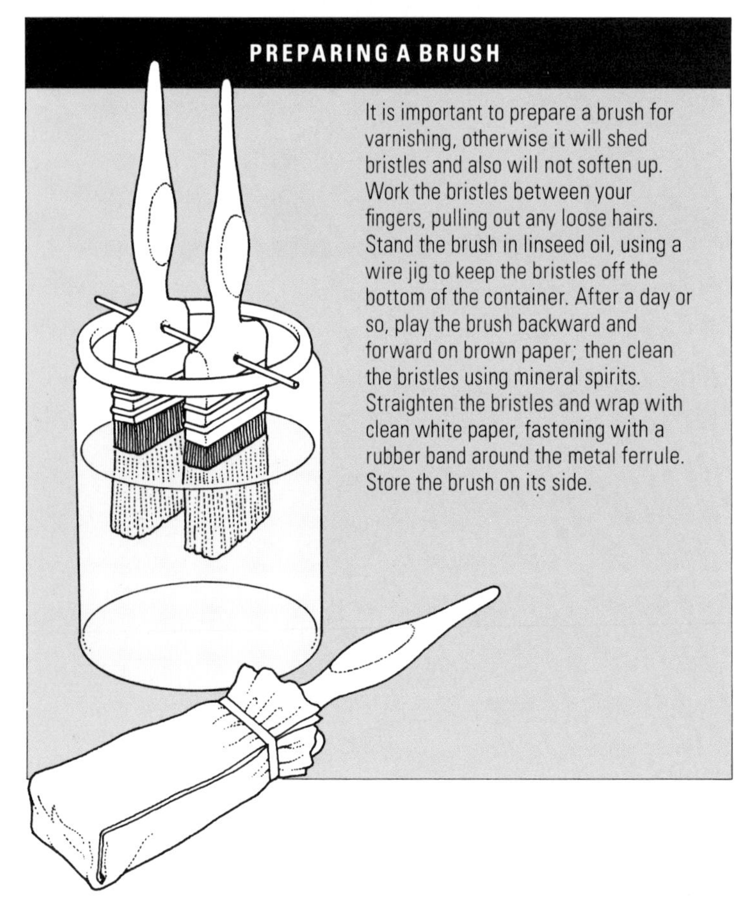

It is important to prepare a brush for varnishing, otherwise it will shed bristles and also will not soften up. Work the bristles between your fingers, pulling out any loose hairs. Stand the brush in linseed oil, using a wire jig to keep the bristles off the bottom of the container. After a day or so, play the brush backward and forward on brown paper; then clean the bristles using mineral spirits. Straighten the bristles and wrap with clean white paper, fastening with a rubber band around the metal ferrule. Store the brush on its side.

applied by brush – though the final coat must be laid on with as little brushing as possible to avoid streaking.

Water-borne varnishes

Water-soluble varnishes are faster drying and, because of their water base, are non-flammable. Woodworkers intent on finishing their work in an environmentally friendly manner are experimenting with these varnishes. Use a brush for application.

Two-part polyurethane varnishes

These varnishes need an acid catalyst for hardening, and are stronger than standard polyurethane. They are particularly useful for floors and bar tops. They do, however, give off terrible fumes when first applied, by brush, and may react with stains. To achieve a high gloss apply three or four coats and rub down the last coat before burnishing with cream and a cloth. Two coats are sufficient if the lacquer is being rubbed to a satin or flat finish with fine steel wool and wax polish.

Applying varnish

As with other finishes, make sure any defects in the surface have been dealt with, filling holes and cracks and sanding the surface flat. Varnish is more forgiving than other finishes in that it is a coat that can be cut back flat – but it will exaggerate any blemishes through the refraction of light. Clean the piece first with mineral spirits to remove wax or grease, especially if the surface has been stripped.

Stain the wood, if required. But note that oil-based varnishes will pull off oil dyes. Check the base of the varnish before starting. Make sure any stain is dry before applying varnish, and lightly sand with fine silicon carbide (see pages 20-22) if a water stain has been used.

Manufacturers of varnishes do not recommend thinning, but varnishes based on mineral spirits are best mixed with about 10 per cent mineral spirits to aid penetration. Dip the brush in the varnish and work thin coats from the center of the panel outward. However, to avoid drips and runs, varnish the edges first. Brush with the grain, then across it, and finally follow the grain, in order to produce an even coat. Try not to brush too hard, as that may leave marks if the varnish is fast-drying, and may also produce bubbles in the finish. If possible, keep the working edge wet all the time, to reduce the chance of an uneven finish.

When the surface is completely dry, cut back with fine paper. Sanding will produce fine white dust; but if the varnish starts to tear up into little balls, it is still too soft and you may need to strip it off and start again. So be careful. Varnish takes time to harden – and though the surface may seem to have set, the same may not be true underneath.

Dust off using a cloth dampened with mineral spirits, then apply the next coat. Continue until the required depth is achieved, making sure that the last application is even and follows the grain, letting the varnish flow. Most pieces will need two or three coats.

If a satin finish is required when only gloss varnish is available, dull the surface using pumice powder applied with a shoe brush. Apply pumice powder to the brush, then work in straight strokes along the grain. To produce a flat finish, use fine steel wool and wax.

Providing a protective finish
▶ *Varnish is a protective finish favored by joiners and carpenters. It is suitable for fittings that will be exposed to continual wear and tear, such as staircases, windows and doors.*

Restoring old finishes

SEE ALSO

18–19 POWERED SANDERS

20–21 ABRASIVES

36–39 CHEMICAL STRIPPING

40–43 HOW TO USE WOOD FILLERS

58–65 FRENCH POLISHING

70–72 OIL FINISHES

73–75 WAXED FINISHES

There comes a time when old furniture and other wooden items need a good cleaning, without resorting to the drastic action of stripping. Indeed, more often than not there is value in retaining the original finish, since it will have developed a mellow patina that cannot be re-created. A patina that has been built up over the years is one of the most attractive features of antique furniture – but, as with paintings, the surface tends to dull with age and the finish may need to be rekindled by thorough cleaning.

The aim should be to give new life to the finish, not to make the piece look new. The beauty of antique furniture lies partly in its used appearance, in the shades and tones of the wood developed over the years. Cleaning and restoration must therefore be done with great care. It is relatively easy to strip or sand back to the wood, but that destroys the finish and detracts from the character of the piece. Always try to conserve, restore and enhance, rather than remove.

Identifying the finish

Before cleaning or embarking on any restoration work, try to identify the finish. This is not always easy. Something about the finish can be deduced from the age of the piece, but previous restorations and renovations may have replaced the original finish with a more modern version.

If the piece was made earlier than the middle of the nineteenth century, then the odds are it was not French-polished originally and is more likely to have been given a finish based on tree resins or fossilized resins. French polishing became common around 1850; later, as furniture production

Cleaning off dirt
▼ 1 *The underframe of this mahogany table needs to be restored. However, dirt has built up over the years, and it must be removed before structural repairs or restoration can be started.*

▲ 2 *Use fine 000 steel wool and a proprietary cleaner to clean off the dirt. Pour the cleaner onto a hand-sized ball of steel wool, using enough to dampen it thoroughly.*

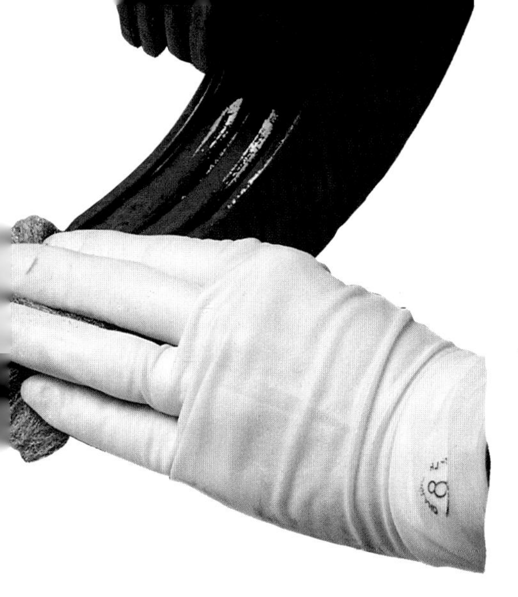

▲ **3** *Rub off the dirt and old wax, following the grain. Make sure you work the steel wool into all grooves and corners. Rewet with fresh cleaner regularly. Ensure that the cleaner cleans the surface of the piece, but that it does not strip off the finish.*

▼ **4** *The cleaning fluid produces a sludge, some of which will get caught up in the steel wool. The rest must be cleaned from the surface with a soft clean cloth. Do this frequently as the sludge can discolor the wood. More than one session of cleaning may be necessary to remove stubborn grime.*

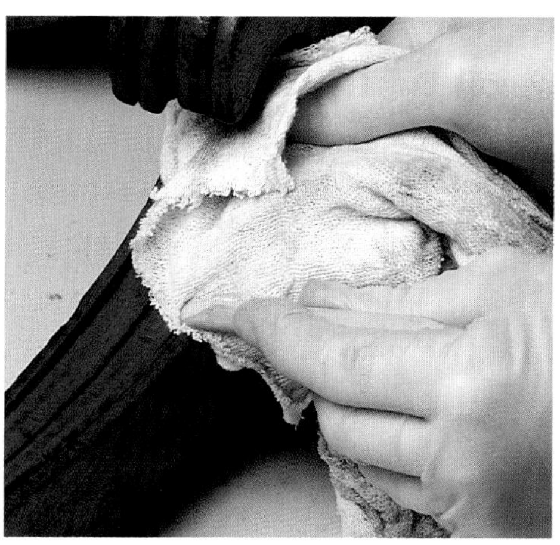

moved into the twentieth century, sprayed lacquer finishes were increasingly used.

For a thorough identification, test a small area on a hidden part of the piece, such as the underside of a table or the back of a rail. Apply mineral spirits with steel wool: this will soften oil or wax, but will not affect French polish or varnish. Always rub carefully and select a spot that will not be easily seen; do not soften the finish too much, or damage may be caused. If mineral spirits have no effect upon the surface, then the piece has been varnished or sprayed and will have to be stripped with chemicals or sanded back.

Cleaning an old finish

The aim is to clean off dirt and grime that has accumulated over the years. Grease and vestiges of food build up on table tops, while oil from hands has to be removed from the arms of chairs. What is required for cleaning is a formula that will pick up the dirt but leave the patina.

Much grime can be removed with soap and water. Gently wash the surface, but do not overwet it, otherwise the wood may move and joints come apart. For more stubborn areas, use a proprietary cleaner or mineral spirits applied with fine steel wool (000 or even 0000). However, do not use this technique if there are any cracks, as the oil may spread under the finish and lift it off or make the surface murky later.

During the cleaning a sludge will form. Wipe this off with a cloth or with paper towels. This sludge must be removed before it dries.

Renewing the finish

After cleaning, where appropriate a French-polish finish can be rubbed onto the surface with a polishing pad – having first filled any small dents with colored or clear beeswax, touching in with pigments or dyes and an artists' brush (see pages 26–27). Oiled finishes can be restored using linseed oil (see pages 70–72).

If the finish has deteriorated so far

MEMO

Tools and materials

Fine steel wool (000 or possibly 0000)

Soft cloth and rags

Polishing pad

Mineral spirits or proprietary cleaner

Beeswax

Linseed oil

Soap and water

French polish

Common problems

If the finish does not react to testing, it is probably a spray finish and needs to be stripped.

HINTS AND TIPS

- Always test on a hidden area.
- Work slowly and carefully. The aim is to clean the finish, not to remove it.
- Do not sand the surface.
- Do not polish to a high-gloss finish.
- Try not to make the piece look as if it is newly made.

▲ 5 *Once the piece is dry, apply polish with batting. There is no reason to build up a finish – just wipe over to bring back the sheen.*

that it cannot be cleaned effectively, it will have to be removed. Use a paint and varnish remover containing methylene chloride (see pages 36–39). Do this with great care – and do not attempt to sand the wood, as sanding would break through the fibers and reveal a new surface. Once the finish has been removed, the surface is ready for oiling, waxing or French polishing, as appropriate. When polishing old furniture, dull the polish to produce an aged look (see pages 73–75).

▶ 6 *The mahogany table is now clean. Note how the color is stronger and the lines more exact.*

Restoring an armchair

▶ *The most obvious areas of this armchair that need attention are the screw holes on the back and peg holes at the corners on the rails. These should be filled with wax. The arms must be polished to clean off the dark oil from hands. Check the legs – especially the intricate turning – for marks and dirt.*

Restoring a Davenport

▼ *Ink stains found on the lid of this Davenport (used as a desk) have been removed with bleach or oxalic acid during restoration. Loose veneers on the pen tray have been repaired and glued down, and old wax and dirt have been cleaned off the legs.*

Restoring an inlaid piece

▲ *Inlay, as on the top of this occasional table, often needs minor repairs. Remove loose pieces of veneer, replacing if necessary and then color matching. Chips on the edge of the piece can be filled with wax. The table may have been used as a plant stand, so check for water marks, which can be removed by gentle rubbing with denatured alcohol and linseed oil.*

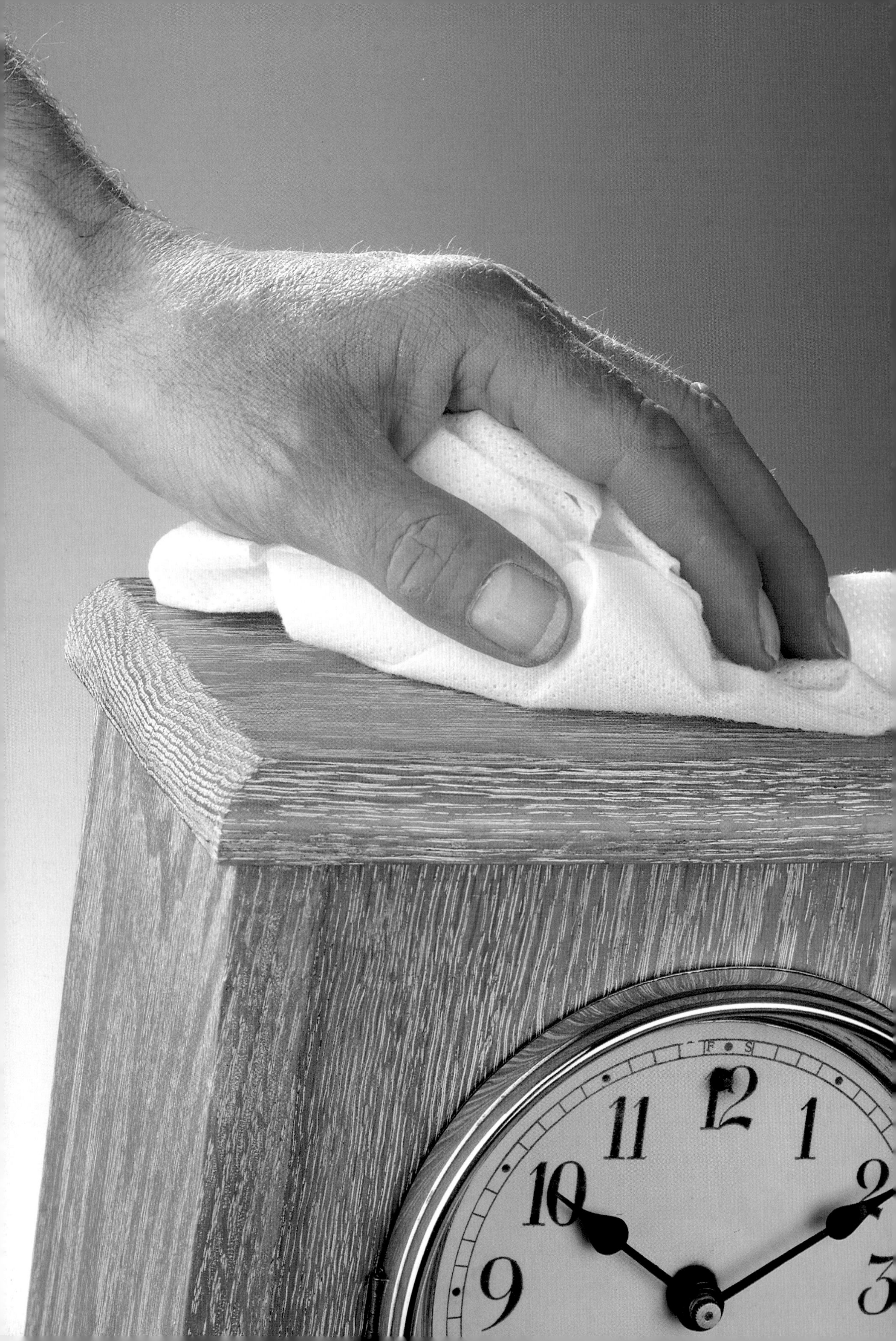

4

Decorative finishes

Decorating wood – especially materials such as MDF (medium-density fiberboard) – with special effects is a craft that has developed with the demands of the market. Fashion and ideas from interior designers have influenced the use of these finishes, and craftspeople have evolved their own techniques and designs. As a result, a wide range of processes and effects is available for the finisher to emulate or use as a medium for innovation.

Stippling

SEE ALSO

18-19 POWERED SANDERS

66-69 WORKING WITH COLORS

76-79 VARNISHING

Stippling (sometimes referred to as sponging) is probably the simplest of paint effects to produce on wood, fiberboard and walls. By far the best substrate for stippling is MDF, which is smooth and takes finishes perfectly.

Unlike MDF, wood and particleboard need filling with plaster of Paris before stippling (see pages 53-55). Mix the plaster to a paste with water and apply it with burlap, rubbing well into the pores of the substrate. Leave to dry and sand flat, using sandpaper on a block. The surface is then ready to take the background color.

The background color is a matter of choice, so experiment with pastel and darker colors. To mix the color, blend artists' oil paints with household undercoat or eggshell. Apply the background color with a flat brush. Leave it to dry, then sand with fine sandpaper.

For the stipple itself, use latex paint, which is easiest to apply. Pour it into a shallow container and mix with other latex colors, bearing in mind the shade of the undercoat. Matching colors, only distinguished by a slight difference in shade, may be most suitable – but startling results can be achieved with a contrast.

Applying stipple

Various materials can be used for applying the stipple finish. Each produces its own distinctive effect. Upholstery foam, sponges and paper towels work well; and there are special brushes, available from decorating suppliers, that are designed to produce individual patterns.

Applying the stipple will need some practice; try it first on a scrap piece of board. Cut up the stippling material into pieces that fit comfortably in your hand. Dip into the color and squeeze out the excess, so that the pad is damp rather than dripping wet. Dab it over the surface, producing a speckled pattern, replenishing the pad with paint as it dries out. An even pattern is probably the most desirable, but there is no reason why the pattern should not be irregular. If you wish, use more colors and change to different pads.

Alternatively, you can use scumbles or glaze instead of latex paint. Scumbles are sold off the shelf, ready-mixed with color, or you can make your own; glaze can be mixed with artists' oil colors, gold size, mineral spirits and driers. Mix the colors to suit, and apply with a pad. Both glaze and scumbles take longer to dry than latex paint.

Whichever method you choose, once you are certain that the paint is dry, seal the surface with a coat of flat or gloss varnish applied with a flat brush. Polyurethane or oil varnish will alter the color of the paint.

HINTS AND TIPS

- Practice on scrap board and test effects before stippling.
- Do not apply the stipple too wet.
- Dab the stipple on gently. Do not use too much pressure.
- Make sure scumble or glaze is completely dry before varnishing.
- Vary the way you dab the stipple for a random effect.
- Try different materials for stippling – almost anything will do.

Making a scumble for stippling

▶ 1 *Scumbles can be bought ready-mixed or you can mix your own. To make it, you need artists' color (sold in a tube), gold size, turpentine or mineral spirits and linseed oil. You will also need a spatula and a container.*

Select the color you want to use and place a small quantity in the container. There is, of course, no reason why more than one color cannot be mixed together. A rough guide to the proportions required is: 1 part color to 1 part turpentine, 2 parts linseed oil and 2 parts gold size.

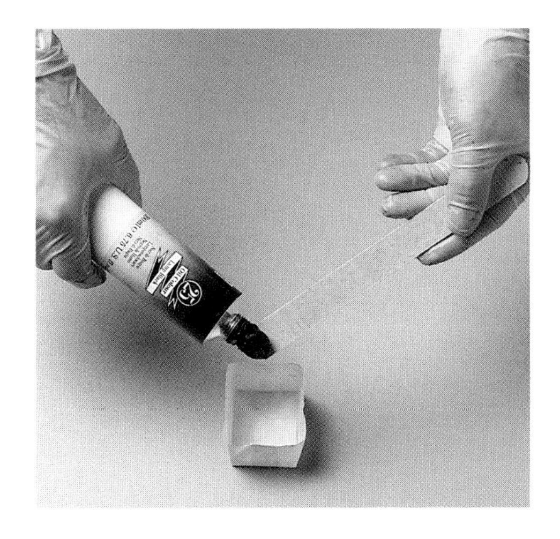

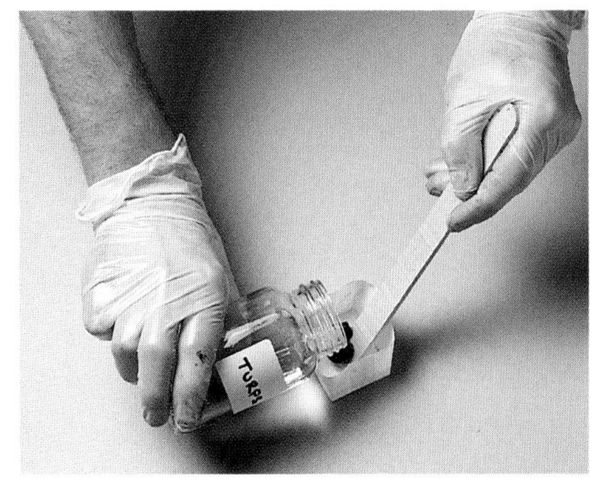

▲ 2 *Thin the color with turpentine or mineral spirits. Do not use too much, and stir it all the time.*

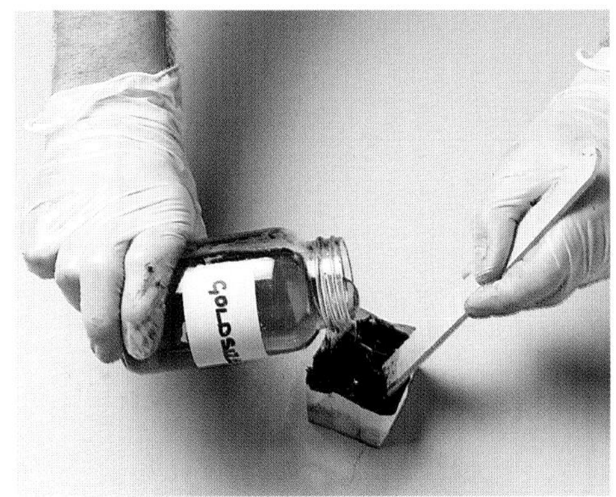

▲ 4 *Add gold size to act as a binder and drying agent.*

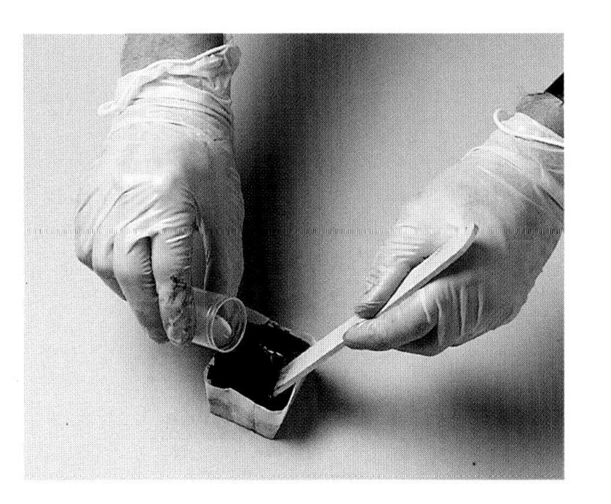

▲ 3 *Mix in the linseed oil to make the scumble glaze "flow out" when you come to use it. At this stage the mixture must not be too thin, but remember that it has to be manipulated with the stipple brush, and so must not be too thick.*

▶ 5 *With time, you will develop your own recipe for scumble glaze.*

MEMO

Tools and materials

Flat brush

Shallow container

Sponge, foam or paper towels

Undercoat

Latex paint, scumbles or glaze

Flat or gloss varnish

Common problems

If the sponge or stippling tool is too wet or too dry, it will not produce an even pattern and will be difficult to use.

Drying time

Wait for 2 hours before stippling, after applying undercoat.

Leave stipple for 8 hours before applying varnish.

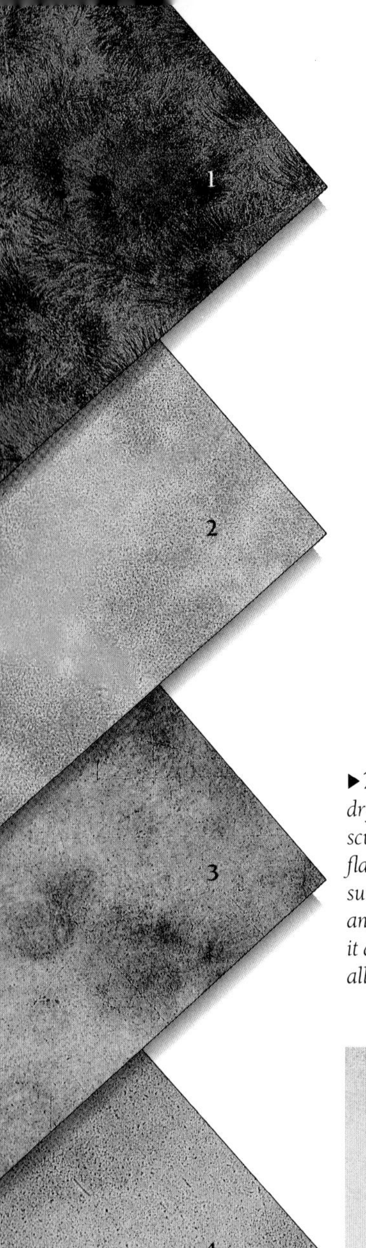

Creating a stipple finish

▶ **1** *Prepare the surface – in this case MDF – with undercoat, applying it evenly. Start by using a lighter undercoat than the scumble for stippling, but on future pieces experiment with a dark groundwork.*

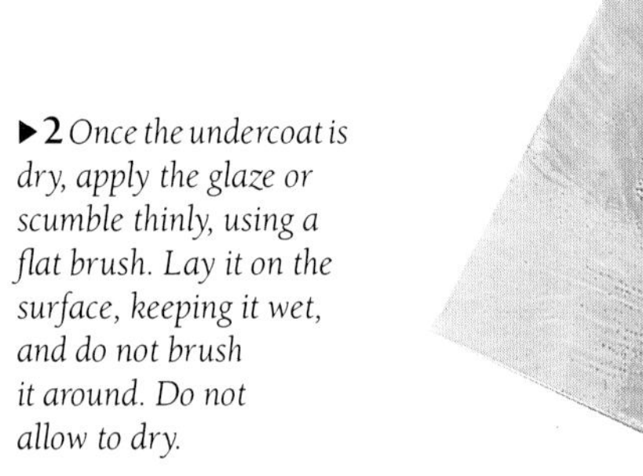

▶ **2** *Once the undercoat is dry, apply the glaze or scumble thinly, using a flat brush. Lay it on the surface, keeping it wet, and do not brush it around. Do not allow to dry.*

◀ **3** *Hold the stipple brush firmly, and dab over the surface. Maintain an even action as you move around the surface, ensuring that the pressure of each dab is similar. Try not to go over one area more often than others. Keep going until the whole surface has been stippled.*

A selection of different stipple finishes

▲ *Experiment with combinations of color to produce a range of stippled finishes. Try both contrasting and complementary colors.*
1 *Black background and gold stipple.*
2 *Cream background and orange and yellow stipple.*
3 *Cream background and raw sienna and black stipple.*
4 *White background and green stipple.*

▶ **4** *If desired, use a clean cloth to wipe off a narrow border before the stipple has dried. This gives a more professional finish. Once the glaze has dried, protect it with gloss or flat varnish.*

Adding interest
▲ *The wall above the basin unit has been stippled with a gray glaze. Note how the surface is more varied and interesting than a painted gray wall.*

Creating contrasts
▶ *The stippled gray walls above the chair rail contrast well with the heavier effect on the door and woodwork. Below the chair rail, the stipple has been augmented with veins, applied using an artists' brush.*

Graining

SEE ALSO

18-19 POWERED SANDERS

20-21 ABRASIVES

66-69 WORKING WITH COLOR

76-79 VARNISHING

86-89 STIPPLING

94-97 MARBLE EFFECTS

98-101 RAG ROLLING

HINTS AND TIPS

- Remember when testing scumble colors that the idea is to move wet coats around, combining the various colors, in order to produce the grain pattern.
- Test on scrap materials.
- Look after specialist brushes, as they are expensive.
- Most standard scumbles will need tinting with pigments.
- Make sure each stage has dried before attempting the next application.

Before attempting to reproduce the grain of any wood, take a good look at the natural wood – compare it with other woods, to identify its distinguishing characteristics, and try to memorize its grain pattern and color. You will notice, for example, that the medullary rays of oak are unique (their appearance depends on the way the wood has been milled); and that mahogany has a distinctive range of red, brown and pink shades. When graining, it may also help to have a piece of the relevant wood available to act as a guide.

Graining is done with scumbles. You can buy these in a range of wood colors, ready-mixed with pigments, gold size, mineral spirits and driers. Alternatively, you may prefer to mix your own (see pages 86–87). Scumbles are similar to glaze but dry more slowly, which allows time for graining. They are also of higher viscosity, so thinning may be necessary.

Simple graining tools, which have grooves to simulate grain, are available from paint stores. Apply the scumble with a flat brush – then, while it is still wet, draw the graining tool across the surface to reproduce the lines of the grain. Bear in mind that grain does not always run straight, but has waves.

Oak graining

Having smoothed the surface and sealed the wood with shellac sanding sealer, use a flat brush to lay down the background color. For oak, the undercoat should be beige. Leave the

Creating a simple open-grain finish
▼ **1** *Having smoothed the surface and sealed the wood with shellac sanding sealer, apply the colored scumble using a flat brush, laying the finish on evenly over an undercoat. Use long straight strokes, the full length of the piece.*

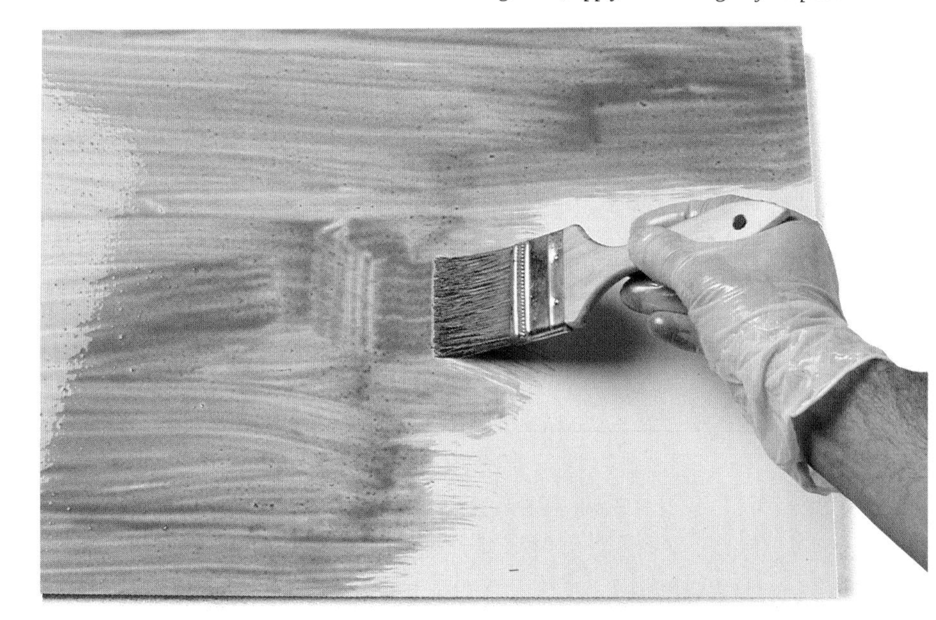

▶ **2** *Use a comb to etch an open grain pattern into the colored scumble. Draw the comb across the surface, tipping and rolling it from end to end. Remember that the grain does not always run straight, and has shakes and knots. By rocking the comb from side to side wider patterns are produced.*

▶ **3** *This open-grained effect is designed to imitate pine and other softwoods. Notice how the grain pattern widens and narrows, and contours are produced. Increase the depth of graining with other colors. Once dry, protect the surface with varnish, or stain it.*

MEMO

Tools and materials

Flat brush

Graining brush

Badger brush

Artists' brush

Combs

Graining tools

Scumbles

Gold size

Linseed oil

Mineral spirits

Cotton cloth

Undercoat

Varnish

Appropriate surfaces

The ideal surface for a grained finish is MDF, which has no obvious grain and needs minimum preparation.

undercoat to dry, then sand it lightly with fine sandpaper.

Next, lay down some oak-colored scumble with a flat brush, using a badger brush to take out the brush marks. Draw a steel graining comb across the surface, making lines in the scumble. Continue right across the surface, making sure each stroke is in line with the preceding one. Wipe the comb clean after each stroke.

Creating a simple close-grain finish
▲ **1** *Having put down an undercoat, and let it dry, apply the scumble as you would for a simple open-grain effect, with long, straight strokes. Make sure the scumble is applied evenly.*

Take the comb and draw it across the lines at angles of about 30 degrees. Use a softener or badger to blend the lines in so they match the natural look of wood. Add further figuring with an artists' brush. Make the dark strokes with an artists' brush, softening afterward. This produces the straight grain of oak.

To create fake medullary rays, prepare the surface in the same way and draw the steel comb over the oak scumble. Soften the effect; then take a graining brush (a long, broad-headed, stiff-bristled brush) and, using a dabbing action, follow the grain, with the graining brush laid on its back. This reproduces the flecked appearance of the grain. Traditionally, medullary rays are simulated with the thumbnail, covered with cloth. Alternatively, use the back of a comb wrapped in a cloth. Once the finish is satisfactory, leave to dry and then apply flat or gloss varnish.

Mahogany graining

After preparing the surface as above, apply a pink-beige undercoat. Sand when dry, then apply the mahogany

▶ **2** *Work the scumble with a graining brush to create the tight, straight grain. Hold the brush loosely and use a beating action along the panel, lengthwise, to produce flecks in the grain.*

scumble with a flat brush, using a curling action to produce the appearance of mahogany figure. Soften the brush marks, then brush with a darker scumble, softening the two coats together.

For straight-grain mahogany apply the scumble with straight strokes of a flat brush, dabbing the grain with the tip of the brush and blending with a badger.

Highlight the grain pattern by dragging a Vandyke water stain across the surface.

Graining real wood
▲ *Real wood, such as on doors, which may be in poor condition can be overpainted and then given a painted grain.*

Glaze graining
▲ *A gray-toned paint glaze was brushed on freely. The cross-grains were then scraped out of the wet glaze with a pencil wrapped in a cloth.*

Graining and stenciling
▼ *A combination of graining and stenciling has been used to create the interior decoration in this room.*

Marbled effects

SEE ALSO

18-19
POWERED SANDERS

20-21
ABRASIVES

40-43
HOW TO USE WOOD FILLERS

53-55
GRAIN FILLERS

66-69
WORKING WITH COLORS

The most obvious reason for creating a marbled effect is the desire to imitate real marble, and in grand period houses it is not uncommon to find outstanding examples of marbling that are difficult to distinguish from the real thing. The materials used today, which are available off the shelf, are refinements of those used through the ages, but they are more stable and more consistent. Nevertheless, although one batch varies little from another, it is best not to mix batches – and trial and error is the most reliable way to achieve the desired effect.

Preparing the surface

Prepare the substrate, filling the grain if necessary (see pages 53–55). You may want to continue the marbling around corners for three-dimensional realism, so make sure the edges are cleaned up and that holes are filled and sanded flat. Apply a flat undercoat paint, either acrylic or oil, usually white or pastel. Latex may not be the strongest of paints, but they are good enough for practice. With time, you will probably find that the most vivid colors are produced using artists' oil paints, especially glaze. Leave the undercoat to dry, then sand with fine sandpaper.

▲ 2 *The undercoat is applied as a background color. It does not need to be white – any color can be used, to suit the marbling effect desired. Apply the undercoat with a flat brush. When it is dry, sand it flat to ensure the surface is as even as is possible.*

▲ 3 *Wipe linseed oil over the surface, using a piece of rag, before applying the glaze. This allows the color to float on the surface, so that it can be manipulated before it dries.*

Producing marble effects

▶ 1 *The piece ready for marbling. You will need glaze and undercoat, a sponge to mottle and an artists' brush for the veins, a flat brush and badger brush, and linseed oil and colors.*

Working with glaze

The next stage is to apply a glaze, for manipulation while still wet. At this point the colored glazes are not meant to stick to the undercoat, so wipe the surface with linseed oil.

You can buy glaze in either a colored or a clear form. Clear glaze needs to be mixed with colored oils or pigments, which are supplied in tubes by art suppliers, ready for use. Mix the colors in a shallow container, always using plenty of white. Mix the glaze in equal proportions with gold size and mineral spirits. Apply a thin layer to the surface, using a flat brush.

While the glaze is still wet, lightly soften the surface with a badger brush (see pages 14–15), evening out the brush marks and producing a slightly mottled effect. Stipple the darker areas with a sponge, then soften with a badger brush once more. The result must look natural, without sharp lines or brush marks.

Add further glaze layers while the previous coat of glaze is still wet. Use thin layers with subtle colors, gradually merging the layers together. This can be repeated until the required effect has been achieved. Make sure that the edges are treated in the same manner, to make the piece look like solid marble.

The veins and streaks are applied

▲ **4** *Apply the glaze with a flat brush, laying it on using straight strokes along the length of the piece. Make sure the glaze is laid on evenly, leaving as few brush marks as possible.*

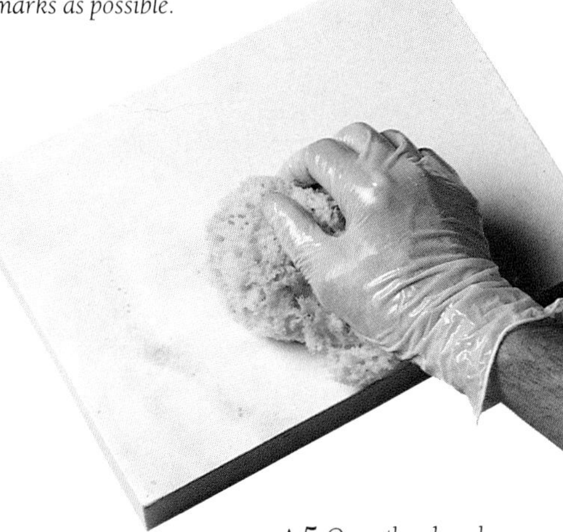

▲ **5** *Once the glaze has been applied, stipple the surface with a sponge. Use gentle dabs of the sponge, without taking too much paint from the surface. This softens the effect of the glaze, giving it a mottled look. It also removes any brush marks.*

▶ **6** *Soften the effect produced by the sponge with a badger brush. Lightly brush the stippled glaze, blending it in with the background color. There must be no brush marks left on the surface once this stage has been completed.*

MEMO

❖

Tools and materials
Badger brush
Artists' brush
Flat brush
Feather
Glaze
Artists' oil paints
Gold size
Mineral spirits
Linseed oil
Sponges and cotton cloth

❖

Common problems
It is easy to make the marble too dark, so use plenty of white and develop the color slowly.

If the softener is not kept clean, it can smudge the effect.

❖

Appropriate surfaces
Use on MDF, if possible, or other flat, grainless materials.

Drying time
The glazes will take about 2 hours to dry.

▶ 7 *Use an artists' brush to work in the veins of the marble. Draw across the surface, manipulating the veins by rolling the brush between thumb and finger. Try to produce a random pattern of veins, imitating the natural feel of marble.*

HINTS AND TIPS

- Have a good look at real marble before attempting to create a marbled effect.
- Always practice on scrap material first.
- Use pastel and subtle shades.
- Blend colors together.
- Apply thin, not heavy, layers of color.
- Wash off failed effects with mineral spirits, and start again.
- Always mix enough glaze to finish the job.
- Carry effects around edges to give an illusion of solidity.
- Rag-rolled borders enhance the effect and make it more interesting.

with an artists' brush or a feather. Hold the brush between finger and thumb, and move across the surface oscillating the brush and making irregular strokes. This will form graduated streaks in the glaze, giving a natural effect. Soften these streaks with a badger, blending the glazes.

Another effect to try is splattering. Use an artists' brush filled with glaze, and flick it over the surface. This is best done in concentrated areas. Use the badger for blending. As with any paint effect, there is no end to experimentation with color and design. Additional glazes can be mixed with dry pigments.

Imitating marble tiles

Real marble is usually stuck in place in panels, like tiles, with thin lines between them. You may want to imitate

A selection of different marble finishes
▶ **1** *Sky blue background, red ocher and black glaze.*
2 *Off-white and pink background, red oxide and yellow and red glaze.*
3 *Off-white background, raw sienna and yellow ocher glaze.*
4 *White background, black and white glaze.*
5 *Black background, gold glaze.*
6 *Dark green background, white scumble glaze.*

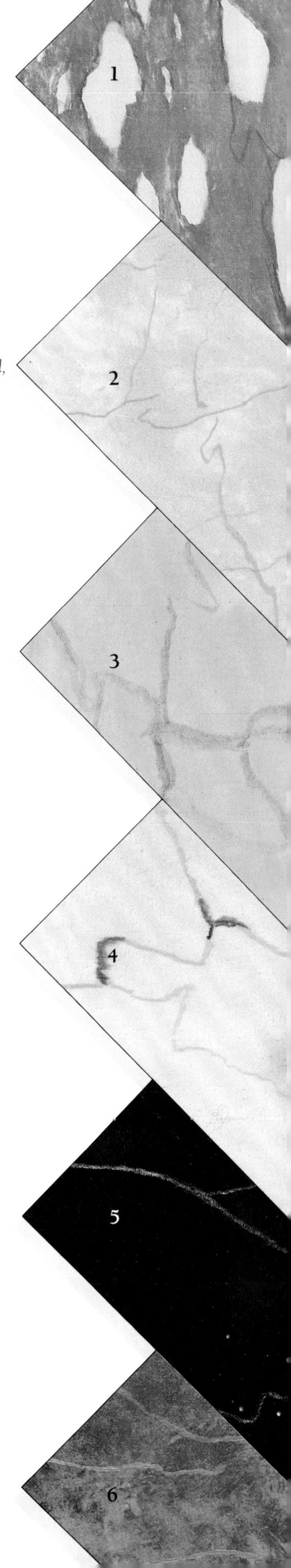

▲ **8** *Soften the veins – again with the badger brush – to blend into the overall marble effect. Brush the surface lightly, moving the color in the veins into the background color. Do not wear away the lines too far as they will become indistinct.*

this pattern, in which case paint dark lines in a grid formation. Marble tiles vary in size, but are often about 12 to 15 inches square. Using a straightedge, draw on the grid before marbling the area. The tiles need not necessarily all be the same, and an interesting effect can be achieved by altering the color and grain of the marble.

▲ **9** *Varnish the finished piece to protect it from wear and tear. When experimenting with creating a marble effect, use pale colors at first, and try blending them together, as if building up layers. Look closely at real marble to see what you are attempting to copy. When you understand how to manipulate the glaze, move on to more dramatic marble effects, using stronger colors.*

Rag rolling

SEE ALSO

18-19 POWERED SANDERS
20-21 ABRASIVES
40-43 HOW TO USE WOOD FILLERS
53-55 GRAIN FILLERS
66-69 WORKING WITH COLORS
76-77 VARNISHING
86-89 STIPPLING

A traditional way of creating a mottled paint effect on furniture, paneling and walls is to roll the surface with rags before the finish dries. There are any number of techniques used to achieve this decorative effect, from literally rolling cloth across the surface to dabbing the substrate with a rag or other closely knitted cloth.

From a furniture-maker's point of view, MDF is the best substrate on which to work. Other materials need filling with plaster of Paris (see pages 53-55) mixed to a stiff paste, applied with burlap and left to dry before sanding flat (see pages 18-21).

Apply an undercoat and sand back flat. Acrylic paint dries well, but oil-based paints give stronger adhesion. White or pastel eggshell is probably the best base over the undercoat, and can be mixed with artists' oil colors.

When choosing the material for rag rolling, select paints that are compatible with those applied as a base – for example, oil on oil or water on water. Alternatively, mix up paints with glaze and oil colors. The glaze flows more easily, as it contains linseed – but, because of the oil content, take care when drying rags, which can heat up and combust.

Creating a rag-rolled finish

▲ 1 *Check the surface of the piece for faults. When any faults have been dealt with, apply the background color. An oil-based paint, such as eggshell, gives the best surface for rag rolling, but others can be used.*

▲2 *Coat the surface with colored glaze, using a flat brush and laying the glaze onto the piece, rather than brushing it around. Cover the surface evenly. You are going to move the material around, so do not work so slowly that it dries.*

▼3 *Any material can be used for rag rolling, including cotton cloth, polyethylene or, as in this case, paper towel. Make sure the "rag" is clean before use.*

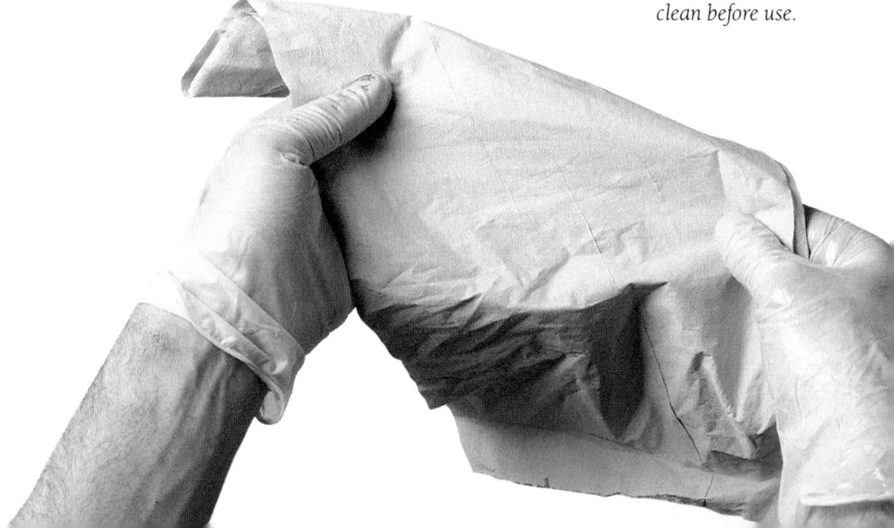

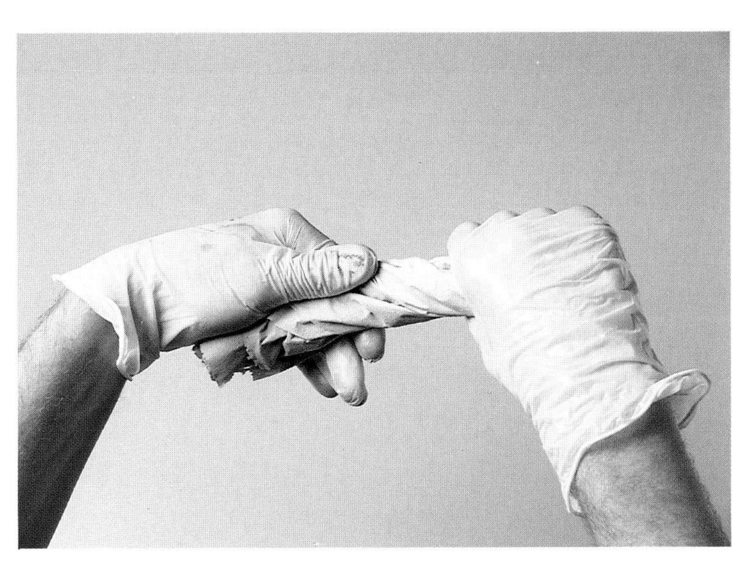

◀ 4 *Roll the paper or cloth into a long roll. It is important that it is not rolled too tightly, and that the surface remains uneven. Different effects can be produced by changing the tightness of the roll, and it is worth experimenting.*

Applying the glaze

Apply the wet coat to the surface thinly. It is important to work fast while the paint is still wet, otherwise it will be difficult to manipulate. The key is to work small areas at a time, having tested the color on a piece of scrap. Use a soft flat brush, maintaining an even coat.

Do the rag rolling with a piece of cotton cloth rolled around some dowels. Alternatively, you can simply roll up the cloth, making sure that the outside is uneven in order to produce the mottled effect. Keep the effect even across the surface, and always maintain a wet edge as you work.

Once the paint is dry, further

Rag-rolled paneling
◀ *The paneling behind and around the bath has been rag-rolled. Notice how the effect has been extended up onto the walls. The straight lines are achieved by removing any excess finish using a piece of cloth dampened with mineral spirits, following a light pencil line.*

MEMO

Safety precautions
Never leave rags containing linseed oil rolled up, as they can spontaneously combust.

Tools and materials
Flat brush

Badger brush

Cotton cloth

Undercoat and eggshell

Plaster of Paris

Colored glaze

Flat or gloss varnish

Common problems
It is easy to let the color and effect vary over large areas. Try to keep it even and constant throughout – especially when, after working around a large piece, the first edge meets up with the last.

Appropriate surfaces
You can use rag rolling on furniture, paneling or walls.

Drying time
Leave the eggshell overnight before rag rolling.

Leave the glaze a day or two, to dry thoroughly, before varnishing.

applications can be made for contrasting color. Apply a further layer of color and continue the rolling process. One way of varying the finish is to soften the mottled effect, before it dries, with a softening brush or badger. This is a long-haired brush made from badger hair. Use it to brush the surface lightly with short strokes, just touching the surface. Once it is dry, apply a coat of flat or gloss varnish. Polyurethane or oil varnish will alter the color of the paint.

Alternative techniques along the same lines include ragging on and ragging off. The first involves applying the colored glaze directly to the surface, using a wadded-up rag. Ragging off is identical except that the glaze is applied thin and wet to the surface by brush then mottled by dabbing with the rag. They are both similar to stippling (see pages 86-89).

Which technique is chosen is a matter of ease and convenience, though you are bound to find visual distinctions between the methods.

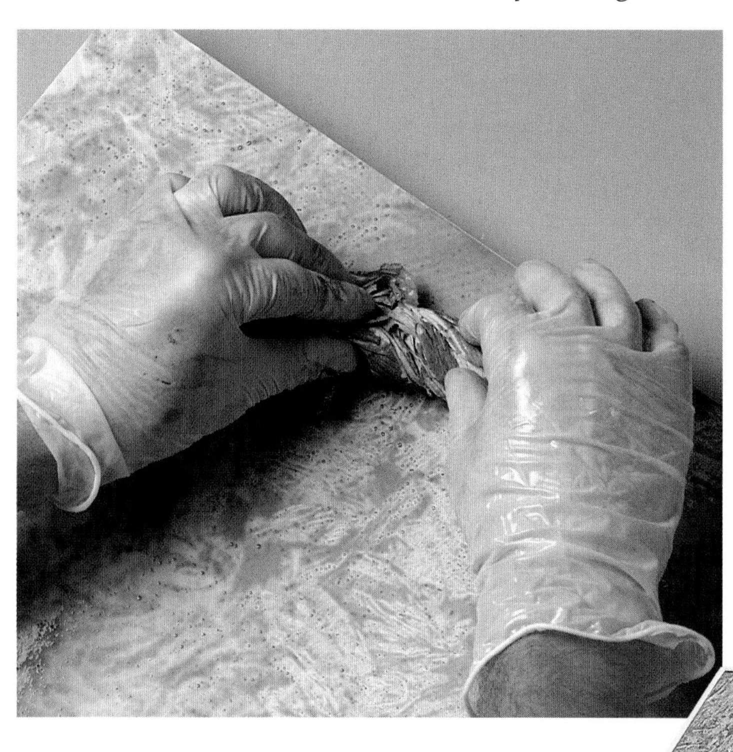

◀ **5** *Hold the "rag" in both hands and roll it across the wet surface, to produce a mottled effect. Use a badger brush to soften the effect, and leave to dry before applying further glazes.*

▼ **6** *While the final glaze is still damp, if required, wipe off a border around the rag-rolled area, using a clean cloth dampened with mineral spirits. When the glaze has dried thoroughly, apply a coat of gloss or flat varnish to protect it. Bear in mind that polyurethane or oil varnish will alter the color of the paint.*

HINTS AND TIPS

- Try out color on scrap before rag rolling.
- Apply thin coats.
- Use new cotton cloth.
- Only attempt small areas at a time.
- Do not let the cloth get too wet.
- Always clean your softener or badger before and after use.

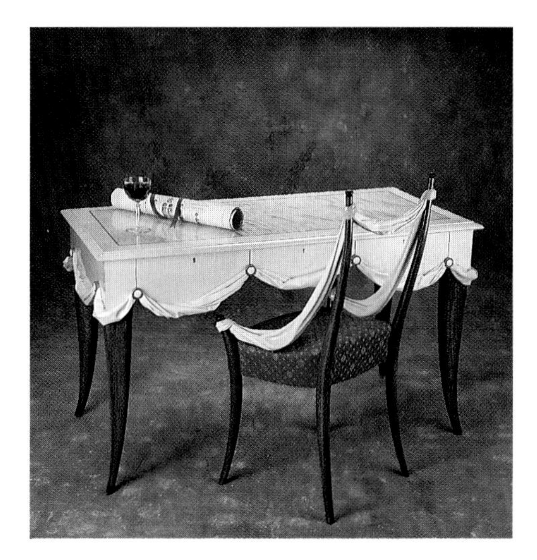

Rag-rolled furniture
◀ *A table and chair in figured birch and fiddle back sycamore, with a rag-rolled panel on the table top.*

Subtle shades
▼ *The colors used on these rag-rolled walls are very subtle, giving a soft feel to the room.*

Ebonizing

SEE ALSO

18-19 POWERED SANDERS

20-21 ABRASIVES

44-49 STAINING WOOD

53-55 GRAIN FILLERS

58-65 FRENCH POLISHING

66-69 WORKING WITH COLORS

The rarity and expense of ebony as a natural timber has made ebonizing a popular imitative finish, especially on reproduction Regency furniture and as a substitute for black Chinese lacquer. Today, ebonizing has become synonymous with a uniform finish, with no graining, except for the pores, showing through. Nevertheless, any color can be used, and often the aim is to create a very dark gray finish with lighter streaks. On mass-produced furniture, a black ash finish is commonly used – usually sprayed on for an even texture, though using black polish instead of spray adds depth to the finish. To simulate the grain structure of ebony and produce a smooth surface, use close-grained woods such as beech, sycamore or mahogany. There is no reason why the grain should not show through the ebonized finish, though that may make color matching more difficult.

With ebonizing, the slightest imperfection is magnified, so prepare the surface assiduously (fingers are often the best judge of preparation) and take extra care throughout the finishing process.

Ebonizing a small chest

▶ **1** *Ebony is a very dense wood, with very little grain. It is therefore essential that any piece to be ebonized is prepared thoroughly with all the holes and pores filled in and sanded flat. The slightest blemish will be shown up, and exaggerated by the finish. Any idea that black will mask faults is unfounded – indeed it shows up mistakes more than any other color.*

Application

Traditionally, a nigrosine water stain is used for staining the wood. Nigrosine water stain is available by mail order from finish suppliers (see the back of this book for some useful addresses). It's best to avoid using alcohol stains for this purpose, especially on a large area; because they dry so quickly, they are difficult to apply. If using a water

▲ 2 *Stain the prepared piece with a nigrosine water stain, or a black alcohol stain, which is being used here. Apply the stain wet and rub well into the grain until an even effect is achieved.*

▲ 3 *You will need to apply plenty of stain to ensure the finish is not patchy. Keep a wet edge at all times, and then wipe off any excess stain with a clean piece of soft cloth. Wipe the surface completely clean and then leave the piece to dry.*

▲ 4 *Once dry, lightly sand the surface to remove any specks of dust. Then apply black grain filler to fill any open pores. Wipe the filler across the surface with a piece of burlap. Clean off any surplus grain filler and leave to dry.*

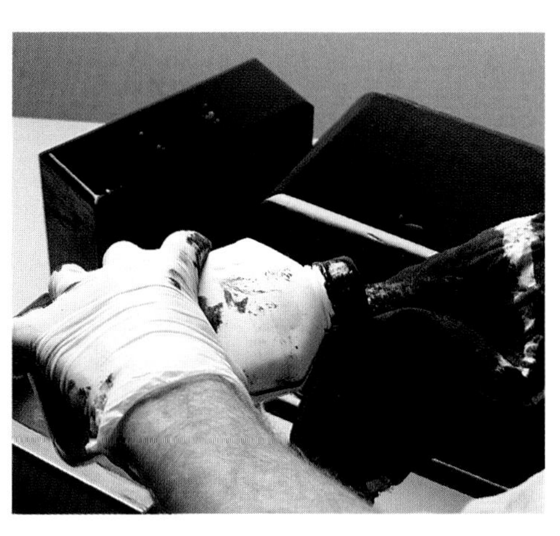

▲ 5 *Once the filler has dried, lightly sand and wipe clean. It is now time to start applying the black polish. Use a black alcohol stain dissolved in white shellac polish. Use 10 parts of polish to 1 part of stain. Load the polishing pad with the black polish, and apply as if French polishing.*

MEMO

Tools and materials

Polishing pad

Soft cloth

Batting

Black water stain

Black alcohol stain

Denatured alcohol

White or blonde polish

Common problems

Using too much denatured alcohol when removing the oil can cut the polish back too far, creating patches and streaks.

Make sure all the oil has been worked out with the polishing pad before finishing off, otherwise it can cause sweating and, later, cracking.

Appropriate surfaces

Wood with a close grain structure is best for ebonizing – although interesting effects can be accomplished on more open-grained surfaces.

Drying time

Water stains takes 30 minutes to dry.

Leave the first coat of polish to dry for 20 minutes.

Topcoats take 8 hours to dry.

The finishing polish takes 5 hours to dry.

▼ *6 Build up the surface with polish, using a combination of circular, straight and figure-eight strokes. Use a drop of linseed oil as a lubricant if necessary. Make sure that the finish is even, checking for patchy areas. Once the polish has been built up, leave to dry.*

stain, wet the surface first to raise the grain, then allow it to dry and sand it flat.

Once the stain has dried, apply white or blonde polish mixed with black alcohol stain, using a polishing pad as for French polish (see pages 58-65). Make a saturated solution of black stain (black in denatured alcohol), using about ½ cup of stain to 2 cups of polish. If you want to add lighter streaks, use a coloring mop to apply alcohol stain mixed with denatured alcohol.

Build up a body of black polish, then leave to dry hard before flatting down with 320 grit garnet paper or silicon carbide of the same grit. Make sure the surface is sanded flat.

To give depth to the finish, apply a final coat of white or blonde polish, using a touch of linseed oil as lubrication. Once the finish looks full enough, remove the oil with denatured alcohol in the polishing pad to produce a deep gloss. Leave to dry, then burnish with a soft cloth and pumice powder.

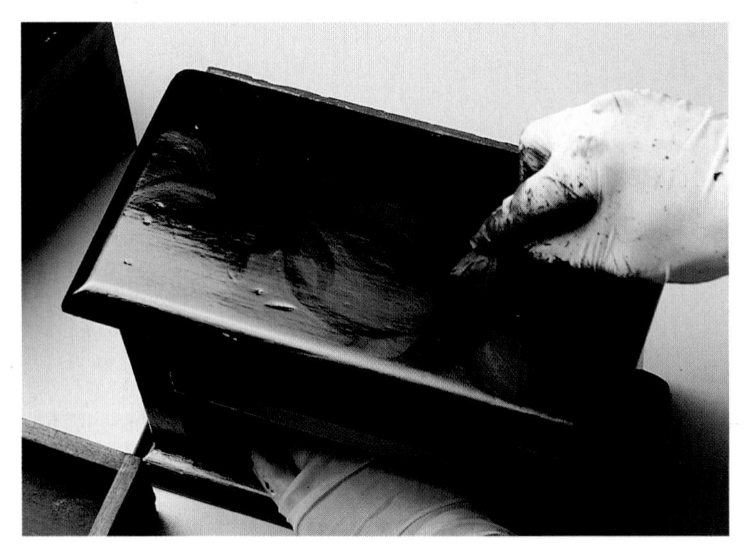

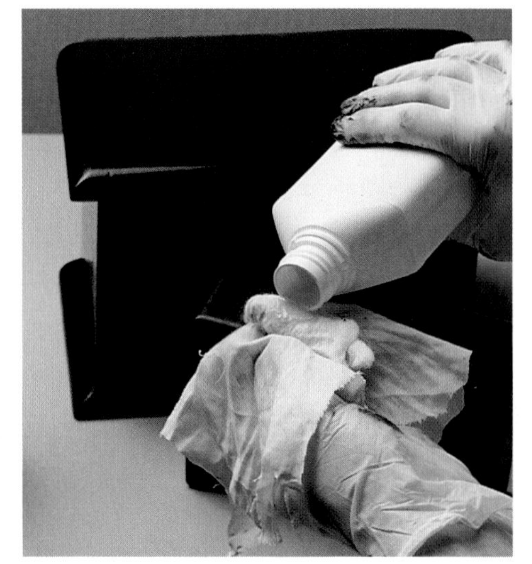

▶ *7 When the build of black polish is completely dry, cut it back with 320 silicon-carbide self-lubricating sandpaper. The surface must look satin as well as flat – any unevenness will be apparent later. Wipe off the dust and clean the surface.*

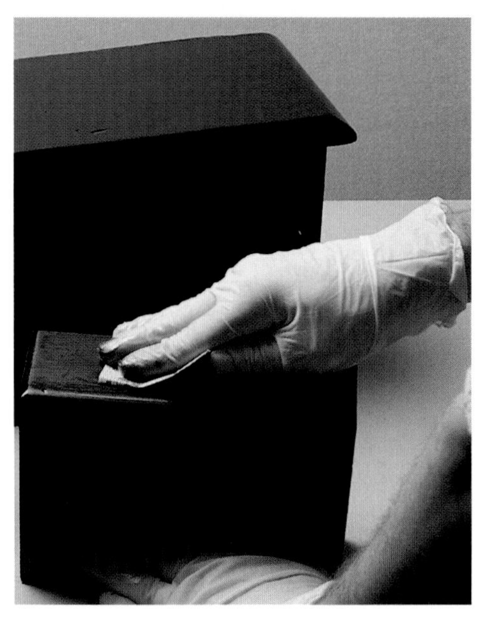

▲ *8 To produce greater depth to the ebonized surface apply white polish. Load the polishing rubber with white polish and build up the surface as if French polishing, until a full gloss finish has been achieved. Leave to dry. If you want a gloss finish, nothing more needs to be done.*

HINTS AND TIPS

- Preparation is the key, as defects will be amplified by the finish.
- Use grain filler on open-grained wood.
- Only use alcohol dyes for coloring with polish.

▲ **9** *For a satin finish, rub the piece with fine 000 steel wool and wax polish. Rub with the grain and always apply the same pressure, otherwise the finish may look patchy and uneven.*

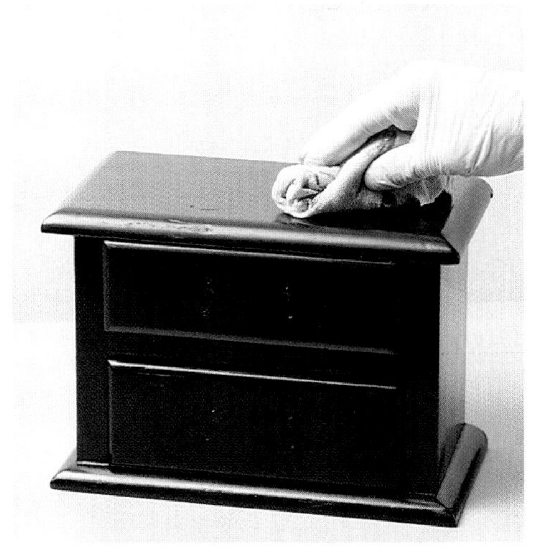

▲ **10** *For a final sheen, rub the polished surface with wax and a soft cloth. Rub with the grain, covering the whole piece.*

◀ **11** *What was once pine is now ebony. It is at this stage that you realize that any blemishes will show up the piece for what it really is.*

Stenciling

SEE ALSO

66-69
VORKING WITH COLORS

86-89
STIPPLING

The beauty of stenciling is that it allows anyone, from a complete novice to the most artistic and experienced finisher, to enhance the simplest of finishes with elaborate and attractive decoration.

American settlers decorated their homes with stenciling, and the effect became a measure of status. The patterns, which were usually done on a pale background, were taken from pictures or drawn and cut freehand. Today, patterns for stenciling can be bought ready-made from craft stores, and you can use a photocopier to enlarge or reduce images for tracing.

Cutting a stencil

Almost any material can be used for the stencil, but clear acetate is best. It allows the paint or finish to be wiped off easily. Acetate can be difficult to cut, as it has a tendency to split – but, being clear, it can be used for direct tracing.

Make sure there is at least a 2-inch border around the pattern, for support. Large motifs may need a wider border. Also, bear in mind that you may want to use the edges as a reference when you are applying the finish. Position the decoration in the center, and trim the edges later.

Use a razor-blade knife or craft knife for cutting the shapes. It is best to use a sheet of glass as a cutting board (pad the edges with masking tape) or special self-healing rubberized board. This prevents the board blade being deflected by old cut marks, which can happen on cutting boards made from other materials. Only the point of the knife is used for cutting the stencil. It can be sharpened by grinding the back of the blade to create a new tip.

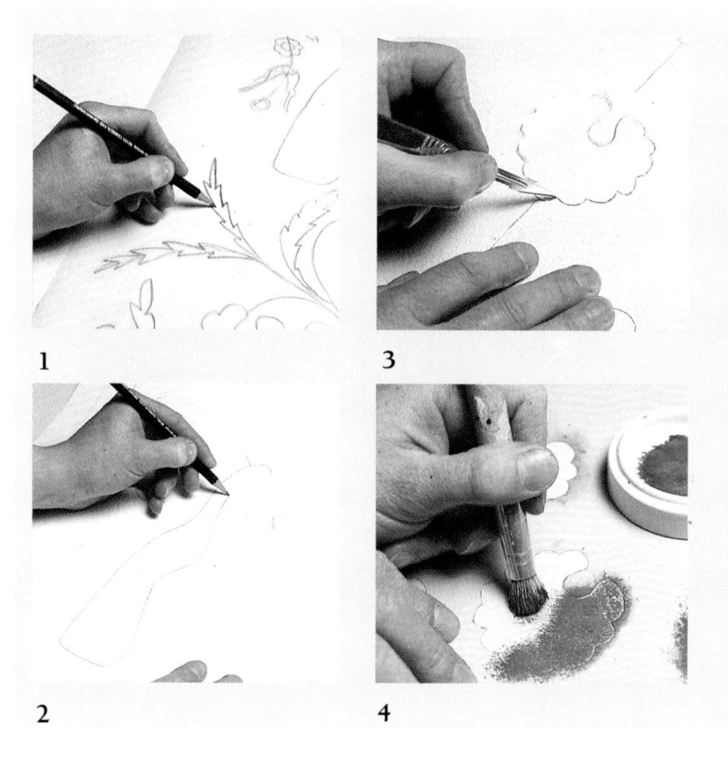

Making a stencil
1 *Draw out the motifs for the design on tracing paper, using a soft, dark pencil.*

2 *Transfer the motifs to acetate film and go over them to mark the outlines clearly.*

3 *With a fine, sharp knife, cut carefully around the outlines.*

4 *Place the stencil firmly on the surface and fill the shape with color using a stenciling brush.*

Start with simple designs, without cutting out large areas of the stencil. If too much rigidity is lost, you will find that it is difficult to manage the stencil while applying the finish. Indeed, as the patterns become more complex, bridges will be needed to keep the stencil stiff. Cut these bridges as thin as possible, as the unpainted areas will need to be touched up after stenciling.

Multi-colored patterns are produced by using a number of stencils. The important thing is to make sure all the stencils are compatible. Do so by punching holes in the corners of each stencil, then line the holes up with marks on the original drawing or tracing. The holes can also be used as references when applying the finish.

Applying the finish

The groundwork for stenciling can be any color or material – but for walls a flat undercoat or eggshell is best, though latex works well. The advantage of water-based paints is that they dry fast; although that does not matter for the background, it is vital when coloring the stencil shapes. Stencils are generally applied on a light or pastel background, but there is no reason why the pattern should not be picked out in bright colors against a darker background. On wooden objects, seal the piece first with flat varnish (gloss has less key) or a sanding sealer.

The position of the pattern is important, so try it out first, marking off reference lines along the edges with

Stenciling a chest of drawers using a ready-cut stencil

◀ **1** *Painted furniture is a common recipient for stenciling, though natural wood can also provide an excellent background for subtle patterns and colors. Make sure the painted piece is thoroughly prepared before application, using an undercoat as a base. The undercoat does not have to be white – pastel colors are the best alternative.*

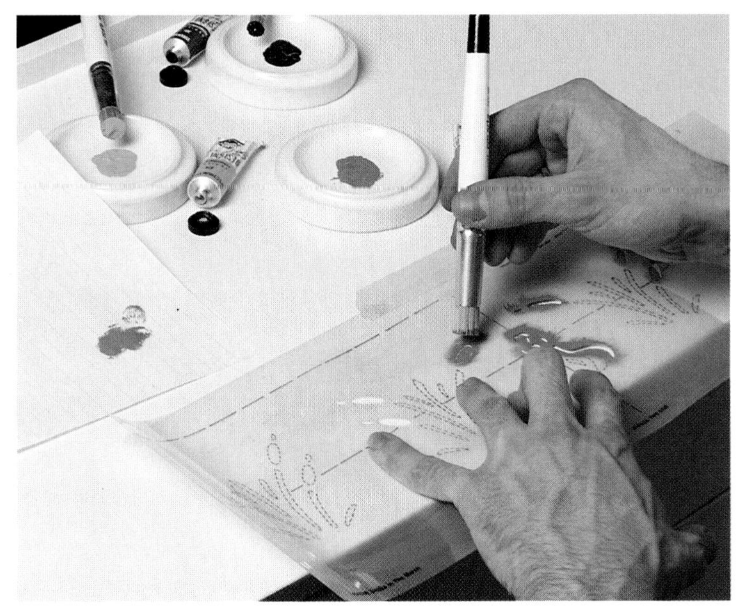

▶ **2** *For these small patterns, on a painted surface, use artists' colors mixed in shallow dishes. Test the color on white paper. Position the stencil and tape it down firmly. Apply the color by dabbing with a stencil brush. Press down hard on the stencil, and do not use too much paint, to ensure that none of the material creeps under the stencil. Sharp lines are essential.*

MEMO

Tools and materials

Soft pencil

Flat brush

Stipple or stencil brush

Craft knife or razor-blade knife

Straightedge

Acetate or ready-cut stencils

Cutting board and palette

Marking pen for acetate

Masking tape

Oil paints or stains

Mineral spirits

Varnish

Common problems

The finish will creep under the stencil if the stencil is not pressed hard enough. This also happens if the finish is too thin, or too much finish is applied.

Do not split a motif in half at the end of a stencil. The line will always show.

Appropriate surfaces

Furniture, doors, drawers, walls and floors. Also, boxes, toychests and other decorative items.

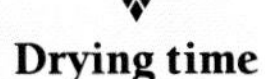

Drying time

Leave the finish for 30 seconds before removing the stencil. Allow it to dry overnight before varnishing.

CHOOSING STENCIL DESIGNS

- Stenciling can be used on almost any surface, from walls, floors and ceilings to small boxes. The ability to produce repetitive designs is one of its most obvious features; stenciled borders are therefore particularly popular. Equally, single identical motifs on a series of doors or drawers can look most effective.

- Floral and ribbon designs are widely available, and can easily be copied from pictures or even wallpaper. Use a photocopier to enlarge or reduce a design to suit the requirements of a particular piece. Geometric shapes work well as borders, or as rug patterns on floors; and a twisted rope effect can be achieved with proprietary stencils or by cutting out a series of leaf shapes. Look at woven or printed designs on rugs, curtains, wallpaper and linen for ideas and tracings.

- Try to use a stencil that is appropriate for the piece. Animals always look good on toyboxes and on cupboard doors. A string of camels, like a frieze, around a child's room is fun, as are almost any well-defined animals. Children's books are a good source for designs, but animal stencils are sold by most craft stores and by some stationery and toystores. Fruit and other everyday objects are equally suitable and especially rewarding for children, who can pick out the different images. A sequence of shapes can be made to look more interesting if no one image is painted in a particular color more than once.

- As far as possible, blend the shape of the design to the shape of the piece or area being decorated. The idea is to enhance the piece, not to impose an unsuitable image that confuses the eye. However, there is plenty of opportunity for imaginative stenciling. For instance, the silhouette of a window can be stenciled on a floor to create the illusion of sun streaming into the room.

▲ **3** *Once the first color has started to dry, remove the stencil. Try to avoid dragging the color, as it will be difficult to touch up. Leave the motif to dry.*

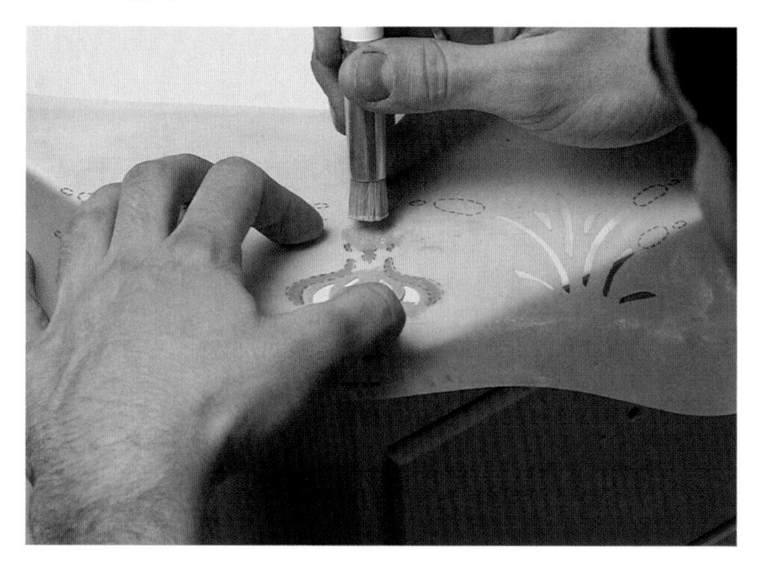

▲ **4** *Apply a second color by dabbing with the stencil brush.*

◄ **5** *Select the next motif to be applied, and mix up a suitable color. Make sure that the colors match, and that enough is mixed to complete the stenciling – mixed colors are difficult to repeat.*

chalk. These can easily be wiped off later – but you must remember to do so, as a coat of varnish would seal the lines in forever. Do not start applying the stencil before the background is completely dry; similarly, never add further stencil colors until the previous one is dry.

The best means of applying the paint is with a special stenciling brush. These are not expensive and have short bristles shaped rather like those of a shaving brush. Use the stenciling brush with a dabbing action, as if stippling (see pages 86–89). First, though, you need to attach the stencil to the workpiece, making sure that it fits as snugly against the surface as possible. Any gaps will allow the paint to creep, producing a poorly defined and untidy finish. When applying the paint, have an instrument such as a paint scraper ready for pressing down the stencil in place, using your spare hand.

Mix the color to suit, using artists' colors in an oil paint or glaze. Mix

▶ **6** *Three colors have now been applied, and the pattern is taking shape. Notice how the stalks of the flowers are a dark color, and the emphasis is given to the flowers or seed pods, which are brighter.*

▲ **7** *Use a simple repetitive pattern to join up the more detailed shapes. This livens up the piece, without making it fussy. Try to follow the shape of the piece being stenciled; highlight edges, corners, door panels and drawers. Stencils can have a number of patterns cut in them, but too many make the stencil weak.*

▼ **8** *Stenciling is particularly effective for brightening up a nursery, bathroom or kitchen. Any combination of colors can be used, but always make sure each application is dry before attempting the next, and keep the stencil clean at all times.*

Coordinating stencils
▲ *Although these stencils are both simple two-color patterns they brighten up surfaces by following the line of the stairs and by picking out the drawer fronts on the chest.*

enough for the job, as it will be difficult to reproduce the exact color later (see pages 66–69). Do not make the paint too thin, or it will run. Decant a small quantity of the finish onto a palette of some sort (glass works well). This helps to keep the amount of paint on the brush to a minimum, and so also reduces the chance of creep.

After painting the pattern, leave the stencil in place for at least 30 seconds and then remove vertically in one action. This may need some practice. Wipe off any excess from the stencil, using mineral spirits, before applying more paint. This is why acetate is so good. When creating a repetitive pattern, make sure that the stencil does not disturb the previous motif as you move on. Sometimes the stencil will have to overlap; in which case wait until the paint is dry, and in the meantime work on another area. It is important to have marked out the position of each pattern with chalk before starting. Try to keep

HINTS AND TIPS

- Special marking pens are needed for drawing on acetate.
- Attach tracings to acetate with masking tape.
- Keep stencil clean.
- Try out patterns with colored paper shapes first, or with paint on scrap material.
- Do not use absorbent material for stencils.
- Apply the paint lightly, with a dabbing action.

Combining decorative techniques
▶ *Before stenciling, this shelf unit was rag-rolled to give the background a garden feel. The eye is drawn toward the two painted plant pots, but notice how the repetitive patterns above the shelves and along the leading edges balance the design.*

the spacings and borders regular.

Wait until the pattern is dry before applying another layer or a protective coat of gloss or flat varnish. One effect worth trying is a single coat of flat varnish over two coats of gloss. This softens the glossiness a little. Use polyurethane for a tough coating for floors, but make sure before application that it doesn't react with the colors.

"Antique stencils"
▼ *This buffet has been painted, though some of the wood's grain has been allowed to show through. This effect is enhanced by the light patterns on the rails and end panel.*

USING COLOR FOR STENCILING

- When stenciling, you are attempting to produce an overall effect – so make sure the colors used are compatible. Do not use too many colors, as that means cutting or buying more stencils. Floral stencils often look best in pastel shades, while silhouettes and geometric patterns generally benefit from strong contrasting colors.
- Try also to keep the stenciling sympathetic to the piece. Old items may need faded colors, to suit their age, while modern furniture with hard lines can take stronger colors and bold decoration. When applying a stencil pattern to wood, bear in mind the color and figure of the grain. Stains will let the grain show through but tend to creep and to spread rapidly, though pigment stains can solve the problem.

Repetitive stenciling
▼ *This is a fine example of repetitive stenciling. The floorboards have been given a thin wash. The larger pattern has been stenciled in a darker shade and the smaller stencil is picked out in a more contrasting white. Notice how the faults and holes in the floorboards complement the repetition of the stencil, softening its effect.*

Crackle finishes

SEE ALSO

Crackle finishes are used for two quite distinct reasons. The first is to age a piece, simulating the cracking of finish over the years. Alternatively, an interesting decorative effect can be created with contrasting colors. This is sometimes used for imitating leather. In both cases, a coat of crackle glaze (a clear glaze available from finishing suppliers) is applied to the piece. As the glaze dries, surface tensions are produced, causing the finish to craze. It is possible to apply this finish by spraying (see pages 148–149), but the technique and materials used are different.

Apply a coat of oil varnish. Leave until tacky then apply the glaze to the surface with a flat brush, laying it on the surface, without working it at all, as the cracking will appear at once.

To highlight the effect, once the glaze is dry, rub paste wax into the cracks, using a soft cloth, then lightly burnish the surface. Alternatively, brush a thin scumble (see pages 86-87) into the cracks and wipe off the excess. You can either buy the scumble ready-mixed or mix your own, using gold size, pigment and mineral spirits. Once the surface is dry, burnish with a soft cloth. Crackle glaze needs no further protection – in fact, coating it with varnish would be pointless since that would cover up the cracks.

Colored crackle finish

For a decorative effect, apply a colored crackle glaze over a contrasting color. Experiment with combinations of color and shade. First, apply the colored "undercoat," making sure the surface is smooth. Then mix the second color with the crackle glaze and apply it to the dry surface; as the glaze cracks, thin lines of undercoat will appear.

The best effects are created with complementary colors – for instance, red and black or blue and red. Some colors look best as the top coat; others, especially the brighter colors, work better underneath. Lime green with gold cracks looks good, as do dark maroon with gold cracks, black with white, and gold with silver. Try all sorts of combination. Mix the background color with standard glaze, and apply it to the prepared surface with a brush. As with the clear crackle glaze, seal the wood with shellac sanding sealer first.

For an antique gilt effect, apply a silver background and cover it with a clear glaze tinted slightly with brown. Once the crackle has dried, rub dark-brown scumble or wax into the cracks. This works well for gilt picture frames, which often crack with age – either because the original finish was low in resins and substance or because oil is buried below layers of French polish.

HINTS AND TIPS

- Always test effect on scrap board of similar consistency.
- Make enough colored glaze to finish the job.
- Let each coat dry before applying the next one.
- Do not skimp on preparation.

CRACKLE PATTERNS

- Small boxes take a crackle finish well, whereas a dining table is probably too big. When applying a crackle finish to large items, lay the crackle glaze on heavier and wetter than for small pieces, in order to produce a generous "crazy paving" pattern.
- It is important to create a crackle finish that suits the piece. Never exceed 2 inches, even on large areas, as the finish can start to peel if the pattern is too wide. On rails and slender frames, a ¼ inch pattern looks best.

A selection of different crackle finishes
▲ **1** *White background and pink crackle.*
2 *Brown background and pink crackle.*
3 *Dark green background and yellow crackle.*
4 *Yellow background and turquoise crackle.*
5 *Black background, and blue crackle.*

Applying a crackle finish

▲**1** *The crackle is going to be used to age a mirror frame. In other circumstances crackle works for decorative effect. Make sure the surface is thoroughly prepared. In this case, the frame has been wiped with mineral spirits.*

▲**2** *Having prepared the surface, and masked off any areas that do not need to be cracked, apply a coat of oil varnish. Do this with a flat brush, laying it on so that there are no brush marks.*

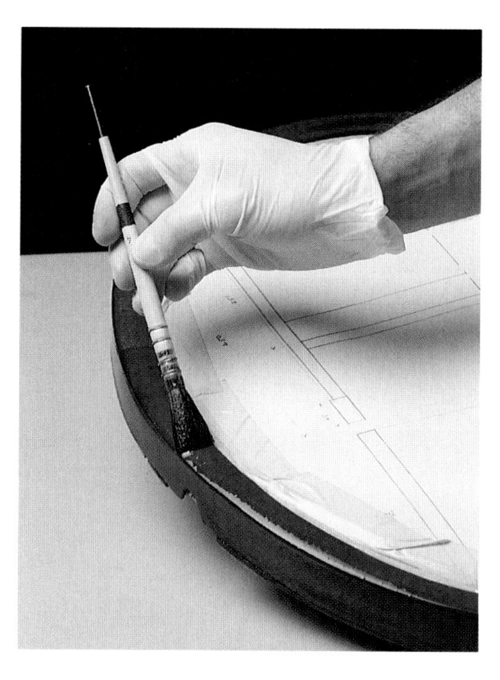

▲**3** *When the varnish is tacky apply a coat of crackle glaze. This is supplied ready for use. The size of the crazy paving pattern produced depends on how much glaze is applied. A thicker coat results in a wider crackle. As with the varnish, lay on the glaze, allowing it to flow freely.*

▼**4** *As the glaze dries it cracks, producing the distinctive pattern. This can be enhanced by rubbing the cracks with dyes or pigmented wax, which can be made to contrast or complement the undercoat color.*

MEMO

Tools and materials
Flat brush

Oil varnish

Undercoat or eggshell paint

Paste wax and pigment

Artists' oil colors

Crackle glaze

Common problems
Uneven application produces an uneven pattern.

Too much color will make the finish too dark.

Drying time
Let shellac sealer dry for 15 minutes.

Glaze takes about 30 minutes to dry, but leave longer.

Leave crackle glaze to dry for 1 hour.

Distressing

SEE ALSO

18–19 POWERED SANDERS
20–21 ABRASIVES
26–27 BRUISES, DENTS AND SCRATCHES
36–37 CHEMICAL STRIPPING
44–49 STAINING WOOD
58–65 FRENCH POLISHING
66–69 WORKING WITH COLOR
80–83 RESTORING OLD FINISHES

Distressing, also known as antiquing or faking, is used to "age" contemporary furniture or new components of antique pieces. The simplest guide is to look at furniture of the relevant period and try to imitate the markings.

When preparing the surface, bruises and knocks can of course be ignored – but do not be tempted to ignore machining marks, which will betray the youth of the piece. The distressing is done with hard objects, such as bags of nuts and bolts, bicycle chains and hammers, often softened by cloth. Water marks can be reproduced by using a cup with stain smeared on the bottom. When distressing, make sure the marks are deep enough to break the fibers thoroughly, so they will take plenty of water stain. This makes the dents look even darker, as if they have collected dirt over the years.

Without holding back on distressing the surface as a whole, concentrate on the areas likely to suffer with time. Legs get bashed regularly, as do edges and table tops. A small bag of nuts and bolts works particularly well and helps create a random pattern of bruising. Mass-produced reproduction furniture often exhibits distressing that looks too systematic, since it follows a pattern, having been done by machine. Try to keep the effect as natural as possible, and practice first on some scrap wood or even on a rejected piece of furniture that is beyond repair.

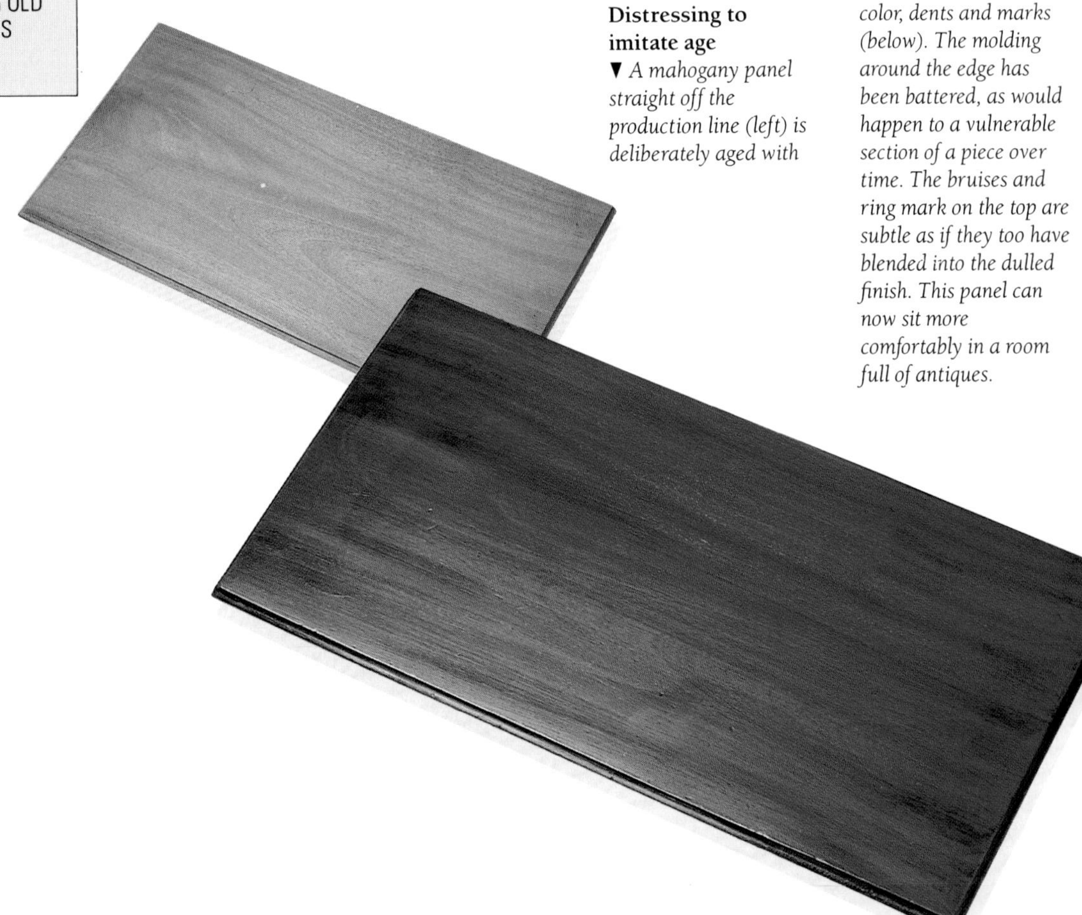

Distressing to imitate age

▼ *A mahogany panel straight off the production line (left) is deliberately aged with color, dents and marks (below). The molding around the edge has been battered, as would happen to a vulnerable section of a piece over time. The bruises and ring mark on the top are subtle as if they too have blended into the dulled finish. This panel can now sit more comfortably in a room full of antiques.*

◀ **1** *Use a bag of nuts and bolts to make bruises and dents on the surface. The contents need to be heavy enough to do some damage. Make sure you move the bag around in a random motion; mass-produced reproduction furniture can be identified by a regular pattern. Concentrate on edges and legs.*

▶ **2** *Once the surface has been distressed, apply a water stain. Use plenty of stain, keeping it wet as you manipulate it around the piece. Rub the stain into the damaged fibers of bruises and dents so that they show up darker.*

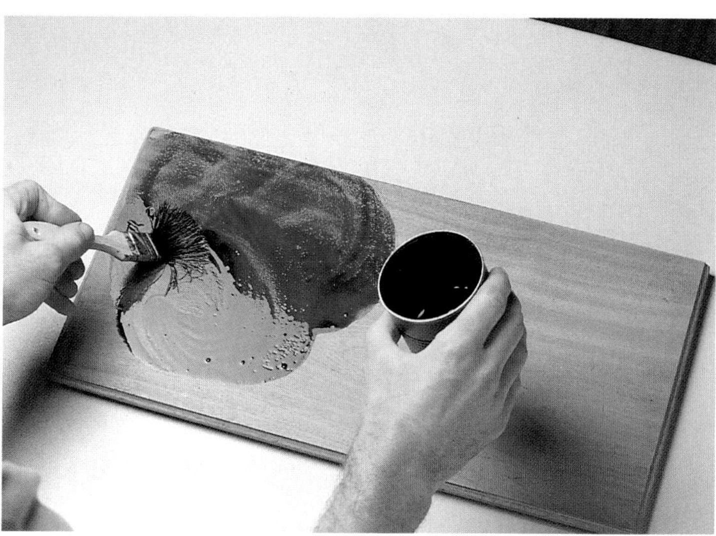

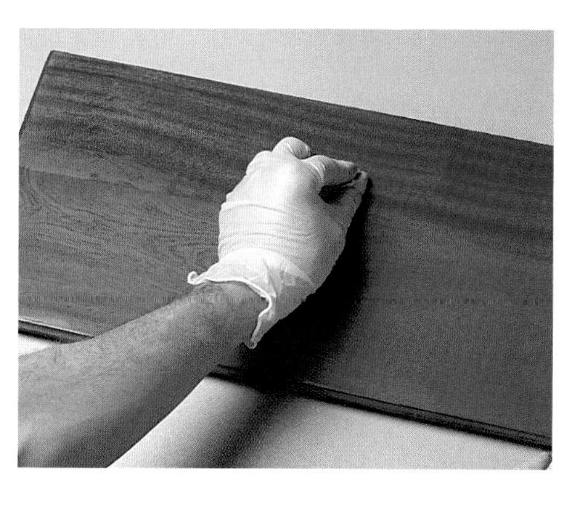

▲ **3** *When the stain has dried, seal the surface with a shellac sealer. Wipe the sealer across the surface with a soft cloth, using straight strokes along the grain.* 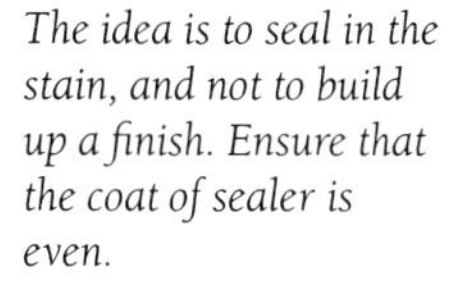 *The idea is to seal in the stain, and not to build up a finish. Ensure that the coat of sealer is even.*

▲ **4** *Many old pieces have ring marks, from alcohol on glasses or hot water under cups and mugs. To imitate such a mark, fill a metal container with hot water and wet the bottom. Leave this on the surface for five to ten minutes to make a dark ring.*

MEMO

Tools and materials

Brushes

Metal objects

Polishing pad

Soft cloth

Stains

Blonde polish

Paste wax

Common problems

The distressing pattern will not look natural if it is too regular.

Do not distress an existing finish. Pieces must be stripped back first.

Appropriate surfaces

Any piece can be given an antique finish. However, an antique or distressed finish is obviously inappropriate for contemporary furniture.

Drying time

Water stain takes about 40 minutes to dry.

▶ **5** *Stain is not sufficient to give the piece a color that reproduces the effects of ageing. Mix alcohol stains and pigments with French polish in a container, and apply with a brush. Cover the whole surface liberally with color and rub into the wood, to produce a darker finish. Try to produce a slightly opaque color mix.*

HINTS AND TIPS

- Use deliberate strokes when distressing.
- Rub in the stain well.
- Look at antique furniture and see how it wears.

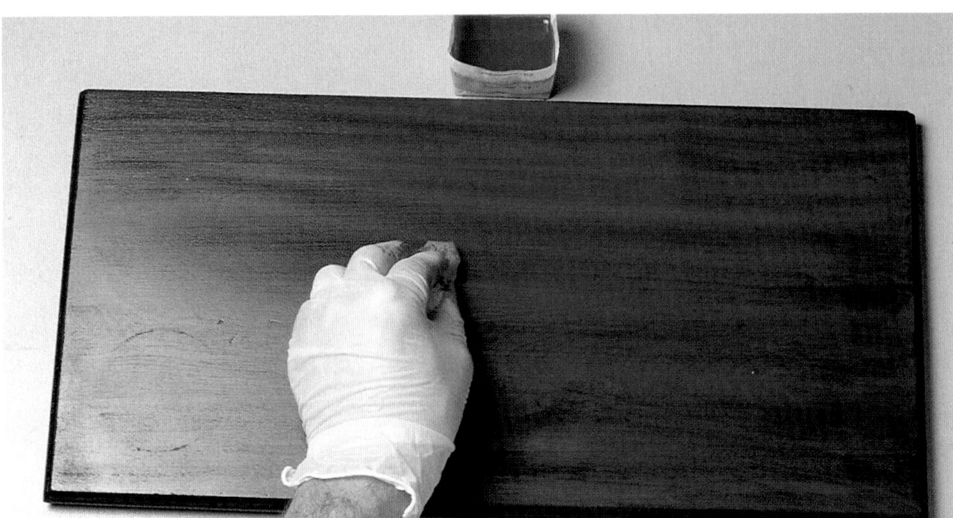

◀ **6** *After the color has dried, apply a coat of transparent polish using the polishing pad. Work up a build until a finish just short of full grain has been produced. Start with a circular pattern, moving across the surface. Finish with straight strokes following the grain.*

▶ **7** *An antique piece will have lost some of the shine of new polish, so dull the surface once the polish has dried. Use fine 000 steel wool to rub the polish with straight strokes along the grain. Finish with a coat of dark colored paste wax to enhance the aged appearance.*

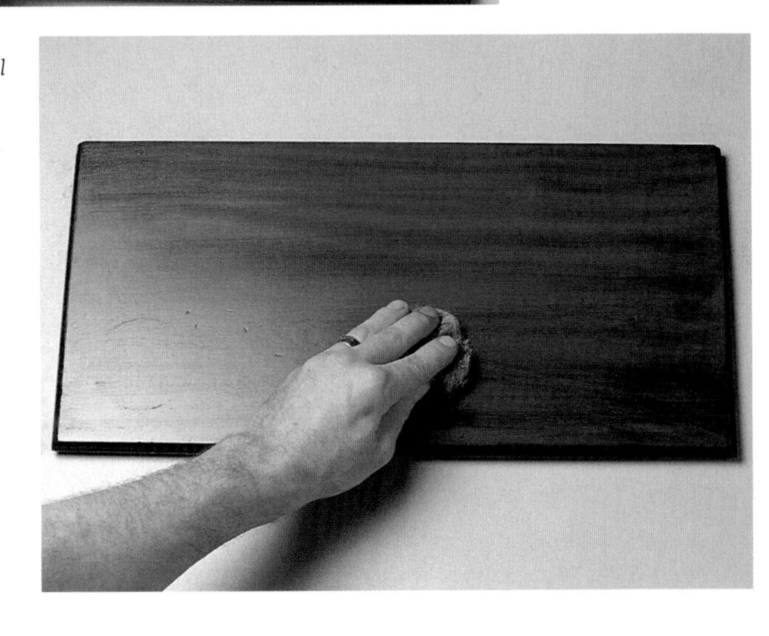

Finishing distressed furniture

Once you are satisfied with the distressing, stain the piece dark then wipe off the surplus. The stain will bite into the marks, making them show up dark, as old marks would. Use water stain, as it gives you plenty of time to fool around with the finish. Leave any odd splashes to simulate splashed marks made over the years – but rub the stain off the corners and moldings, as would happen with time. Seal with a shellac sealer.

Lightly sand the dried stain with fine sandpaper (see pages 18–21) and begin the polishing process with blonde polish, which tends to make the surface look faded (a tinted polish would liven it up and make it look newer). Work up to a semi-filled finish, with the pores partly filled, but do not try to produce a high gloss. Dull this finish using 000 steel wool, rubbing evenly in the direction of the grain. Finally, apply a tinted wax with a soft cloth, before burnishing. Or use a shoe brush and pumice powder, sprinkling the surface with the powder and sweeping the brush with the grain, then polish with wax.

Corner cabinet with distressed finish
▲ *Andy Holmes' corner cabinet, made from recycled materials, is a fine example of how marks and dents give a piece age.*

Combining distressing and colored wash
◀ *A combination of distressing and a colored wash gives this chest of drawers a feeling of age. Particular attention has been paid to the vulnerable parts of the piece, especially the edge molding.*

Rubbed finishes

SEE ALSO

26–27 BRUISES, DENTS AND SCRATCHES
44-49 STAINING WOOD
58-65 FRENCH POLISHING
66-69 WORKING WITH COLORS
73-75 WAXED FINISHES
80-83 RESTORING OLD FINISHES
114-117 DISTRESSING

A rubbed finish is used to simulate the effects of age on a piece of furniture or paneling, by rubbing stain selectively to produce the highlights and dark patches of wear. The technique is most commonly used on oak reproduction furniture, particularly reproduction Jacobean items, but it can be used on other woods too.

Start by preparing the surface in the normal way – though, since the aim is to achieve an antique feel, it will look more convincing if you leave some of the blemishes and bruises. Which faults you leave will depend on the degree of distressing (see pages 114–117) you hope to accomplish. But make sure any conspicuous machining marks are removed, as a genuine antique piece would be unlikely to exhibit the telltale ripples produced by a power planer!

Stain the piece using Vandyke crystals mixed with water, to create a dark color. Water stains are available by mail order from finishing suppliers, (see back of book for some useful addresses).

Once the stain has dried, sand lightly to remove any roughness. Then overstain, using a dark oil dye. Work the stain into the grain, but leave corners and moldings unwiped, so that they are darker than the rest. Leave to dry before starting the rubbing.

Using 000 steel wool, make a pad to fit in the hand. Work on the highlights until the dark stain has been rubbed off, then continue rubbing until the patchy effect has been subtly blended in and there are no definite lines remaining between the light and dark areas. On panels, rub the center, easing the color off without making a sharp line. Always work in the direction of the grain, gradually easing the color. Once the desired effect has been achieved, clean the shreds of steel wool and wood dust from the surface.

The idea is to remove the finish from those areas that over the years would be worn away by wear and tear. The tops of beads on moldings and the edges and corners of chairs and tables are, for example, particularly liable to wear. Conversely, more inaccessible areas collect dust and dirt, and so darken with age. To simulate that effect, mix pigments and alcohol dyes with polish and touch up the low points (around raised panels, on inside corners, and anywhere out of everyday reach), using a brush. Take a good look at old woodwork to see how it ages.

Use a dark garnet polish for finishing the rubbed effect. Apply at first with a soft cloth, and then leave to dry. Sand, using fine paper (about 320 grit), then dust off and continue to apply polish with a pad (see page 60). Shade in any parts that show up too distinctively, using an alcohol color with small amounts of pigment, applied with either a soft cloth or a brush. If a deeper finish is required, use white polish as a final coat. Leave to dry and continue polishing, but do not build up a high-gloss finish, which would be inappropriate on antique furniture.

Once the polish has dried, use 000 steel wool to dull the finish, to create a satin or semi-flat effect, always following the grain. After dulling, apply a wax finish with a soft cloth, using a pale colored paste wax. Finish off by lightly burnishing.

HINTS AND TIPS

- Remove the stain gradually, by rubbing in progressive stages.
- Do not make sharp lines – the rubbed effect must blend in subtly.
- Make sure the surface is smooth at each stage.
- Dampen before starting to polish or apply stain.

Producing a rubbed finish

▲ 1 *Pieces such as this mahogany stool acquire rubs with age. After years of use, the color is no longer even — lighter areas appear at the center of panels, on seats or on chair backs.*

▲ 2 *Prepare the stool to produce a smooth surface and then apply color. In this case a dark water stain (Vandyke) is used; it penetrates well, and can be worked into corners and crevices to give a darker color. Rub the stain into the moldings.*

▲ 3 *Once the stool has been stained, wipe off the surplus and leave to dry. Then sand lightly and overstain using dark oil dye. Note the darker areas on legs and corners.*

▲ 4 *When the piece is dry, rub off the stain with fine 000 steel wool or flexible abrasive (as here). Start from the center of a rail or panel and work toward the corners. Rub off more stain in the center than in the corners, blending gradually toward them.* *Use alcohol dyes, mixed with French polish and applied with a brush, to enhance the rubbed effect. A dark oil dye will help the contrast, but make sure the color blends in. Use a dark garnet polish for finishing the rubbed effect.*

▲ 5 *Give the finished stool a coat of white polish, working up to a semi-full gloss finish. Then wax polish the piece, to bring out the color and add depth. Distressing at an early stage will enhance the impression of age.*

MEMO

Tools and materials

00 and 000 steel wool

Soft cloth

Brushes

Polishing pad

Vandyke crystals

Dark oil stain

Alcohol colors and pigments

Garnet polish

Fine sandpaper

White polish (if a deep finish is required)

Dark colored paste wax

Common problems

The gradual shading of a rubbed effect can be difficult to achieve, but is important.

Remember to raise the grain before staining.

Appropriate surfaces

Rubbing is most commonly done on oak and mock-Jacobean furniture – but there is no reason why it cannot be used on other furniture or on items made from other woods.

Drying time

The water stain will take about 40 minutes to dry, but leave it for 3 or 4 hours before applying the oil stain.

Leave the rubbed oil stain overnight before polishing.

Pickling

SEE ALSO

16–17 SCRAPERS

18–19 POWERED SANDERS

44–49 STAINING WOOD

53–55 GRAIN FILLERS

58–65 FRENCH POLISHING

66–69 WORKING WITH COLORS

73–75 WAXED FINISHES

The principle of pickling is similar to that of grain filling (see pages 53–55). It is used on open-grained woods (most commonly oak), a pickling paste being worked into the pores of the wood. When the surface is fully finished, pickling enhances the grain pattern, by emphasizing the pores and leaving a contrasting color.

Although it is possible to make your own pickling paste, buying a container of pickling paste is worthwhile in the long run. Proprietary pickling pastes include drying agents, which help to speed up the process.

If you want to color the paste, decant a quantity into a shallow container (never contaminate the paste in the original container with color). It may be difficult to repeat the color – so mix plenty for the task. Most colored pickled finishes are pastel shades (pink and green are popular choices), so avoid making the paste too dark.

Open the grain with a stiff wire brush, working in the direction of the grain. If you need to stain the piece, use a water stain, before pickling, and

Producing a pickled finish

▶ **1** *An oak clock case, which has been chemically stripped of previous finishes ready for pickling. Oak is particularly appropriate for pickling because of its open grain, but other woods can also be used.*

▲ 2 *Take off any hardware, and sand the piece with 240 grade sandpaper. Check all the surfaces to ensure that they are free from dirt and grease.*

▲ 4 *After opening the grain, stain the piece with any color. It is best not to use oil dye because this can cause patchiness at a later stage. Leave the stain to dry.*

▲ 3 *Open up the grain to take the pickling paste by rubbing the surface with a stiff wire brush, using straight strokes along the grain. Try to open the grain evenly, and not more deeply in some areas than in others. Check the results regularly against the light, making sure the whole surface has been worked with the wire brush.*

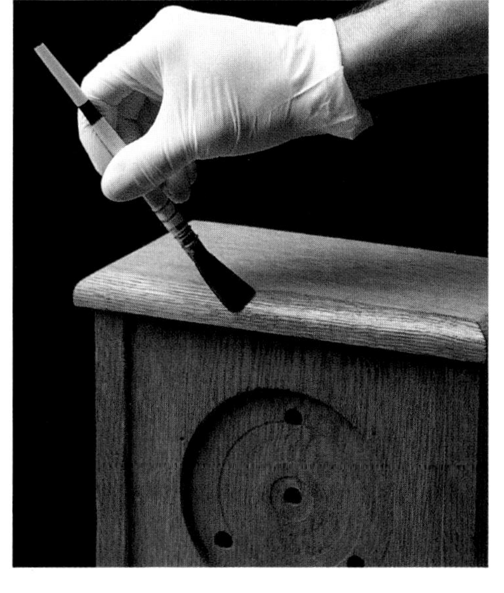

▲ 5 *Seal the stain with a pale or white polish to ensure the pickling paste does not dry patchy. If a harder, more durable finish is required seal the stain or the bare wood with teak oil or even a coat of varnish that has been thinned with white spirit.*

MEMO

Tools and materials

Scrapers and abrasive for preparing the surface

Burlap and soft cloth

Pickling paste

Water stain

Dyes and pigments

Shellac sealer

Wax

Wire brush

Common problems

Do not wipe off until the surface is dry, otherwise paste will be pulled out of the grain.

Do not color the paste too darkly.

If pickling paste is applied in the direction of the grain, it will not fill the pores consistently.

Appropriate surfaces

Open-grained woods, especially oak, also elm and ash.

Kitchen furniture and cupboards, paneling, staircases and restored furniture.

Drying time

Leave pickling paste to dry overnight before finishing off.

seal with a shellac sealer. Leave overnight to ensure that the sealer is thoroughly dry and hard before rubbing in the pickling paste – otherwise the stain can be worked away, resulting in a patchy effect.

Rub in the paste with burlap, working across the grain. If you work in the direction of the grain, the paste will not hold as well in the pores. Do not use too much paste at any one time. After letting it dry for about 10 minutes, gently wipe off the excess, working in the direction of the grain. Then leave overnight before applying further finishes.

On oak, a wax finish is most appropriate. There is no reason why other finishes cannot be used – but rub carefully with the polishing pad if applying French polish, so that none of the pickling paste is raised from the grain.

▲ **6** *When the polish has dried it will have sealed in the stain. The pickling paste needs to be rubbed in, which would affect the stain if it was not sealed.*

◀ **8** *Pickling paste is a combination of wax and white pigments, and is supplied ready-mixed. If desired, other colors can be added to the paste before it is applied to the piece. Apply the paste with a cloth, before rubbing it into the pores using a piece of burlap. Work across the grain.*

▲ **7** *Smooth the sealed surface with a flexible abrasive, or use fine 320 grade sandpaper.*

▼ **9** *Before the paste dries, wipe off any excess with burlap, across the grain. Make sure the grain is filled evenly, and that not too much is wiped off.*

◀ **10** *Gently wipe with the grain to remove any cross-grain marks that were made by the first wiping session. Do not wipe any of the paste from the grain.*

A selection of pickling effects

▶ **1** *Spirit blue stain and pickled.*
2 *Natural oak color and pickled.*
3 *Red pigment stain and pickled.*
4 *Alcohol green stain and pickled.*
5 *Red and yellow pigment stain and pickled.*

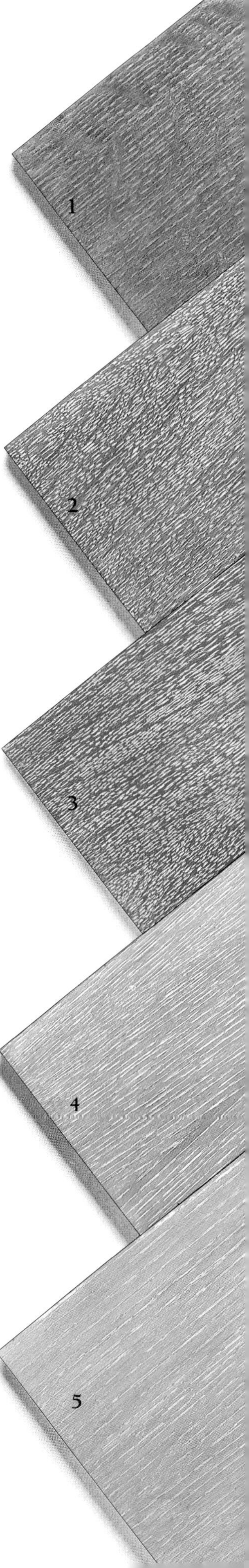

HINTS AND TIPS

- Always apply pickling paste across the grain.
- Prepare the surface thoroughly with scrapers and abrasive, working up the grits.

▶ **11** *Leave the paste to dry overnight and then burnish the surface with a soft cloth. Apply a coat of white or pale polish but seal the paste. Do not use too much polish – allow the natural sheen of the wood to show through.*

5

Spray finishes

At the turn of the century, as mass production of furniture grew, so demand increased for finishes that would be easy and quick to apply, hard-wearing, and maintenance-free. As a result, a whole new industry evolved, devoted to simulating traditional finishes. The scope and range of modern finishes is as wide and varied, and the preparation of the surface with abrasives, fillers and stains every bit as important

Spray guns and the spray workshop

SEE ALSO

133–137
ADJUSTING AND USING A SPRAY GUN

138–143
SPRAY FINISHES AND THEIR APPLICATION

144–149
CREATING SPECIAL SPRAY EFFECTS

164–167
TROUBLESHOOTING

168–169
HEALTH AND SAFETY

HINTS AND TIPS

- Always select a good quality spray-gun. Buy the best one you can afford.
- Try out the gun to see how it feels.
- Always clean out after use, making sure the holes are not blocked.
- Lubricate all parts with general-use oil.

The principal feature that distinguishes the various types of spray gun is the way the finish is held and then passed to the nozzle for atomizing with compressed air. There are basically only three options – and unless bulk spraying with a pressure-feed gun is required, the choice is really limited to gravity-feed and suction-feed guns. For small jobs such as stenciling, the range can be extended to aerosols, but they are rarely used by professional finishers except for touching up damaged spray finishes on site.

Convenience, economy and the types of finishes to be used are the criteria to consider when choosing a spray gun. For the small workshop, gravity-feed guns are normally the most convenient. They are easy to handle, economical (as small quantities can be mixed for short jobs), and suitable for most finishes.

Suction-feed guns are less convenient, as the underslung reservoir makes them unwieldy. However, they only need small quantities of finish at a time; and they are the most popular option when using heavy pigmented finishes for spraying cars and other metallic surfaces.

All of these guns (with perhaps the exception of aerosols) produce the smooth finish associated with spraying, so long as they are maintained properly (see page 135) and the materials and workpiece are thoroughly prepared. Aerosols are more difficult to use, because they cannot be adjusted and the material is not atomized as consistently.

Gravity-feed guns

Most woodworkers wanting to fit up their workshop for spraying are likely to buy a gravity-feed spray system. If, on the other hand, you are mainly going to spray metal with colored paints, then you will probably choose the suction variety. Gravity guns are simple and easy to use. The finish is

CHOOSING A SET UP

- Each gun can be adapted to suit the needs of differing finishes by changing the set-up of air cap, nozzle and needle. These are supplied in various shapes and sizes, with all sorts of hole configurations in the air cap. Each component is marked with a code, and manufacturers publish a chart to show which air cap should be used with which nozzle and needle for any particular finish. It is important to use the correct combination of parts.
- Tell your supplier what finishes you expect to be spraying. The chances are that you will be able to use one versatile set-up for all wood finishes, but you may need a special air cap and nozzle for high viscosity finishes such as polyester and filling primers. Needles are usually standard, but check that you have one that is suitable.
- The viscosity of a finish affects the set-up you choose. High viscosity finishes require a larger set-up.
- Stains and polyurethanes have the lowest viscosity; and nitrocellulose the highest, though this depends on how much thinner is used (in order to produce a thin or thick coat). Whenever possible, use two thin applications rather than one heavy coat.

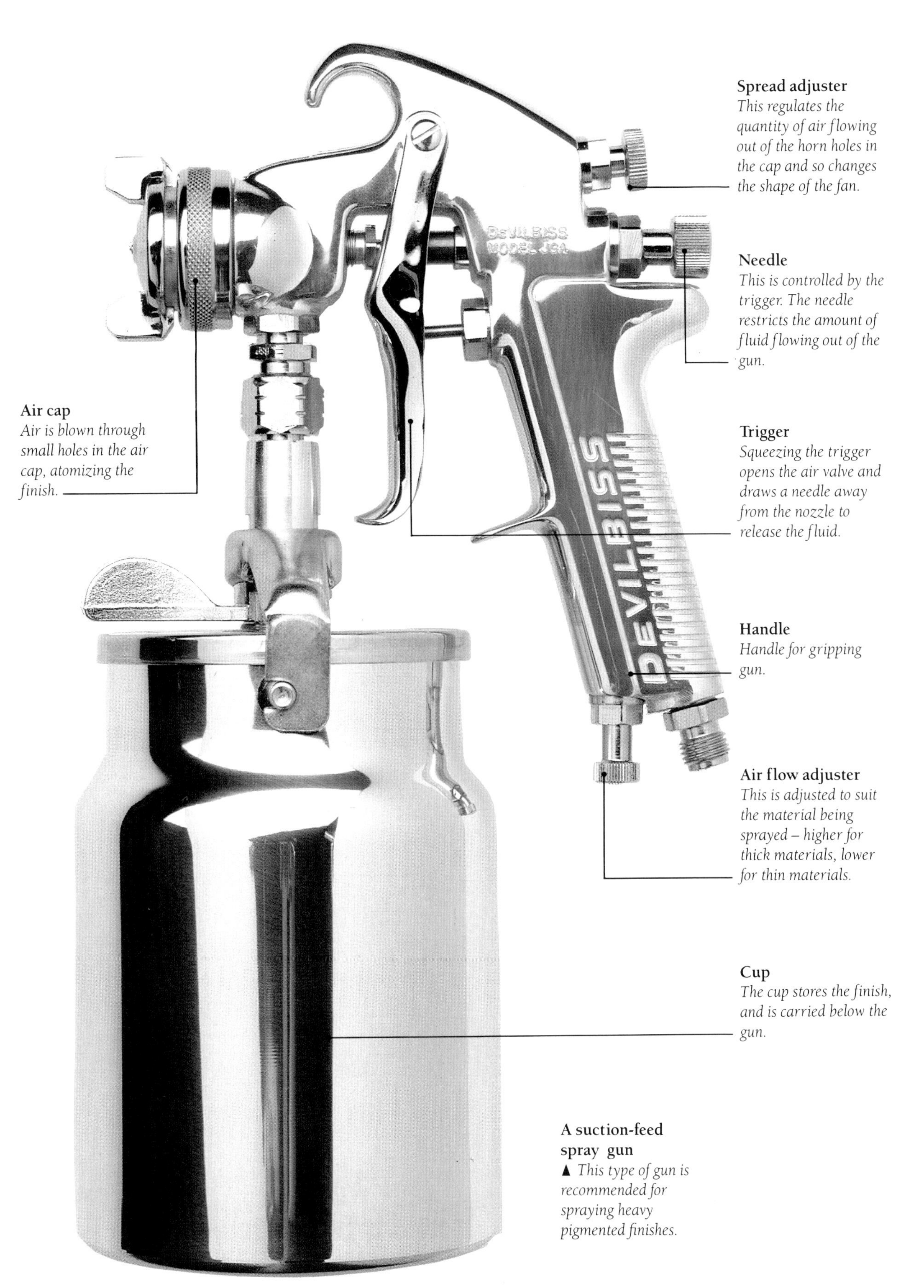

A suction-feed spray gun

▲ *This type of gun is recommended for spraying heavy pigmented finishes.*

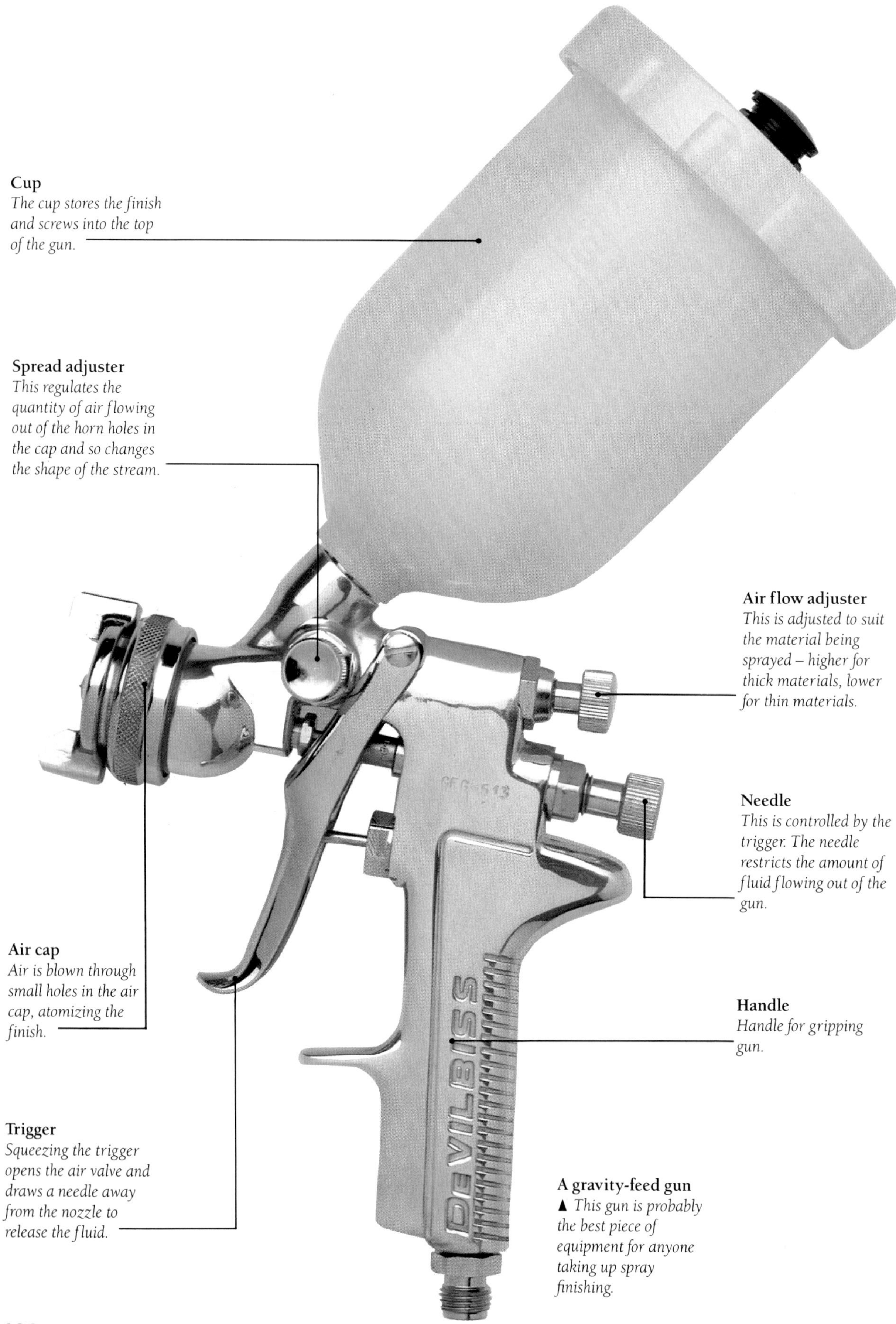

A gravity-feed gun
▲ *This gun is probably the best piece of equipment for anyone taking up spray finishing.*

mixed and stored in a cup that screws onto the top of the gun. The cup takes just over a pint, which is ample for spraying both sides of a 6-foot table top with one coat of finish.

It is important not to run out of material midway through spraying a large surface such as a table top. Spray finishes dry within minutes and the gun must be kept on the move all the time, so trying to spray a surface in stages can result in a patchy finish. There are few wood-finishing operations that will use up a full cup for one coat – but always err on the side of generosity when measuring finish, so you do not run out at a critical moment. Equally, do not overfill the cup on a gravity-feed gun, as it can then spill finish over the piece as you spray, leaving conspicuous droplets that take time to flatten with sandpaper.

When assembling the spray gun, make sure that the small plastic filter at the bottom of the cup is in place, to stop dirt getting into the gun and blocking the nozzle. In use, the finish flows down into the gun and out of the nozzle. There the finish is atomized by air blown through small holes (called atomizing holes) in the air cap, which surrounds the nozzle, and through the horn holes that stand proud on each side of the air cap.

With the compressor working, the gun is constantly ready; but the compressed air will only flow when the trigger is squeezed. Squeezing the trigger opens the air valve and draws the needle away from the nozzle to let the finish out. However, the initial pressure on the trigger opens the air valve only a little, without allowing the finish to flow, thus ensuring that material does not drip out of the gun onto the workpiece without being atomized.

The beauty of the gravity-feed gun is that it is so easy to use. The cup does not get in the way as you spray, and you can work with small quantities of finish at a time. If you are planning a long session of spraying with stain, mix plenty of stain in a larger container, as you will not be able to repeat the color exactly. Gravity-feed guns are susceptible to clogging and slow flow when spraying heavy paints because of their high solid content, especially those that produce a metallic effect. Suction-feed guns are better for such work, but are generally not as convenient to use.

Suction-feed guns

Suction-feed spray guns are broadly similar to gravity-feed types, but the finish is siphoned up from a cup slung below the gun. The nozzle of a suction-fed gun protrudes further through the air cap than on gravity-feed or pressure-feed guns. As the air rushes out through the air cap, a vacuum is formed that sucks up the finish from the reservoir. Adjustments are much the same as on the other guns, though the set-up of nozzle, needle and air cap is different.

One advantage of suction guns is that the reservoir can be larger than on a gravity gun. You therefore don't have to refill it as frequently, which saves time. It also helps when mixing the finish. As the cup holds that much more, mixing up in another container may be unnecessary. However, the size of the cup and the fact that it is often made of metal (rather than plastic as for gravity-feed guns) does make the gun heavy. Also, if you lose concentration, the cup tends to hit the surface and mark the finish.

Another advantage is that you can mix the finish in the cup before attaching it to the gun (whereas on a

MEMO

GRAVITY-FEED GUNS

Common problems

If the flow is too slow for atomizing, the finish is probably too heavy and a suction-feed gun is needed.

Appropriate finishes

Any finish can be used in a gravity-feed gun, except for heavy paints with a high solid content.

SUCTION-FEED GUNS

Common problems

If the finish fluctuates and stutters when you are spraying, the reason may simply be that the suction tube is not bent forward.

Appropriate finishes

Suction-feed guns work well with any finish, but are particularly good for heavy metallic paints.

HINTS AND TIPS

- When using a gravity-feed gun do not fill the cup too full, or it will drip finish over the surface.
- On a suction-feed gun, make sure the filter is in place and the suction tube is bent forward.

gravity gun the cup has to be screwed in place before it can be filled, which is less convenient). When fitting the cup to the gun, make sure the filter at the bottom of the tube is in place.

When you look at a suction gun, you will notice that the tube that picks up the finish from the cup is bent. This is a design feature. When the gun is tipped forward, as often happens while spraying, the tube needs to point toward the front of the cup, to ensure that it sucks up finish and not air. If air is sucked up, then the finish is likely to be uneven.

Why suction-feed guns are particularly suitable for spraying finishes with a high solid content, such as metallic paints, is that heavy particles of finish tend to sink to the bottom of the reservoir, where they will not be sucked up – whereas they would be the first to drop into the workings of a gravity-feed gun, slowing the flow or even blocking it up. Suction guns are, in fact, equally suitable for thin-flow coats. These are used when a thin final coat of finish is needed that will flow smoothly across the surface. They may have as much as 15 percent thinners content.

Compressors

For efficient spraying, air must be supplied to the gun at a constant pressure. It is also vital that the air is clean and dry. These requirements are achieved by two items of equipment: a compressor and an air regulator.

When buying a compressor, the specifications to look for are the volume of air supplied and the maximum pressure that the compressor is capable of providing. Spray-gun manufacturers produce set-ups of air cap, needle and nozzle to suit any air supply from 6 to 20 cubic feet per minute. For first-time buyers, they recommend a compressor that supplies 12 cubic feet per minute at 60lb psi pressure.

Once you have chosen a compressor, tell the spray-equipment supplier which kind you have selected and they will offer a set-up to suit your system.

Compressors work by drawing air through a filter and pumping it, under pressure to a receiver tank, to the air regulator. The pump can be driven by a diesel or electric motor, but the cheaper ones plug into a socket and are much easier to maintain. The air regulator which needs to be as near to the spray booth as possible, regulates the air pressure and extracts any moisture or oil. It incorporates a series of filters, and a meter to measure and adjust the air pressure.

While compressors can be bought or rented relatively cheaply from many manufacturers, it is best to purchase an air regulator from a spray-equipment supplier. It is important to buy a reliable one that will ensure a steady flow of compressed air. When you are spraying, there's nothing worse than a fluctuating air supply. If the air supply falters, the gun will splutter momentarily and will fail to atomize the material, allowing drops to fall on the surface.

A drainage tap on the air regulator

HINTS AND TIPS

- Open the drain taps on the receiver tank and air regulator at the beginning and end of each spraying session to let out moisture and excess air.
- When buying your first spraying system, opt for a compressor that supplies about 12 cubic feet of air per minute at 60lb psi pressure.
- Try to position the air regulator as close to the spray gun as is conveniently possible.

provides an outlet for collected moisture. Before each spraying session, open the tap to let out any water – otherwise it may percolate through to the gun and cause the finish to be ruined (see pages 164–167).

There is also a drainage tap on the compressor's receiver tank. When the compressor has been turned off, open this tap and let the water drain out (water tends to build up in the tank because air heats up and condenses it as it is subjected to pressure). The armature of the pump can burn out if it has to run against too much pressure – so if you are doing a long run of spraying, turn off the compressor at lunch time and drain the tank before resuming work.

Organizing a spray workshop

Very little equipment is needed in a spraying workshop – indeed, the less clutter the better, as it only collects dust. There are, however, a few important accessories that aid successful spraying; and, as in any finishing workshop, natural north light makes it so much easier to check the surface thoroughly.

Turntables and pin boards

For the spray booth (see page 132), buy or make a turntable on which the piece to be sprayed can stand or lie. If you have a swivel chair that is beyond repair, you can make a turntable by salvaging the swivel mechanism and placing a platform on top. It is useful to be able to adjust the height, and to have larger platforms for bigger pieces. Thin sticks of wood help to raise the piece off the turntable and reduce the likelihood of marking the finish. Longer, thicker battens can be used to extend the table.

Another way to support workpieces without marking them is to make a pin board. This resembles a fakir's bed of nails. Take a piece of ply and drive nails through it so that the points protrude by ½ in, spacing the nails at 3 in intervals.

Drying racks

Especially in a cramped workshop, drying racks are handy for stacking panels. You can also hang chairs from these racks, spacing the arms further apart than the standard 4–6in gaps. Make a homemade rack, using 2 × 2in wood, with long feet to which uprights are joined by angle brackets. Use dowels for the arms, fixing them into holes drilled in the uprights.

Cleaning facilities and materials

Make sure there are cleaning facilities in the workshop. This does not mean you need a drain – in fact, never pour waste finishes or cleaning material into the main drains. Keep a sealable metal container for waste materials, and take it to an approved site for disposal. Spray-gun manufacturers provide special brushes for cleaning spraying equipment, but a good supply of rags is useful too.

Lacquer thinners will clean all modern finishes, so always have plenty to hand. They can be bought in large quantities – but, rather than continually opening large containers, decant thinners and finish into smaller more manageable bottles, using a funnel. Pouring from barrels of finish is difficult, and there is a risk of wastage as they miss the target.

Spray-gun brackets

Once spray guns have been cleaned, they need to be hung up out of the way. There are special brackets available from gun suppliers, shaped like bicycle clips but sturdier and wider, into

MEMO

COMPRESSORS AND AIR REGULATORS

Safety precautions

Do not open the drainage tap on the receiver tank while the pump is working or with the electricity supply turned on.

Common problems

If the air supply fluctuates and produces an uneven finish, check that the tank and air regulator are drained and working properly.

If water or moisture gets to the surface, blisters and blushing (see pages 164–167) are likely to form in the finish.

HINTS AND TIPS

- Keep a stock of thin sticks for resting panels on.
- Position plenty of hanging points for the spray gun.
- Have a good supply of rags for mopping up.
- Old swivel-chair actions make good turntables.
- Store finishes, thinners and other materials in a lockable cupboard.
- Keep rags and cloths away from dust.
- Position the air regulator for the compressed air near to the spray booth.
- Run an extra line from the compressor to use for blowing away dust.

which the guns fit after cleaning and while in use. Take care when using full gravity-feed guns, as they sometimes tip back in these brackets, allowing the finish to leak out of the top. Most guns are produced with hooks worked into the body, in which case you can use a nail instead of a bracket.

Spraying tints

You will need a selection of spraying tints, which are based on lacquer and can be mixed with any modern finish for color matching or special effects. Red, black, green and yellow are sufficient to start with.

Spray booths

The environment for spraying needs to be free from dust. It must also be well ventilated, as the solvents and atomized solids used for spraying are harmful and need to be kept away from the finisher.

Factories have sealed booths that provide a dedicated spraying area, with powerful exhaust fans to clear the air in the booth of dangerous fumes. The solids are filtered off by water or fiber filters, so that only the solvents are blown out into the open air. Few woodworkers, however, can afford the space or expense of an industrial spray booth.

Homemade spray booths

One possibility is to erect a homemade spray booth in your workshop. It can be any size to suit your work, and does not necessarily have to be sealed. In fact, many industrial spray booths are open on one side. You can build a small booth with a simple 2 × 2 inch wood framework clad with thin plywood. Cut a hole in the back of the booth, and fit an exhaust or fan to extract the fumes from finishing materials and expel them from the workshop. Cover the hole with a fibrous filter to catch solids. If the filter clogs up periodically, that means it is working satisfactorily.

Line the sides of the booth with paper, so you can simply strip it off and replace it when it gets coated with finish. It's vital to keep booths and spraying workshops clean – as dust, besides marring sprayed finishes, is also a fire hazard. Dampen the floor to trap dust. Since the exhaust fan in your spray booth will draw dust toward it, it is important to keep the whole area clean.

When using a booth, never spray with the gun pointing away from the exhaust – otherwise the spray will be diverted away from the area you are aiming at and may cover you instead. A revolving stand for the workpiece is therefore essential in a spray booth, so the piece can be turned and you don't have to move around it. You can either buy a turntable, as used by sculptors and potters, or make one of your own (see previous page).

Adjusting and using a spray gun

SEE ALSO

126–132
SPRAY GUNS AND THE SPRAY WORKSHOP

138–143
TYPES OF SPRAY FINISH AND THEIR APPLICATION

144–149
CREATING SPECIAL SPRAY EFFECTS

164–167
TROUBLESHOOTING

168–169
HEALTH AND SAFETY

There are four adjustments to any type of spray gun. However, the air flow adjuster normally stays fully open all the time, as it is much easier to alter air pressure at the air regulator (see pages 130–131), where there is a gauge. This is useful for adjusting the size of the particles borne in the air flow. Most finishes run at 30 to 35lb psi, but by cutting the pressure right back splattering effects (see pages 144–145) can be achieved.

The fan adjuster (also called the spread adjuster) is much more important, as it regulates the quantity of air flowing out of the horn holes in the cap and so changes the shape of the stream. With this valve fully open, the flow is a very flat ellipse. The flow returns to a funnel shape about 2 inches wide when the air is cut off from the horn holes. Use a wide ellipse (as wide as the gun will allow) for flat surfaces. A more cylindrical flow is needed for rails, legs and narrow surfaces.

It is also possible to adjust the fluid flow carrying the finish. This is done by limiting the travel of the trigger, which restricts the needle's movement away from the nozzle. Close up the fluid adjuster for finishes that have been thinned for easy flow; open it up for heavy pigmented finishes. You know that too much material is being applied if runs appear on the surface.

The final adjustment is to direct the fan of finish vertically or horizontally.

Adjusting a spray gun

◀ **1** *Adjusting the needle travel to alter the flow of material from the gun.*

▲ **2** *Unscrew the knurled knob to allow more material out of the gun, and tighten to restrict the flow.*

▲ **3** *Test the flow of material through the gun, and keep adjusting the needle stop until the required flow is achieved. Spray a piece of scrap as a test. If the coat is heavy and runs, too much material is being used. If the surface does not look wet, not enough lacquer is passing from the nozzle.*

CLEANING A GUN

- Proper maintenance of a spray gun is essential. It will not work efficiently if any of the tiny air and fluid holes are even slightly blocked – and as modern spraying finishes dry very fast, this can happen quickly. Smooth results may be jeopardized by foreign bodies in the spray gun; and, especially if you use more than one type of finish for spraying, consistency of color is likely to be marred by any residue left in the reservoir.

- Immediately after spraying is completed, pour any finish that remains in the cup into a waste container, for disposal at a toxic-waste disposal point. It is not advisable to pour the residue back into a can containing fresh finish, as that may contaminate it. This is certainly true of any material mixed with a catalyst or thinners, but you may find that there is no adverse effect on finishes that are used straight from the can.

- Clean all parts of the gun with thinners, paying special attention to the holes in the air cap and nozzle. It is not necessary to remove the nozzle, but take off the air cap and clean it thoroughly. Use a brush to clean the inside of the gun; and make sure that all holes are clear. Do not leave the gun to soak in thinners overnight, as the packing may shrink and dirty solvent can block vital air passages. After cleaning, reassemble the gun and oil all moving parts.

With the horn holes horizontal, the fan will be vertical. Most of the time you will be spraying from side to side, and so want the finish to be directed in a vertical swathe, as if you were painting with a flat brush. You will therefore only need to alter the setting when you are going to spray up and down.

Using a spray gun

Modern finishes are popular not only for their qualities of resistance, but also because they can be applied consistently at an economic rate. Indeed, a professional spray finisher will say that a consistent finish is the most important characteristic of a job done well. Some practice is needed in order to fully understand the formula for a fine finish and to learn the hand-to-eye coordination required when working with a spray gun. Even so, you will be surprised how easy and quick it is to get started – and you will soon appreciate the potential of a spraying system.

The important variables to experiment with are the fluid, spread and air-supply adjustments on the gun and air regulator, and the viscosity of finish being used. There is no benefit to be gained from high air pressure, as high pressure makes the air and atomized finish bounce back onto the finisher – so keep the pressure as low as possible, without creating globules of finish. About 30lb psi is sufficient for most finishes. If the flow of fluid is too fast, you will be unable to keep up and the finish will start to run. Always use two or more thin applications, rather than one thick coat.

The distance between the gun and the surface, along with the smoothness of the sweep as you are spraying, is critical for the finish. This is where the skill of the finisher really tells. Generally, unless the manufacturer of the finish recommends otherwise, spray with the gun about 8 inches from the surface. Too near will result in runs; too far spreads the finish too wide.

Keeping the spray consistent

Consistent spraying is accomplished with smooth, steady sweeps of the gun, parallel to the surface. When learning to spray, there is an almost irresistible tendency to keep the wrist firm, as if putting in golf. When putting, the arms form an arc, with the hands further from the ground at the beginning and end of each stroke than at the moment when the club hits the ball. So, if you keep your wrist rigid when spraying, the part of the work closest to you will receive a thick coat of finish (often with runs), whereas the areas furthest away from you will be more thinly coated.

The trick is to flex your wrist as your arm moves. Try not to move your body unless absolutely necessary. If you move your body, that will upset the consistency of the sweep – so keep your body still and only move your arms. The aim is to keep the spray gun

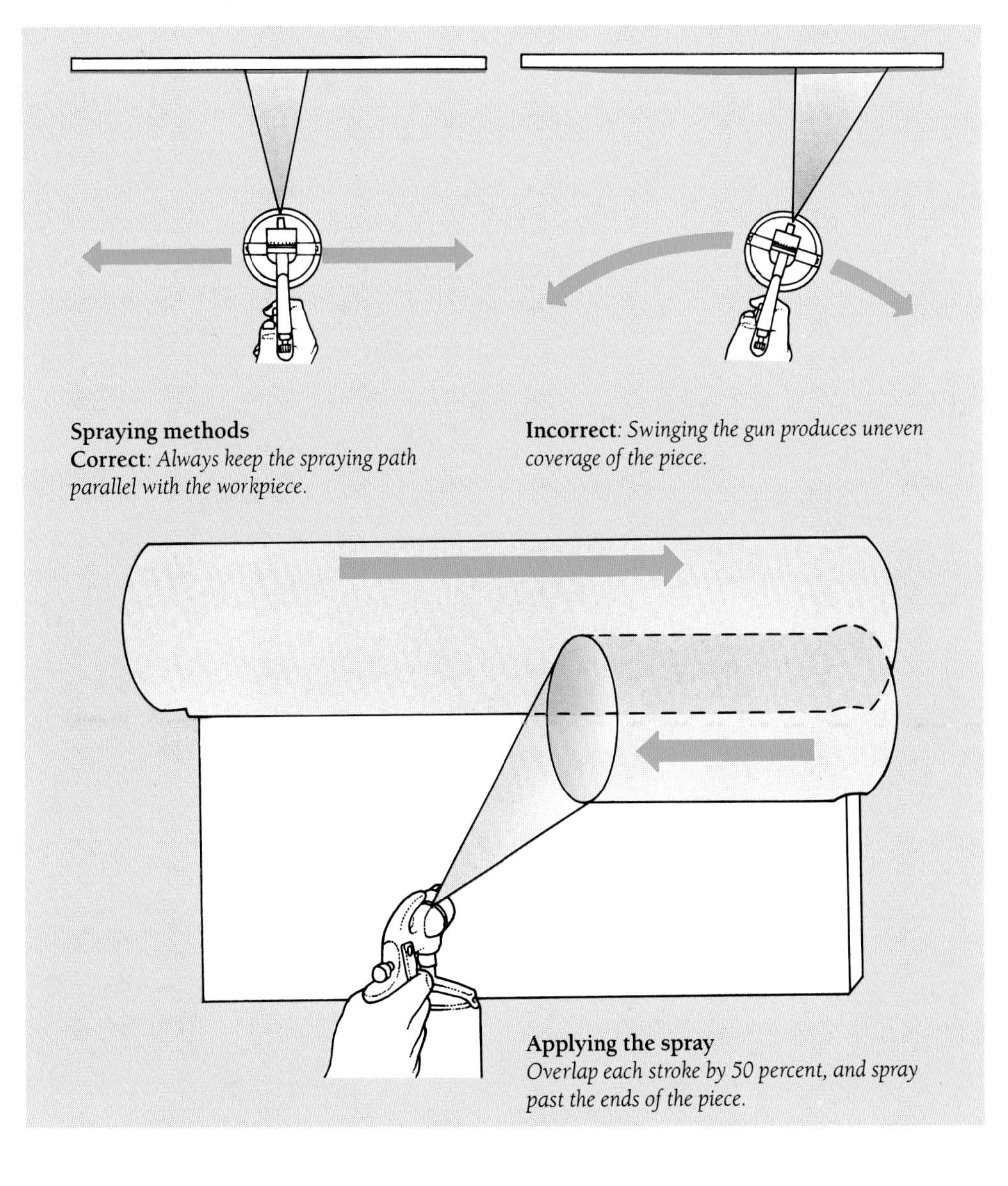

Spraying methods
Correct: *Always keep the spraying path parallel with the workpiece.*

Incorrect: *Swinging the gun produces uneven coverage of the piece.*

Applying the spray
Overlap each stroke by 50 percent, and spray past the ends of the piece.

MEMO

Safety precautions
When spraying, always wear goggles and a mask or, if possible, a respirator.

Wear protective gloves when working with acid catalysts.

Wear overalls at all times.

Tools and materials
Spray gun

Compressor and air regulator

Goggles, mask or respirator, overalls and protective gloves

Spray booth

Sealable metal container for waste

Spray finishes and thinners

Common problems
Spraying too close or with too much fluid causes runs.

Spraying too far away or with too much air results in a thin, uneven finish.

Appropriate finishes and surfaces
Do not use shellac finishes with a spray gun, as they tend to cobweb.

Drying times
Most spray finishes are dry within 20 minutes, though some take hours or days to cure fully.

HINTS AND TIPS

- Test colors by spraying them on scrap wood (if possible, similar to the wood of the workpiece), to get a true idea of the finish.
- Always spray parallel to the surface, flexing the wrist and keeping the gun an even distance from the workpiece. Most finishes should be sprayed about 8 inches from the surface.
- Keep the air pressure as low as possible, and the fluid flow at a rate you can keep up with.
- On wide surfaces, overlap each sweep of the gun by about 50 percent.
- Continue each sweep beyond the end of the piece to ensure complete coverage.

parallel with the surface all the time. Flex your wrist as if ironing a pair of trousers or painting a door.

Spraying a table

When you are spraying, there is always going to be some overspray that does not hit the desired spot. Most will be sucked out by the exhaust system, but some of this material is bound to fall upon areas already finished. Do not, however, be frightened to overspray at the end of each sweep, and do not be tempted to take the pressure off the trigger. A constant flow of finish is vital, even if, momentarily, the gun is not aimed at the surface. It is important to start and end each sweep with the spray at full blast. Do not alter the flow with the trigger. Instead, adjust the gun. Always spray with the trigger full on. To ensure an even coat across a wide surface, such as a table top, overlap each sweep by about 50 percent.

Because some of the overspray will always fall on finished components, leave the most visible parts till last and start with the most inconspicuous areas. On a table, that means spraying the inside of the legs or underframe first, and then the outside. When it comes to the table top, always spray the edges first, even though they are more obvious to the eye than the underneath. This is because more overspray is created when spraying the edges than when working on the bottom or top. After the edges, spray the bottom and, finally, the top.

Finishing with spray is rather like veneering. If only one side is sprayed, it may "cup" (distort) due to the pull of the drying finish. So always finish both sides, even if the top is fixed in place.

Aiming a spray gun
When spraying a curved chair leg, spray directly at the center of the piece, using a narrow fan shape. For square-shaped legs, direct the spray at the corners of the piece, again with a narrow fan shape.

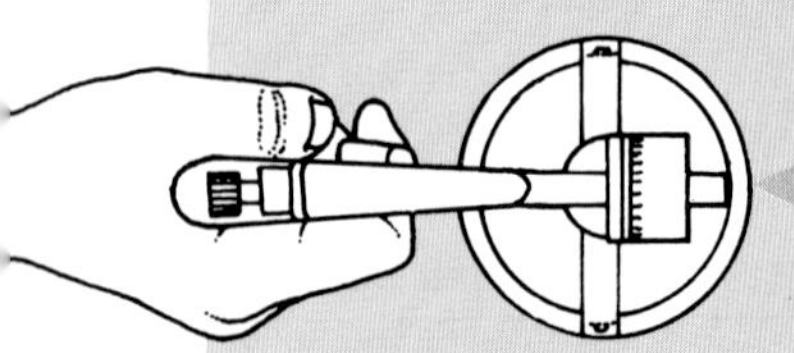

Spraying a chair

Before starting to spray, check the spread adjustment on the gun. Test this by spraying on a piece of scrap or against the side of the booth (see page 132). A wide fan, which is ideal for spraying a table top, would produce too much overspray on the rails and legs of a chair. So reduce the amount of air channeled to the horn holes; and spray a cone-shaped fan, spreading to about 2 inches as it hits the surface.

It does not matter how you spray rounded chair legs and rails, but try not to point the spray gun directly at the face of square components. Instead, position the gun so that it is aiming at an edge and two faces. This way you can spray both faces simultaneously, which saves time and consumes less finish. However, do not use this method when spraying components wider than about 1½ inches, as that could result in an uneven finish.

When spraying a chair, start with the legs. Spray the inside of a leg first, then the outside. Spray the rails in the same manner. Next, spray the outside (i.e. back) of the chair's backrest, then the front of the backrest, and last of all the seat.

Types of spray finishes and their application

SEE ALSO

126–132 SPRAY GUNS AND THE SPRAY WORKSHOP

133–136 ADJUSTING AND USING A SPRAY GUN

144–149 CREATING SPECIAL SPRAY EFFECTS

164–167 TROUBLESHOOTING

168–169 HEALTH AND SAFETY

In this section we look at how to prepare surfaces to take spray finishes, then we look at specific spray finishes and their application.

Preparing surfaces for spraying

When it comes to preparing the surface for spraying, the usual rules for producing a smooth, blemish-free surface apply. Unless an alternative method is recommended, all the spray finishes described here are compatible with the various wood fillers, grain fillers, waxes, stains and sealers used for non-spray finishes.

Use shellac or two-part wood fillers where appropriate (the latter are recommended for larger repairs). Paste-wood fillers should be used for a full-grain finish. It can be used between coats of lacquer finish to fill dents that have been missed during preparation.

Oil dyes should not be used for staining pieces that are to be sprayed. Catalyzed finishes in particular are likely to react with these stains, changing the color of the wood radically. A dark oak, for example, may suddenly turn rose red.

Water and alcohol stains can be used under spray finishes, though before applying a water stain, remember to raise the grain by wetting the wood then sanding it flat. NGR stains and alcohol stains can be sprayed on, though the results are unlikely to be superior to application by hand.

Sealing and color matching

Most woods will need to be sealed before the first spray coat. The type of sealer varies from finish to finish, and can be determined by the wood type. Once the first spray coat has been

Stripping a chair for spraying
◀ **1** *The gloss finish on this chair needs to be stripped off before preparing to spray. It is quicker to strip with chemicals rather than trying to cut back the old finish using sandpaper.*

▲ **2** *Always wear protective gloves, overalls and goggles when working with chemical strippers. Decant a little stripper at a time into a coffee can. Ventilate the workshop or work outside.*

▲ **3** *Using a flat brush, lay the stripper onto the surface, keeping it wet as it is applied. Do not brush it around – this will only speed up evaporation and reduce the effectiveness of the stripper.*

▲ **4** *Use a paint scraper to test to see if the old finish is ready to be scraped off. Always scrape with the grain. Remember to wrap waste scrapings in newspaper, and dispose of them carefully.*

▶ **5** *Use a bunch of coarse steel wool to rub off any of the finish that is left on the surface. Always wear heavy gloves when working with this grade of steel wool, and do not try to tear it from the roll – instead, cut it with shears or a pair of old scissors.*

◀ **6** *Apply another coat of stripper, and rub off waste with more coarse steel wool, using a stick or spatula to remove finish from nooks and crannies. Do not use a metal point because it is likely to scratch the wood. Check the manufacturer's instructions to see if the stripper needs to be neutralized. Follow their instructions for doing so.*

▶ **7** *The finished chair, ready for sanding through the grades with garnet paper, from coarse to fine.*

applied, some color matching may be necessary. In all cases this can be done using alcohol dyes, either mixed into lacquer and sprayed onto the workpiece or simply rubbed on. The alcohol base will bite into all spray finishes, even catalyzed lacquers.

Alternatively use dyes especially prepared for use with lacquer. They are powerful – so use them in small quantities. Apply more than one color to obtain the right match, spraying on and leaving to dry for about 5 minutes. They are the most suitable option for shading (see pages 146–147), for which they are best used after the first sealer coat.

How many coats?

Depending on the effect or protection required, one or two coats of finish will be sufficient. It varies from one piece to another. An average-size kitchen-table top will need about 1½ pints for spraying both sides with one coat of finish, while a chair will need about 1¼ pints.

Spray finishes dry quickly (within 20 minutes), but take longer to cure. It is important to apply the second coat as soon as possible after the first – once the surface is touch dry and has been lightly sanded (denibbed) – so that it can bite in before the curing process starts.

Burnishing

Although they are available in flat or gloss, you may want to boost the gloss of spray finishes further. Use rubbing compound and a lambs-wool pad attached to a drill. Last of all, buff by hand with burnishing cream and a soft cloth.

Nitrocellulose lacquer finishes

Nitrocellulose lacquer is the oldest of modern spray finishes. It was first used

Staining with a spray gun

◀ **1** *Alcohol stains can be sprayed, though rubbing stain in by hand is likely to produce a superior result. Use a gravity-feed spray gun to apply the stain. This type of gun is the easiest to handle around the chair. Regulate the pressure at 20lb psi, and apply a wet, even coat. Work from the inside of the legs outward. Then stain the edges and the underneath of the seat before starting work on the top. The idea is to stain the most visible areas last.*

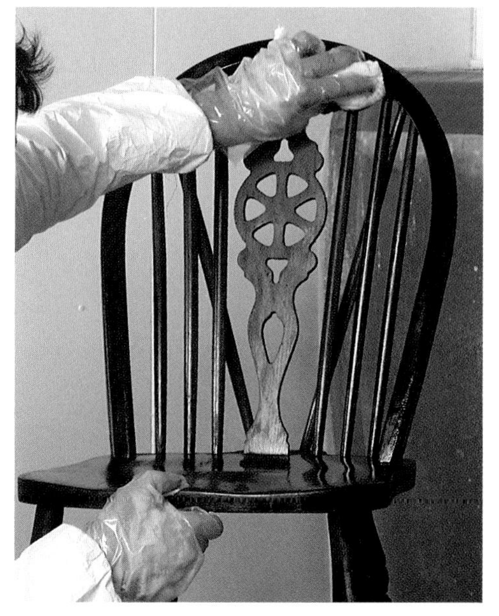

◀ **2** *Wipe off any surplus stain using a clean cloth until an even color has been achieved. Leave to dry.*

HINTS AND TIPS

- A makeshift spray booth can be erected from polyethylene sheeting, but make sure it is well ventilated.
- Check filters regularly for clogging.

at the beginning of this century as "dope" to stretch and strengthen the canvas covering of early aeroplanes. It was favoured for its quick-drying qualities. The cellulose compound, which remains a base ingredient of many spray finishes, is extracted from the cotton plant.

Nitrocellulose finishes are about the simplest to spray, as they are used directly from the can, without having to mix them with catalyst or thinners. Only add thinners to lacquer finishes when they are not atomizing properly – and even then they should be thinned by no more than 10 percent. Globules of finish on the surface are evidence of the lacquer being too thick.

Before spraying, seal the wood by hand with a shellac sealer and leave it to dry for 30 minutes before lightly sanding with fine silicon-carbide paper. There are also various sanding sealers available with a lacquer base, which include an agent to make sanding easier. However, this sanding agent is a soapy material and may create problems with adhesion of subsequent coats of finish, so try it out first. Sanding sealers can be used on open-grained woods such as oak, ash and elm.

Other sealers are available, too, which suppliers recommend for particular finishes. If you are not sure which to choose, ask the manufacturer for a compatible finish and sealer. Polyurethane and shellac sealers are good for oily wood, followed by any other finish, and also for refinishing when there is a risk of silicones in the grain. Do not use more than one coat of any sealer.

Having sealed and denibbed the surface, spray the first coat of lacquer. Leave this to dry for about 20 minutes before sanding it and applying the next coat. However, it takes 2 or 3 hours before lacquer is ready for rubbing. For a quick, cheap finish one coat of lacquer is sufficient, but a thin-flow coat on top adds depth and strength.

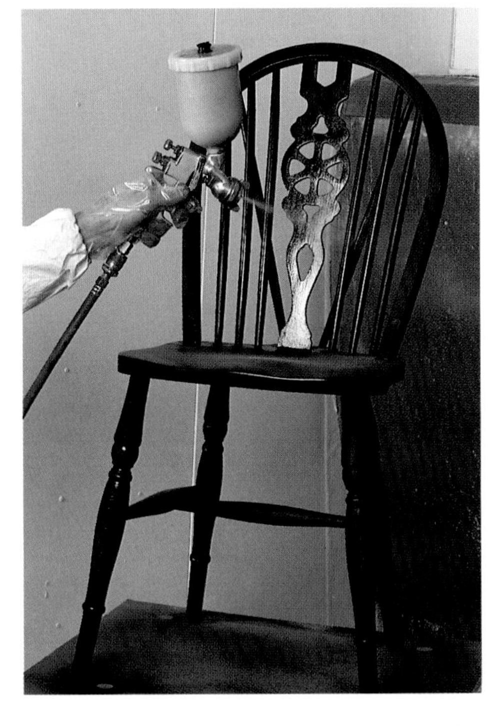

Spraying on sealer
▶ **1** *Use a gravity-feed spray gun to apply the sealer. Set the pressure at 25lb psi. Apply an even coat, making sure that all areas are covered. Again, work from the least visible toward the conspicuous parts. Do not apply too heavy a coat – this is only meant to be a sealing application.*

▶ **2** *Leave the sealer to dry for about 20 minutes at 65°F. The surface is then slightly rough and will need smoothing. Use fine 320 grit self-lubricating silicon-carbide sandpaper, always following the grain and taking care not to break through the sealer and stain. Be especially gentle on the corners, and hold the paper flat in the hand, with the center two fingers pressing it down onto the surface.*

PROS AND CONS OF NITROCELLULOSE LACQUER FINISHES

Pros

- Moderate cost
- Fast drying
- Easy application

Cons

- Susceptible to "blushing" (moisture makes surface white).
- Sensitive to temperature – needs at least 65°F.
- Not resistant to water. Unsuitable for exterior use.

Catalyzed lacquer finishes

The main drawback to catalyzed lacquer finishes is that they have to be mixed with a catalyst, which adds to the setting up time. The catalyst needs to be handled carefully, wearing protective gloves. Catalyzed lacquer finishes have been in use for about 40 years, and are supplied with either a melamine-formaldehyde or urea-formaldehyde base in flat or gloss. Their great advantage is that they are hard-wearing, being especially popular for table tops.

However, their power does have detrimental effects upon stains and some woods. Brown oil stains are often turned red by catalyzed lacquer finishes, and red streaks are sometimes produced in sycamore and certain fruit woods, such as pear. Catalyzed lacquer finishes are also sensitive to silicones and waxes on the surface, so use a detergent to clean the piece before spraying and preferably seal with a shellac sealer when refinishing old wood. Make sure any stain is completely dry before applying the finish (a dry surface will look flat). Follow the recommended drying times on the side of the stain container.

Paste-wood fillers are not compatible with catalyzed lacquer and should be avoided. Catalyzed lacquer finishes have a high solid content, so will fill the grain to a greater extent than other spraying lacquers.

When spraying catalyzed lacquer, try not to apply it as wet and thick as other finishes. Turn down the flow rate slightly, and sweep a little faster with the gun. Always use two coats of catalyzed lacquer. The proportion of catalyst to base varies from manufacturer to manufacturer. However, adding more catalyst than recommended does not speed up the curing time and will produce a brittle finish; it is also more likely to react with stains. If you use too little catalyst, then the finish will not cure at all. So always follow the instructions provided with the finish.

Because catalyzed lacquer has a high solid content, it may be necessary to thin it, with thinners recommended for catalyzed lacquer finishes. This helps produce a more flowing coat.

A catalyzed lacquer finish takes ½–1½ hours to dry, depending on the room temperature, and can be recoated as soon as it is touch dry. The hardness

Spraying color and lacquer

◀ **1** *Once the sealer has dried, lightly sand the chair and then wipe off any dust. There will be parts of the chair, particularly the highlights, that need to be touched up with color. Turn the pressure down to 15lb psi for touching up.*

PROS AND CONS OF CATALYZED LACQUER FINISHES

Pros

- Catalyzed lacquer finishes are hard-wearing.
- They are resistant to abrasions, and to some acids and alkalis.
- They dry clear, without yellowing.

Cons

- Catalyzed lacquer finishes are slow to cure, and are vulnerable to wet heat.

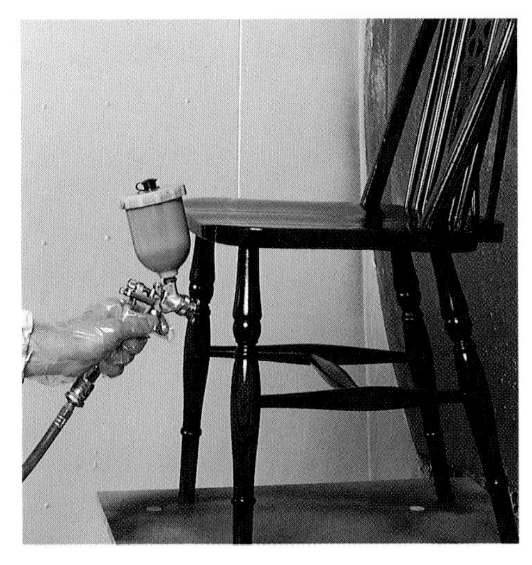

▶ **2** *Picking out the lighter areas, gradually build up an even color. Do not try to use too much color in one pass. Work from front to back, finishing with the back slats. The back usually needs more color than any other part of the chair. Unlike any other spraying operation, touching up the color may require more spray in some areas than others.*

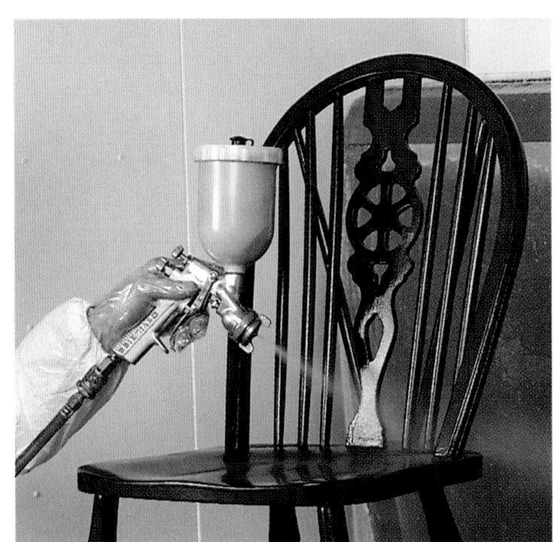

▶ **3** *After the final application of color, apply gloss lacquer. Turn the pressure up to 25lb psi, and plan your route around the chair. Start inside the legs, moving on to the slats, and finishing with the seat. Always spray the most important surfaces last*

of the coating increases over a period of about seven days; the harder the lacquer the easier it is to rubbing. Therefore wait at least 24 hours before burnishing. If the article you are finishing is a table, use table mats for the first seven days and wipe off any water spills immediately.

Paint finishes

Nitrocellulose lacquer and catalyzed lacquer finishes are available in paint form for special effects, such as splatter, and also for simple painted surfaces. Contrary to the expectations of woodworkers hoping to hide the defects of their work, paints highlight errors more than any other finish. A black finish is perhaps the most difficult to produce and the least forgiving. Preparation has to be faultless; and, where possible, it pays to spray paints on medium-density fiberboard, which is smooth and requires no filling.

Use a nitrocellulose or catalyzed lacquer pigmented finish for interiors, and polyurethane for outdoors. When grain-filling, which is often necessary, use a paste-wood filler before spraying with nitrocellulose lacquer.

Once the surface is perfect, apply an undercoat. Finishing suppliers sell special undercoats, which are cheaper than thinning down the finish coat and are specifically formulated to aid adhesion. Leave the undercoat to dry for about an hour, then flatten with fine silicon-carbide paper. Make sure the surface is thoroughly dusted, as the smallest speck or hair will show up later. Apply the finishing coat, in either gloss or flat. If necessary, spray on further coats before rubbing.

◀ **4** *The finished chair has an even glow.*

PROS AND CONS OF PAINT FINISHES

Pros

- Paint finishes are available in a range of colors.
- They will mask discoloration in wood.
- They can be used for special effects.

Cons

- Pigmented finishes dry more slowly than clear lacquers.
- They exaggerate woodworking and spraying defects, and are sensitive to dust.
- Faultless preparation is required.
- Before spraying with them, your gun needs to be cleaned very thoroughly.

Water-borne finishes

With most spray finishes, the solid element is carried from the gun to the surface by a petroleum-based solvent, which then evaporates. In some cases, the solvent comprises as much as 70 percent of the finish. It therefore made sense to try to discover a solvent that was inexpensive and environmentally harmless. The answer was water.

Unlike most spray finishes, water-borne finishes do not liven up the surface; and, although they are available in gloss form if required, they have a flatter, more natural appearance than other lacquers. As a result, they are a common choice for Scandinavian-style pine products. You can buy water-borne finishes in either one-part or two-part form. In the latter type, a cross-linker is used as the hardener. Follow the manufacturer's instructions for mixing this catalyst with the bulk of the finish.

If staining is needed, use water or NGR stains (not oil dyes). Before applying water stains, raise the grain then sand.

A water-borne sealer should be used prior to spraying. Before applying the sealer, dampen the surface to raise the grain, then let it dry and sand it lightly. Do not use a grain filler when working with water-borne finishes, as adhesion is not always satisfactory. After sealing, do any color matching that may be needed, using alcohol dyes.

When spraying, turn the fluid rate down. Most solvents evaporate to some degree between the gun and the surface, but this is not the case with water-borne finishes – so try to use thin coats and keep the viscosity up, in order to avoid runs.

Water-borne finishes are not compatible with other spray finishes. The gun and other equipment must therefore be absolutely clean before use, otherwise the finish is likely to foam.

The final coat can be left as it is or rubbed with 000 steel wool and wax. Rub in the direction of the grain, with even strokes, to produce a satin finish.

PROS AND CONS OF WATER-BORNE FINISHES

Pros

- Water-borne finishes do not harm the environment.
- They do not constitute a fire hazard.

Cons

- Water-borne finishes are still comparatively expensive.
- They are difficult to use, as they tend to sag or run.
- They are sensitive to cold, and are easily contaminated by other finishes.
- Grain filler cannot be used with them.

Creating special spray effects

SEE ALSO

126–132
SPRAY GUNS AND THE SPRAY WORKSHOP

133–137
ADJUSTING AND USING A SPRAY GUN

138–143
TYPES OF SPRAY FINISH AND THEIR APPLICATION

164–167
TROUBLESHOOTING

168–169
HEALTH AND SAFETY

Spraying, as a means of applying finish, has been the product of an industry striving for efficiency. Today, spray guns are fitted to automated machinery and run like robots controled by computers. Moreover, the potential for a more artistic approach has not been lost on professional finishers and illustrators. The airbrush, which is favoured by graphic designers for much of their creative work, is simply a miniaturized version of the spray system found in woodworking workshops.

Although the standard spray gun does not offer the accuracy of an airbrush, there is ample scope for producing special effects. These effects fall into two groups: those that are determined by special materials, and those that require creative use of the gun and its adjustments. In both cases, it is possible to achieve similar effects by hand – but, with practice, you will find spraying quicker.

Splatter finishes

Splatter finishes are among the easiest of creative spray effects to produce. By hand, surfaces can be splattered with a toothbrush, creating an irregular speckled pattern. The same results can be achieved in the spraying shop, by adjusting the air pressure, fluttering the trigger, and altering the distance between gun and surface.

When using a spray gun, globules of finish are dropped onto the surface by

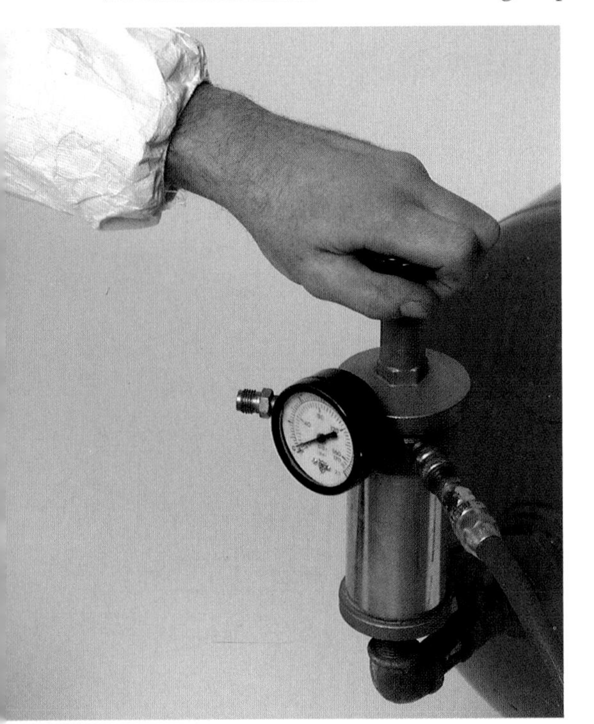

Applying a splatter finish

◀ **1** *Turn down the air pressure at the air regulator until it is just sufficient to atomize the finish. Test the effects of this on a piece of scrap, or the side of the spray booth. The finish must not be mixed too thinly, otherwise it will continue to atomize without forming the characteristic splatter globules.*

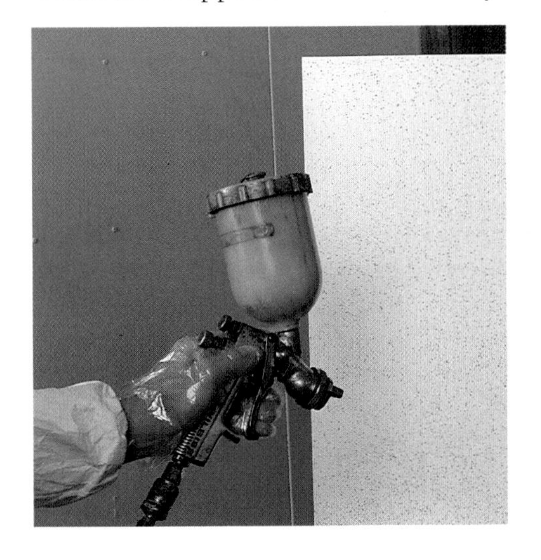

▲ **2** *Patchiness is not always a disadvantage when splattering. If you want an even splatter, keep the gun moving all the time. Vary the distance of the gun from the work surface to alter the size of the splatter globules. The nearer the gun is to the piece, the larger the blobs of finish.*

turning down the air pressure at the air regulator. This means that, instead of the finish being atomized into a thin spray, the material falls on the workpiece in droplets. Pastel colors are normally best for the background, with brighter splattering on top. There are no strict rules to follow, and you may find other color combinations suit the situation better. Choose colors that complement each other.

Any type of paint or pigmented finishes, which are available from finishing suppliers, can be used for the base coat and for splattering. Make sure the surface is thoroughly prepared. Apply one layer of undercoat and then the required base, using fine sandpaper between coats.

Fill the spray gun cup with splatter finish mixed to the same viscosity as the base coat. Turn down the air pressure at the air regulator until it is just sufficient to atomize the finish (test this on some scrap wood). By pulling back the trigger further, more material will flow to the nozzle, creating a thicker splatter pattern. The closer the gun is to the surface, the bigger the speckles will be, as the particles of finish break up in the air.

Once you are satisfied with the effect (and there is no reason why further coats of splatter in different colors cannot be added), protect the surface with one coat of flat nitrocellulose finish. The splatter for this final application should dry almost immediately – but leave for an hour or so, just in case.

▲ **3** *The finished panel shows fine blue speckles on a white background. Light colors are best for the background, but there are no limitations to the number, size and color of the splatter marks.*

Combining colors

▲ *This painted side table shows some of the extreme effects that can be produced with a sprayed splatter finish. Not only have three or more colors been used, but the distance between gun and workpiece has been constantly changed to create a range of globule sizes. Some have become so large that they have distorted so that they look like rockets in flight.*

Shading

While either suction or gravity-feed guns can be used for a splattered finish, the latter are best for shading, as they are much easier to manipulate when trying to replicate the aged look produced by rubbing (see pages 118–119). Though it may take time to develop the skills necessary for accurate shading (especially, creating darker areas in corners and recesses), you will find that gradual shading of a panel from the centre outwards is as easy as by hand.

Stain the piece using a water or alcohol stain. Stain to the color required for the lightest areas. Seal this with a shellac sealer, then sand gently with 320 grit silicon-carbide paper and dust off.

Use spray tints for the shading. Mix to a color about half a shade darker than the original stain. The trick is to use a tint that is not too dark, otherwise it becomes very difficult to produce gradual shading from light to dark. The aim is to avoid any sharp definition between shaded and unshaded areas. Darken those areas that are most likely to collect dust with age, building up the color in recesses and internal corners with coats of spray tint. Finish with a flat nitrocellulose lacquer.

Sunburst effects

You may be excused for mistaking sunburst for shading. The effect is similar, though sunburst is used for decoration as opposed to reproduction and restoration. It is popular on guitars, car dashboards and wooden surfaces that have to blend in with plastic and metal. It is a flamboyant finish, and some artistic flair is needed in order to achieve an attractive result. Stunning effects can be produced with bright yellow, greens, and reds; or more subtle effects with browns and wood colors.

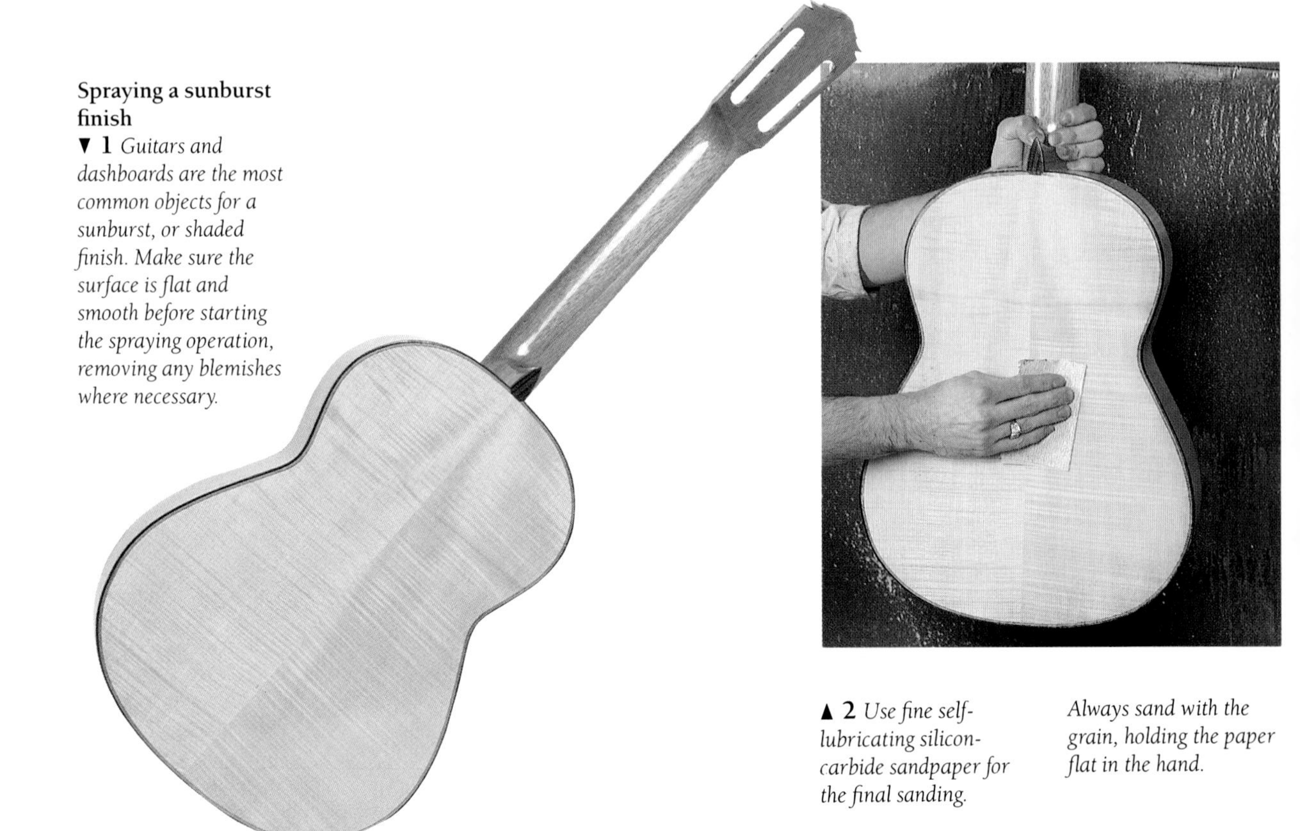

Spraying a sunburst finish
▼ **1** *Guitars and dashboards are the most common objects for a sunburst, or shaded finish. Make sure the surface is flat and smooth before starting the spraying operation, removing any blemishes where necessary.*

▲ **2** *Use fine self-lubricating silicon-carbide sandpaper for the final sanding. Always sand with the grain, holding the paper flat in the hand.*

▲ 3 *Apply the base stain, using a water or alcohol stain. Choose a color that is lighter than the finished color required. Keep the coat as even as possible. If you have a choice of spray guns, use a gravity-feed type for this operation.*

▲ 4 *Start applying the darker, shading spray, gradually building up the color from the outer edges of the guitar. The principle of producing the brightest areas in the center of panels is true for the majority of pieces.*

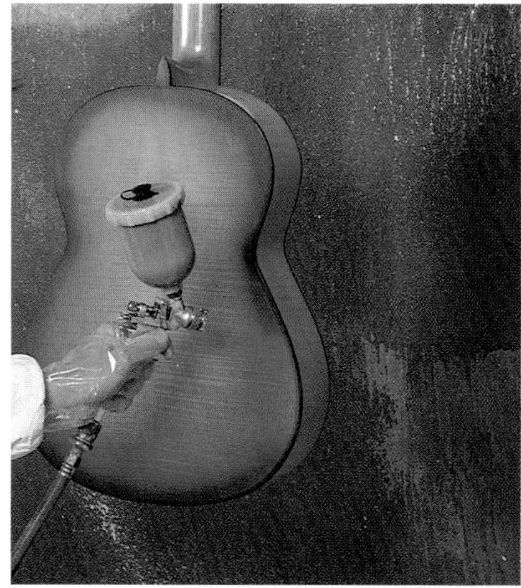

◀ 5 *Build up the shading, blending it with the lighter areas. Although the aim is to produce a darker ring around the edges, it is important that there is no obvious line between dark and light. Build up the shading slowly, rather than applying a single, heavy coat.*

◀ 6 *Protect the sunburst effect with two even coats of clear lacquer. Denib between applications. Dashboards are often sprayed with a high-gloss finish, but it is equally appropriate to use satin or flat lacquers.*

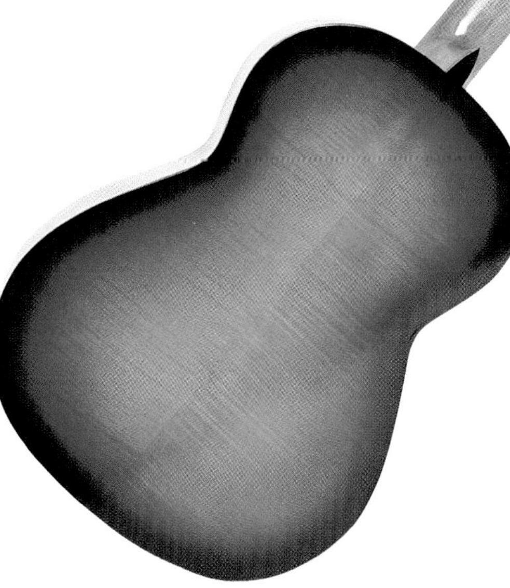

◀ 7 *The finished guitar, showing the gradual shading from light to dark. In this case, the sunburst finish has been used as decoration, but it can also be used to imitate the rubbed quality of older pieces.*

Once the surface is flat and has been thoroughly prepared, stain with a light color, in alcohol or water form (see pages 44–49). Seal the stain in, using a sanding sealer (see pages 44–49), and leave to dry before sanding lightly with 320 sandpaper. Clean off any dust. Select a spray tint a little darker than the stain and spray outwards from the centre, as if shading.

Now choose an even darker tint and shade the outer edges. Leave to dry for an hour or so, then spray on a protective coat of nitrocellulose lacquer – or catalyzed lacquer if the piece is likely to be subjected to wear and tear.

Before and after hammer finish

▲ *An oval panel before and after spraying with a hammer finish, which in this case imitates pewter. The effect is produced by a combination of two spray applications. The second coat is sprayed on when the first is still tacky.*

Hammer finish

The reason a hammer finish is so named is not because a blunt instrument is used to distress the surface, but because the finish resembles hammered pewter or metal. It is a special effect used to make surfaces look metallic. Like wrinkle, it hides the grain of the piece. It can be used perfectly well on elaborately grained wood – but it is a pity to hide the character of an attractive wood, and medium-density fiberboard is probably the best substance on which to work.

A hammered finish is produced by two spraying applications. The first coat is a lacquer based on an aluminum paste, to give the metallic content. Once this has been applied, on a thoroughly prepared surface, leave for 5 to 10 minutes; then apply a splattered coat of ethyl acetate (the appropriate solvent) at low pressure, to break up the aluminium and create the hammered look. The lower the pressure – for example, 5lb – 10lb psi – the wider the hammered pattern will be. Higher pressure – about 10–15lb psi – produces a tighter effect. Use the air regulator to regulate the pressure.

Some skill is required to produce a hammered finish, because the distance of the spray gun from the surface is another factor that determines the degree of hammer. With the gun close to the workpiece, the splatter will be wider. Try to keep the distance constant.

Hammer finish is sold in a variety of colors, and can be mixed with spray tints. Blues, reds, yellows and greens are all popular colors for a hammer effect. Although it is possible to mix your own hammer finish in the workshop, it is more realistic to purchase it ready-made. However, it is expensive and for that reason it is mainly used for small items.

Remember when preparing the surface that you are trying to achieve a metallic effect, so the surface needs to be exceptionally smooth. If necessary, protect with nitrocellulose or catalyzed lacquer once the finish is dry, which takes about 2 hours.

Crackle finish

A sprayed crackle finish is produced in much the same way as by hand, the effect depending largely on the heaviness of the coat. A thick wet application results in a wider pattern. The resins in the crackle are described as "underbound." This means that there is not a sufficient solid content to cover the surface – so, as the solvents evaporate, the solids are drawn together, forming a crazed pattern.

Having prepared the surface, spray or brush on an undercoat and flatten with fine sandpaper, ready for the base coat. This background color will be seen through the cracks of the pattern, so you need to work out in advance what colors are compatible. Mix small quantities of the base and crackle to test the colors. Green and gold work well together, as do gold and silver, white and black, and blue and red. Contrasting colors work best, though subtle shades can be equally effective.

Leave the base coat for about an hour, or until dry, before applying the crackle. Add spray tints to the crackle to produce the desired color. It is possible to make up your own crackle, rather than buy it ready-made. Use dry pigment to suit, together with 2 to 3 percent resin and a cellulose base, plus a solvent (such as ethyl acetate) to thin the crackle for spraying. Start by buying proprietary crackle from a finishing supplier, then progress to homemade finishes once you are familiar with the finish.

Before spraying, turn down the air pressure to about 15lb psi. The cracks form almost immediately, as the crackle hits the surface and the solvents evaporate. The background color breaks through the cracks. As with hand-applied crackle glaze, the heavier and wetter the coat the bigger the pattern. Vary the size to suit the piece. A large table top will need a 2 inches crackle pattern, while rails and small items need a pattern no more than 1 inch wide.

Finally, spray the crackle with either a gloss or flat nitrocellulose lacquer, then leave it to dry for about 10 to 15 minutes.

Before and after crackle finish

▼ *This old shelf unit has been sprayed with a crackle finish to give it more color and a feeling of age. This particular crackle effect was produced using a white background color oversprayed with blue crackle glaze and a flat lacquer coat.*

Guide to woods

The aim of finishing is to bring out the best in wood, enhancing the grain and color, while protecting the surface. It is therefore important to understand wood, and learn to identify the most common species. With that knowledge you will be able to apply the most appropriate finish for any particular type of wood

Introduction

Woods are customarily divided into two groups, hardwoods and softwoods. This classification has a botanical basis. Softwoods have narrow leaves, whereas hardwoods have broad leaves. There is also a difference in wood structure between the two groups. From the woodworking point of view, hardwoods are generally denser and harder than softwoods – but there are exceptions. Balsa (*Ochroma*), for example, which is classified as a hardwood, is one of the lightest and softest woods there is.

The role of finishing in conservation

In addition to the differences between softwoods and hardwoods, and between heartwood and sapwood, wood displays a great deal of variation in terms of color, texture, grain and pattern – each species having its own characteristics and its own particular uses.

In the past this diversity was taken for granted, but nowadays there is increasing awareness that wood cannot be used at the present rate without irreparable damage to the world's rainforests and grave consequences for the entire environment. Unfortunately, the highly figured hardwoods – traditionally the most highly prized woods, used for fine woodwork – are the very ones that are in danger of becoming exhausted. However, by using the appropriate finishes it is possible to upgrade the appearance of woods that are not threatened, and to use them in place of endangered exotic woods.

Substitutes for exotic woods

In the following pages, some of the woods that are most popular with finishers are described in greater detail, together with recipes for traditional and modern finishes. Included are suggestions for ways to finish sustainable woods to resemble exotic woods, so the reader will be able to avoid using tree species that are becoming depleted.

Commercial hardwoods

Oak (*Quercus* spp)
One of the most widely available woods. Its many uses include furniture, boatbuilding and flooring. Harder types are found in England, Western Europe, North America and Japan. Other varieties are grown in Australia and central Europe.

Mahogany (Principally, *Swietenia, Khaya* and *Melia*)
Warm brown to red color. Principally used for furniture, for making pianos and other musical instruments, and for woodcarving. Sources: Central and South America, and Africa.

Walnut (*Juglans* spp)
The color and grain of walnut varies, depending on where it is grown. Uses include fine furniture, gun stocks, turning, woodcarving and veneers. Main sources: Britain, France, Italy, Turkey, North America.

Teak (*Tectona grandis*)
Golden-brown in color. A naturally oily wood, used for both interior and exterior joinery and furniture. Main sources: India and Burma.

Maple (*Acer* spp)
A close-grained wood, the color ranges from white to light brown; the grain pattern varies from burl to straight grain. Uses include flooring and veneers for furniture. Main sources: Canada and USA.

Birch (*Betula* spp)
A close-grained, light-colored wood. Uses include plywood manufacture and furniture. Sources: Europe and North America.

Beech (*Fagus* spp)
A close-grained, light-colored wood. Steamed beech has a pinkish tone. Uses include cabinet-making, bentwood furniture and chair frames. Sources: Europe and North America.

Ash (*Fraxinus* spp)
An open-grained, light-colored wood. Uses include furniture and tool handles. Sources: Europe and North America.

Elm (*Ulmus* spp)
A pale (sometimes pinkish) brown, open-grained wood. Uses include furniture, coffins, pit props and veneers. Availability has fluctuated because of Dutch Elm disease. Sources: Europe and North America.

Rosewood (*Dalbergia, Pterocarpus*)
A hard, purplish wood with dark figuring. Used for veneers and fine woodwork, and often for Victorian and Edwardian furniture. Now an endangered species. Main sources: India and Brazil.

Sycamore (*Acer pseudoplatanus*)
A whitish fine-grained wood with a flash in the grain. Uses include furniture and veneers. Sources: Europe and USA.

Afrormosia (*Pericopsis elata*)
Similar to teak in grain and texture. The color is sensitive to light and can turn almost black. Used for furniture and shop fittings, and often as a substitute for teak.

Makoré (*Tieghemella heckelii*, syn. *Mimusops heckelii*)
Brown with darker markings. Used as a substitute for rosewood. West African in origin.

Obeche (*Triplochiton scleroxylon*)
Yellowish in color. Used for furniture, finished to resemble mahogany. There are several similar woods, including agba (*Gossweilerodendron balsamiferum*), utile (*Entandrophragina utile*) and abura (*Mitragyna ciliata*). Source: West Africa.

Commercial softwoods

Pine
(*Pinus* spp)
Baltic, Scots, yellow, white, pitch and parana (*Araucaria angustifolia*) pines are all used for woodworking, the colors ranging from pinkish to white and yellowish tones. Traditionally used in the building trade, pine is now being increasingly used for furniture.

Douglas fir
(*Pseudotsuga menziesii*)
Red to yellow in color. Used for furniture, paneling, joinery and building construction. Sources: North America and Britain.

Western red cedar
(*Thuja plicata*)
A reddish-brown wood that weathers to a gray color. Used for exterior woodwork, including siding, and for interior paneling. Sources: North America, New Zealand and Britain.

Oak

European oak

American red oak

Oak (*Quercus* spp) has been used by man for hundreds of years for many different purposes and in all sorts of places, ranging from churches, stately homes and castles to boats and ships. It is a tough, hard-wearing wood, with excellent woodworking properties.

Oak is prepared by straight sawing and quarter cutting. When this is done, it shows medullary rays running across the grain pattern. Quarter-cut European oak has particularly pronounced rays.

There are reputed to be over 200 different types of oak, which divide into two main groups – red oak and white oak. The white oaks are considered superior to the red, as they have a finer texture. Within this basic subdivision, differences occur due to variation in growth and climate.

TYPES OF OAK

American oak
Most of the oak from the USA is red, although white oak is grown in North America, too. More than a third of the lumber produced in the USA is oak. American red oak is much underestimated, and with the right treatment can produce some attractive effects.

Yugoslavian and Austrian oak
These are softer and have a straighter grain pattern. They also have a smaller grain and take stains well.

European oak
This is the hardest of the oaks, and therefore tends to be harder to work. It is generally preferred for furniture making.

Pollard oak
Mainly grown in Europe, pollard oak is cultivated by removing unwanted shoots to limit branch formation. As the tree grows, the burrs produced by this drastic pruning are incorporated in the wood – resulting in some particularly interesting grain patterns when the wood is cut and sawn.

FINISHES FOR OAK

Oak lends itself to thin satin or flat finishes, and responds particularly well to waxing. It is often pickled (see pages 120–123). Other open-grained woods, such as ash and elm, can be finished in a similar way to oak.

A number of different terms for oak finishes are used in the wood-finishing trade – such as church oak, Flemish oak and mission oak. Treat these names with caution, as they mean different finishes to different people.

When using red oak, the red tint can be overcome by applying a weak wash of alcohol green before proceeding with any other finish.

JACOBEAN OAK FINISH

Prepare the surface. Stain with Vandyke crystals mixed to a dark shade. Leave to dry.

Apply a dark oil stain, rubbing well into the grain. Leave to dry.

Apply a coat of French polish. Leave to dry.

Sand lightly, using 320 grit paper.

Wax the surface with an antique paste wax. After three applications, burnish with a soft cloth.

This will produce a very dark oak color with a silky finish.

WEATHERED OAK FINISH

Prepare a mixture of soda and lime dissolved in water to a concentrated solution. (Try a builder's supplier for lime.)

Apply this to the grain using a brush. Leave to dry.

Lightly sand off the residue.

The surface can then be waxed, using a white paste wax, or finished with a flat nitrocellulose lacquer.

Mahogany

American mahogany

African mahogany

One of the earliest records of the use of mahogany (mainly *Swietenia, Khaya, Melia*) was by Sir Walter Raleigh, the English explorer, who stopped in Honduras for repairs to his ship. When Queen Elizabeth I of England visited him on his return, she noticed the new decking and remarked how beautiful it was. Raleigh ordered the deck to be removed and had a table made from it for the queen. This generated an interest in mahogany, which increased significantly in the eighteenth century when furniture-makers such as Chippendale used the wood.

Mahoganies come from several parts of the world – including the West Indies, Central and South America, South-East Asia and West Africa. The characteristics, which depend on the wood's origin, range from the hard, heavy mahogany grown in Cuba to the much softer wood found in Nigeria and other parts of West Africa. Mahogany is a favorite wood for pianos, and the deep-red variety used for the backs of guitars and violins and other stringed instruments is known as "fiddleback mahogany." Recently, Brazilian mahogany has become particularly popular; the color varies from golden-brown to pale pink. But very pale mahoganies exist, too, including white mahogany from the eastern USA.

TYPES OF MAHOGANY

Plain
No surface markings.

Stripy figure
The surface is broken lengthwise by stripes of uniform width.

Mottled
The surface looks as if it is mottled, due to the growth of the wood.

Crotch
As the tree grows taller, the larger branches twist and the fibers pull against each other. This produces the most highly figured mahogany. The "crotch" is the fork formed where the branches stem from the trunk.

FINISHES FOR MAHOGANY

Mahogany has a rich color and figure second to none, so should be finished using as little surface coloring as possible. Many furniture manufacturers use coats of color unnecessarily, masking the natural figure and color of the wood. Originally mahogany furniture was waxed or oiled, but in Victorian times French polishing became more fashionable. When staining mahogany, avoid reddening the color too much – it is better to aim for a brown tone. As mahogany is an endangered wood, it should not be used indiscriminately. Instead, you can stain butternut (sometimes called white walnut) to a mahogany shade, using mahogany crystals dissolved in water.

GOLDEN BROWN MAHOGANY FINISH

Prepare the surface.

Stain the wood, using bichromate of potash dissolved in water. Add 2 tablespoons to 1 pint of water.

Leave to dry, then sand lightly with fine sandpaper.

Apply a pale French polish. After building up the finish conclude with straight strokes in the direction of the grain.

This will produce a golden-brown gloss finish.

FULL-GRAINED BROWN-MAHOGANY FINISH

Prepare the surface.

Stain, using 1 tablespoon of Vandyke crystals to 1 pint of water. Apply and leave to dry.

Fill the grain, using a brown-mahogany grain filler. Leave to dry.

Build up, using a garnet polish. Finish off with the grain.

Walnut

English walnut

American walnut

The color of walnut (*Juglans* spp) can range from a dark, almost black, heartwood to a pale-gray sapwood. It is possible to bleach the timber to a creamy color (blonde walnut was all the rage in the 1920s and 1930s), which gives it a rather washed-out appearance. As walnut has such strength, it can be fashioned into attractive shapes – for example, highly figured chair frames, with the grain running through.

Walnut is often used in veneer form, since the irregular growth of the tree produces beautiful veneers. Burl veneer (also known as burr veneer) is formed where there are outgrowths from the trunk, which have intricately grained wood. Butt veneer comes from the stump (or "butt") of the tree. It is cut across the grain to reveal the distinctive twisting grain pattern.

TYPES OF WALNUT

American walnut
The native American walnut (often referred to simply as black walnut) has a distinctive black grain. A strong wood, it is used for gun stocks and airplane propellers.

English walnut
Has a strong dark figure and a fine grayish color, with the dark streaks that are characteristic of walnut. It is now in short supply and is not much used.

French walnut
Has a fine wispy figure. It is used for furniture.

Italian walnut
Very like American walnut. It has a black figure and a fine grain.

Turkish walnut
Has developed its own characteristics, due to the climate. It produces some of the most sought-after veneers because of the highly figured grain patterns.

FINISHES FOR WALNUT

Because of the natural beauty of the wood, the traditional finish for walnut was a wax one. Indeed, since walnut has so many natural colors and attractive grain patterns, there is a feeling among finish designers and woodworkers that these should be preserved by using either satin or flat waxed or oiled finishes. However, although it is considered that a gloss finish detracts from the wood's appearance, it is sometimes necessary and can look just as attractive as a flat treatment.

TRADITIONAL WAX FINISH FOR WALNUT

Prepare the surface.

As walnut has such a close grain and is a hard wood, grain fillers are not necessary.

If there is a contrast between the sapwood and the heartwood, color matching will be needed. Apply walnut crystals with a brush to stain the sapwood, leaving the heartwood its natural color.

Leave to dry, then seal with shellac polish or a sealer. Use a color mop and artists' brush to match the grain pattern.

Apply beeswax, either with a cloth or a flat brush, and leave overnight.

Apply a further coat of beeswax and burnish with a soft cloth.

FULL-GRAIN FINISH WITH A FULL GLOSS

Prepare the surface.

Stain as required, using walnut crystals. Leave to dry.

Apply grain filler as required. Leave to dry.

Sand lightly with 320 grit paper.

Apply white French polish. Work it up until the grain is completely filled. Leave to dry overnight.
Cut back, using 320 grit paper.

Apply a final coat of white polish. Finish with the grain, then leave to dry.

Teak

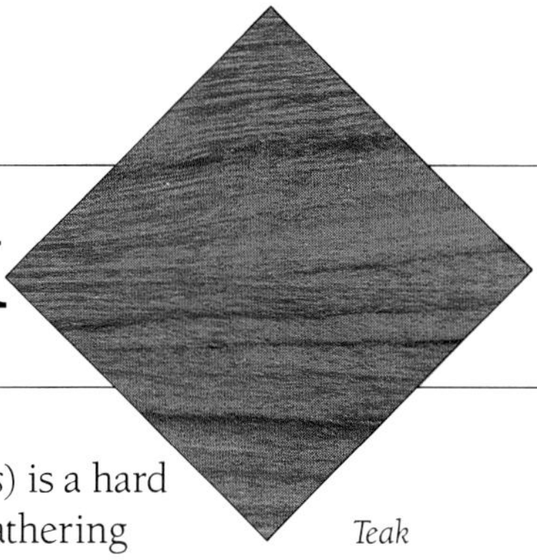

Teak

Teak (*Tectona grandis*) is a hard wood with good weathering properties. It is grown in Burma, India, Thailand, Malaysia and Zambia. The natural color ranges from a golden yellow to a darker brown. Being naturally oily, it is suitable for decking on boats and other situations exposed to moisture. However, the oily nature of teak can cause problems for the finisher – such as poor adhesion, bubbling and, with some two-part finishes, curling.

FINISHES FOR TEAK

Before treating teak with any type of finish, it is advisable to apply a shellac sealer. A thin, flat finish displays the wood's natural characteristics to best advantage. The traditional way of finishing teak was to use several coats of linseed oil. Today, finishes such as teak or Danish oils and tung oil are available. These dry faster than linseed oil, are easier to apply, and provide a more durable finish. Alternatively, for a fine satin finish, you can treat teak with a polyurethane oil.

TRADITIONAL FINISH FOR TEAK

Apply teak or Danish oil (or linseed oil), rubbing it into the grain with a cloth.
Leave it to dry.

Apply further coats of oil.

Sand with fine sandpaper between coats.

Finish with 000 steel wool and more oil.

POLYURETHANE-OIL FINISH

Prepare the surface.

Apply a coat of polyurethane oil thinned by 10 percent, using a soft cloth and rubbing the oil into the grain well. Leave to dry.

Cut back, using 320 grit sandpaper.

Apply a further coat of polyurethane oil, either with a soft cloth or by spraying.
Leave to dry.

Finish with 000 steel wool and more oil.

FLAT FINISH FOR TEAK

Prepare the surface.

Apply a coat of shellac sealer.
Leave to dry for 1 hour at 65°F.

Sand lightly with 320 grit paper.

Spray with a coat of flat catalyzed lacquer.

TIPS FOR TEAK

It is possible to use stains on teak, but they do not take well. When applying water stains, add 1 teaspoon of ammonia to 1 pint.

Use thin coats when finishing teak. A flat or satin finish is best.

For outside use, treat teak with an exterior-grade varnish.

Maple

Rock maple

Soft maple

Maple (*Acer* spp) is a native of North America. Its uses vary from furniture to flooring, and the color ranges from white to light brown. Two varieties of maples are available as commercial timber. Rock maple (also known as sugar maple) is the harder of the two. Soft maple (also known as red maple) has a darker color and is much easier to work. Bird's-eye maple, which makes a highly decorative veneer, is produced when growth buds form but fail to penetrate the bark. As a result, when the wood is cut, an attractive grain pattern, looking rather like watered silk, is revealed.

FINISHES FOR MAPLE

Because of its close grain, maple takes most finishes well. It can be treated with either a flat or gloss finish, as required. A grain filler is not needed.

FLAT FINISH FOR MAPLE

Prepare the surface.

Apply a water stain, using 2 parts mahogany crystals to 1 part Vandyke crystals, then leave to dry.

Apply a coat of sanding sealer.

When dry, apply a coat of flat catalyzed lacquer.

This will produce a golden-brown flat finish useful for domestic furniture.

TRADITIONAL FINISH FOR A NATURAL COLOR

Prepare the surface.

Apply a build of white French polish. Leave to dry.

Sand lightly with 240 grit paper.

Apply a final coat of polish, and finish with the grain.

GLOSS SPRAY FINISH FOR MAPLE

Prepare the surface.

Apply a coat of sanding sealer. Leave to dry for half an hour at 65F (18C).

Sand lightly with 320 grit paper.

Spray with a coat of gloss nitrocellulose finish.

This produces a tough gloss finish.

TIPS FOR MAPLE

Staining maple with mahogany crystals produces a finish resembling cherry.

Other stains can be used, but maple has a good natural color which needs no improvement.

If using two-part catalyzed lacquer finishes, apply a shellac or sanding sealer first, as the acid tends to redden the timber.

Birch

Yellow birch

European birch

Paper birch

A close-grained hardwood, birch (*Betula* spp) is native to both North America and Europe. The grain can be straight or swirling, or an attractive "water-grain" pattern. The heartwood is reddish-yellow, and the sapwood white. Birch is used for furniture, paneling and the production of plywood. It is sometimes finished to imitate other woods, such as mahogany.

Sycamore (*Acer pseudoplatanus*), like birch, is a white wood (though it has a slight flash in the figure) and can be finished in a similar way.

FINISHES FOR BIRCH

Because the grain grows in both directions, careful preparation is needed. The wood lends itself to natural finishes. Birch has an extremely close texture, so very few coats of finish are required.

BLUE-GRAY FINISH

Prepare the surface.

Mix copper sulfate in equal parts, with water.

This produces a blue-gray color, which looks particularly attractive if wood is selected that has a water-grain pattern (resembling watered silk).

Other stains can be used – but alcohol and oil stains tend to produce patchy colors.

ROSEWOOD EFFECT

Stain with mahogany crystals. Leave to dry.

Sand lightly with 320 grit paper.

Apply a coat of white French polish.

Mix alcohol black with French polish and apply with an artists' brush, touching in the rosewood grain pattern to suit. Some practice will be needed to achieve this effect. It is best to copy the pattern from a piece of rosewood veneer.

Use a flat or gloss finish to complete the rosewood effect, either by hand or using a spray gun.

TIPS FOR BIRCH

Apply thin coats.

The grain pattern of birch tends to affect the absorption of stain, resulting in uneven color.

Before you stain a piece, it is therefore advisable to test the effect on an inconspicuous area or a scrap piece of the same wood.

Beech

Beech

Beech (*Fagus* spp) is grown in North America, Europe and Japan. Variations sometimes occur due to climate and growing conditions. With proper forestry control, it is a sustainable wood. Beech is a hard, very versatile, close-grained wood with an even grain pattern. The color ranges from a whitish or pale brown to a darker reddish brown. When steamed, beech becomes pink.

The wood is used mainly for furniture – particularly chair frames, as it lends itself to bending or shaping and takes upholstery well. It is also suitable for turning, and is therefore often used for making turned legs, handles and toys.

For use as a show wood, beech can be stained to imitate other woods, such as mahogany, walnut and oak, and can then be treated with gloss, flat, pigmented, or water-borne finishes.

FINISHES FOR BEECH

Because beech is a close-grained wood, grain fillers are not necessary. However, cross grain sometimes causes problems, in which case a cabinet scraper can be used during final sanding.

If bleaching is needed to lighten the color of the wood, you will find that a two-part bleach gives the best results. Two or more applications may be necessary to bleach the wood white.

Natural beech is attractive in its own right, although pigmented stains can be used to obtain an evenly colored finish or to provide a range of colors, including blue, red and traditional brown. When attempting to match colors using modern finishes, spray colors are useful as they enable you to achieve a very accurate match.

Although beech stains well, oil dyes can bite into it, causing a dark effect in the grain. End grain should be sealed with thinned shellac polish to prevent stain from penetrating too deeply and darkening the wood too much.

MAHOGANY FINISH

Prepare the surface.

Stain the wood, using 2 tablespoons of mahogany crystals to 1 pint of water, then leave to dry.

Sand lightly, using 320 grit paper.

Apply a coat of French polish.

Color matching will probably be necessary. Mix alcohol black and Bismarck brown with French polish to make a warm brown color. Apply with a color mop and an artists' brush.

Build up, and leave to dry.

Cut back with 320 grit paper, then finish with the grain.

This will produce a full-grained, gloss mahogany finish.

ROSEWOOD AND WALNUT FINISHES

The same process can be carried out using other stains and colors. Use alcohol colors and pigments to give an even color.

For rosewood and walnut, stain to the background color and simulate the grain using an artists' brush and alcohol colors.

Practise on a scrap piece of the relevant wood before staining.

Obeche and similar woods

Obeche Jelutong

Obeche (*Triplochiston scleroxylon*) is one of a group of tropical woods that includes jelutong (*Dyera costulata*), ramin (*Gonystylus macrophyllum*) and rubbertree (*Hevea brasiliensis*). They are all now frequently used for furniture, since they are relatively cheap and, as they grow quite quickly, can be replaced by appropriate forestry methods. They machine well and are easy to work by hand. Because they are sustainable and versatile, this group of woods is likely to become increasingly popular in the future.

These woods have a flecked grain pattern rather than a figure. They range in color from white to a yellowish tint. The color of the individual species is fairly consistent, so there is little difference from one piece to another. Since the grain is bland and featureless, the finisher has the challenge of finding the right techniques to make the wood attractive and interesting. Nevertheless, these woods have good finishing properties and are useful for simulating exotic woods that are in less plentiful supply.

A certain amount of practice and experimentation is needed in order to learn how to make the most of these woods – so, unless you have experience of working with them, try out stains and colors on scrap before attempting to finish a workpiece.

FINISHES FOR RUBBERTREE

Formerly, once the latex had been tapped, rubbertrees were cut down and burnt, but now the wood is being used for furniture production. Rubbertree is white with dark-brown flecks, has a close grain, and polishes well. It takes stains but is not very porous, so the best results are obtained with oil dyes. Grain filling is not necessary.

The final finish can either be gloss or flat satin. Modern finishes and matching spray colors can be used to imitate mahogany, oak and walnut. To simulate walnut convincingly, you may need to add figuring, using a mop and an artists' brush.

FINISHES FOR JELUTONG

Jelutong is a soft yellow wood that is good for carving. It can also be used to simulate oak and mahogany. Because of its grain structure, a suitably colored grain filler should be used. Gloss and flat finishes both give pleasing results.

Pine and similar woods

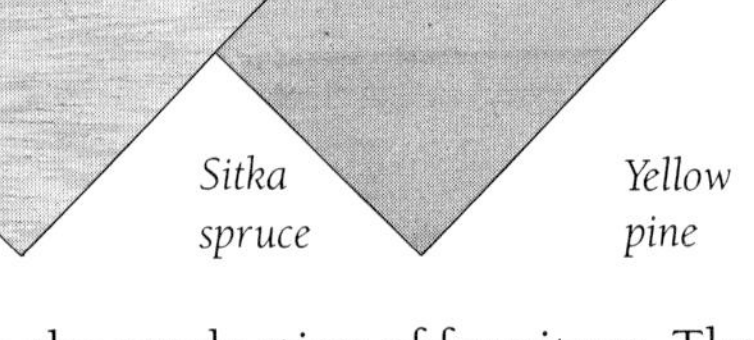

Most pines (*Pinus* spp) and similar woods such as firs (*Abies* spp) and spruces (*Picea* spp) originate in the northern hemisphere, though some species come from elsewhere – for example, parana pine (*Araucaria*) is native to South America. They grow quickly and, with proper forestry management, can be easily replaced. These woods are widely employed in building and joinery, and nowadays are being used more and more in the production of furniture. They can be used in solid or veneer form, or as core woods faced with hardwood veneers. With appropriate finishing it is possible to enhance and improve the appearance of these woods.

TYPES OF PINES, FIRS AND SPRUCES

The commercial woods have a variety of names, which do not always reflect their botanical origin. In fact, sometimes wood sold under a particular name may come from more than one species. Names in common use include:

White pine

Woods sold as "white pine" (*Pinus strobus, Picea abies, Podocarpus dacrydioides*) have a fine grain and can be finished with tinted sealers or French polishes to resemble mahogany. They are used for joinery and for painted or pigmented finishes. Always apply thin coats and rub completely flat, with fine (320 grit) sandpaper to avoid leaving scratch marks as the wood is very soft. Two-part finishes can be used for greater protection.

Sugar pine

(*Pinus lambertiana*) A Californian pine that has practically all the characteristics of "white pine." Used for interior and exterior joinery, piano keys and pattern making. Tends to absorb stains unevenly because of the grain structure, although pigment stains can be used to enhance the natural appearance of the wood. Thinly coated satin and flat finishes are recommended. Wax finishes and lacquers give good results.

Scots pine

(*Pinus sylvestris*) Also referred to as red deal or European redwood, this light-colored pine has a distinctive figure with a reddish or yellowish grain pattern. Scots pine is used for interior and exterior joinery, and for inexpensive pine furniture. It can be stained and takes finishes well, including wax and thin flat finishes. Water-borne finishes are good for producing a natural look.

Southern or yellow pine

(*Pinus strobus, Pinus palustris*) The woods in this group are sold under a bewildering variety of names. The name used depends on where they are grown. They are generally pale yellow to pale brown, but stains do not penetrate the resinous streaks present in the wood, so color matching is often needed. Natural-looking wax or thin flat finishes are recommended. An abraded flat finish looks attractive on these woods.

Douglas fir

(*Pseudotsuga menziesii*) Also known as British Columbian or Oregon pine. Has a pronounced grain pattern and a reddish color. Takes oil dyes well, but not water or chemical stains.

White fir

(*Abies amabilis, Abies grandis, Picea abies*) Has a subdued grain pattern, but with careful selection can be used with brown or mahogany finishes.

Sitka spruce

(*Picea sitchensis*) The wood has a natural springiness. Can be stained, but is better finished naturally as staining tends to look patchy.

Norway spruce

(*Picea abies, Abies alba*) Also known as white deal or European whitewood, this wood is used mainly for interior purposes, as it is not sufficiently durable for outdoor use. It has a distinct grain pattern, with areas of light brown contrasting with the basic white color. The wood tends to look patchy when stained, due to uneven absorption. However, this can be overcome by using tinted sealers or French polishes. Looks best with a thin satin or flat finish. Two-part finishes sometimes produce red blotches.

FINISHES FOR PINE

The color of pine can range from white or yellow to shades of pink, and depends more on the species than on the climate. Light-colored varieties are ideal for painted finishes, since not many coats are needed to produce a white or pastel finish. Some species have a pronounced grain pattern, which is produced by the growth rings.

Preparation is important, as the grain structure varies considerably. Use fine grades of paper during final sanding. When cutting back coats of finish, always sand right back until it looks as if the finish has been removed. The smoother the surface, the better the finish. Before using two-part finishes, apply a barrier coat of shellac sealer or French polish.

Woods like pine can be stained with oil dyes or water stains; alcohol stains tend to look patchy. Pigment stains may be used to simulate other woods, and can produce some interesting effects. Flat or satin finishes are recommended (high-gloss finishes tend not to look so good).

If the wood has a bold grain, color matching may be necessary. Select a natural-brown alcohol stain, to bring out the character of the wood, and apply it with a soft cloth.

Water-based finishes are often extremely effective on pines, producing a natural, "unfinished" look to the wood.

Bright colors such as red and blue can also be used, although it is wise to experiment first. In fact, it is always best before any kind of coloring to try out stains or dyes on a small scrap of the same wood.

NATURAL FINISH FOR PINE TABLES

Prepare the surface.

Apply stain as required. Leave to dry.

Apply a clear sanding sealer. Leave to dry.

Cut back with 320 grit paper.

This produces a tough, natural finish.

SCRUBBED PINE

Prepare the surface.

Apply a coat of button polish or a light-brown oil dye. Leave to dry.

Thin a cream-colored paint to 20 percent and apply it to the surface. Leave to dry.

Sand lightly, using 320 grit paper.

Apply a flat varnish or a wax polish, as required.

This will produce a washed effect, similar to a faded pine finish.

ANTIQUE PINE

Prepare the surface.

Apply a dark oil dye. Leave to dry.

Rub areas such as edges where wear usually occurs with 00 steel wool (see pages 20-21).

Dust off and apply a coat of sanding sealer. Leave to dry.

Denib, using 320 grit paper.

Apply a coat of flat lacquer finish.

TIPS FOR PINE

Always check softwood veneers for glue percolation, which can cause problems, and make sure any glue marks are removed before finishing. Since glue is often light in color, like the wood, it tends to be difficult to see. The best way to detect glue marks is to look across the surface to see them against the light.

Because pine and similar woods tend to be soft, a tough, good-quality finish is recommended when they are used for table tops. Flat polyurethane finishes are suitable for this purpose.

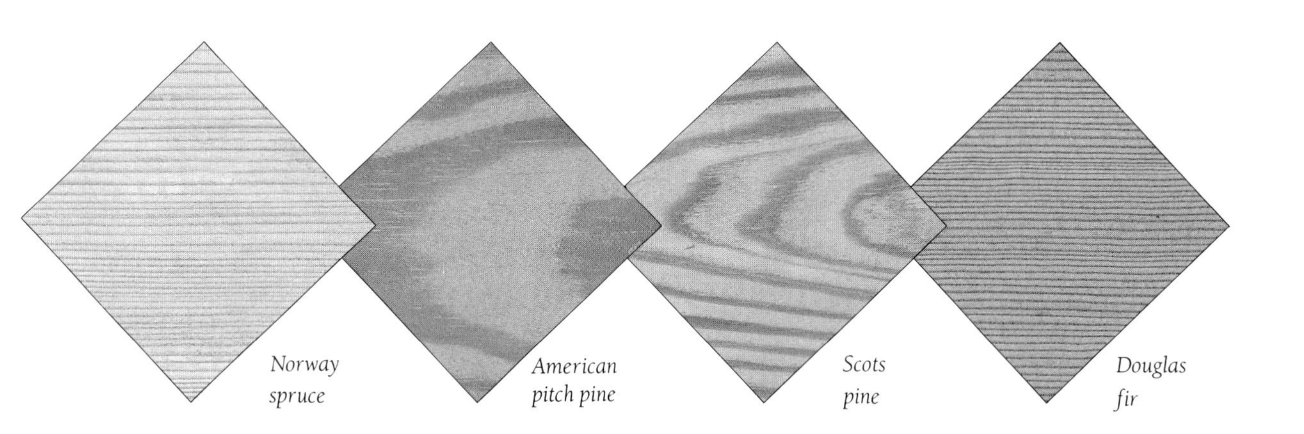

Norway spruce — *American pitch pine* — *Scots pine* — *Douglas fir*

TROUBLESHOOTING

Traditional finishing faults

Although some faults in traditional finishes are due to workshop conditions or the material itself, the majority are caused by human error. Practice is therefore the most effective preventive measure. Fortunately, most traditional finishes (with the exception of varnishes) are reversible and can be rubbed off, without having to resort to stripping and starting again. Oiling and waxing are relatively straightforward finishes, compared with French polishing. The lack of faults catalogued here for those methods reflects their ease of application.

White in the grain

SYMPTOM: White flecks in the grain, under the finish.

CAUSE: Grain filler has not dried, or is too light.

CURE: Rub off polish with denatured alcohol; clean off oil and wax with mineral spirits. Then work out the filler with a stiff brush.

PREVENTION: Make sure filler is dry, or use darker filler.

Ropy surface

SYMPTOM: Waves are visible on the surface after polishing, often in tight circles like ripples. Can also look like rope.

CAUSE: Misuse of polishing pad.

CURE: Cut back with denatured alcohol in the polishing pad and start again.

PREVENTION: Make sure an even pressure is maintained when using the pad. Work with circular motions, trying to keep the pressure the same as you move the polishing pad away from and toward the body.

Cracking

SYMPTOM: Thin cracks show up in the surface after some time has elapsed.

CAUSE: Linseed oil buried under the finish.

CURE: Gently sand the surface with fine sandpaper and repolish. If there is extensive cracking, cut back with denatured alcohol and rework.

PREVENTION: As for sweating, use less linseed oil on the polishing pad and avoid burying oil under heavy coats of polish.

Cracking

Sweating

SYMPTOM: Polish remains sticky, even after some time has elapsed.

CAUSE: Linseed oil has been trapped under the finish. Or old white, blonde or pale French polish has been used.

CURE: Cut back the finish with denatured alcohol in the polishing pad, then leave the surface to dry and rework the finish.

PREVENTION: Use less linseed oil to lubricate the polishing pad, and avoid burying oil under heavy coats of polish.

Blushing

SYMPTOM: A dull whiteness, which can appear in any type of finish.

CAUSE: Damp, cold workshop conditions.

CURE: Cut back and rework.

PREVENTION: Check workshop for damp, and make sure the temperature is not below 65°F.

Blooming

SYMPTOM: A film of condensation appears in the finished surface.

CAUSE: Humidity in the workshop.

CURE: Sand back and rework.

PREVENTION: Check the level of humidity in your workshop and make sure there is adequate ventilation. If necessary, buy a dehumidifier.

Blooming

Crazing

SYMPTOM: Very fine cracks on the surface.

CAUSE: Too much oil has been used to lubricate the polishing pad.

CURE: Sand back with fine sandpaper, and repolish. If the crazing is severe strip off the French polish, and repolish.

PREVENTION: Before tackling the surface with the pad, ensure excess oil is worked out by pressing down with the pad on a scrap of paper or spare piece of scrap wood.

Crazing

Fatty edges

SYMPTOM: Polish builds up along the edges of table tops and the corners of legs.

CAUSE: As the polishing pad is squeezed over the edges, polish builds up there.

CURE: Rub down with fine sandpaper, then touch up and repolish.

PREVENTION: Use the polishing pad to remove excess polish before it builds up.

Whips

SYMPTOM: Polish builds up in ridges, often in circles following the path of the polishing pad.

CAUSE: The polishing pad is too wet.

CURE: Leave to dry. Then sand with fine sandpaper, or use a pad with a little denatured alcohol and work until the surface has been leveled.

PREVENTION: Avoid loading the pad with too much polish.

White edges

SYMPTOM: Edges look as if they are white, where the stain has been worn away.

CAUSE: The surface has been sanded clumsily after applying a water stain.

CURE: Apply polish as normal, then touch up with alcohol colors or pigments once the surface is completely dry.

PREVENTION: Take care when sanding stained surfaces, avoiding pressing too hard.

Flaking

SYMPTOM: Film of finish breaks down with time.

CAUSE: Too much oil in a stain or filler.

CURE: Strip and respray.

PREVENTION: Check that lacquer is compatible with filler or stain.

Chilling

SYMPTOM: Appears as a dull, white semi-opaque film.

Chilling

CAUSE: Cold workshop conditions.

CURE: Repolish the surface using a little denatured alcohol in the polishing pad.

PREVENTION: Ensure the temperature in the workshop does not drop below 65°F.

HINTS AND TIPS

- Always leave the finish to dry before attempting to deal with faults.
- Apply thin coats of finish, rather than fewer thick coats.
- Always use materials as specified by the suppliers.
- Before taking remedial action, think out what may have gone wrong and check possible causes.
- When spraying, only use those thinners recommended by the supplier.
- When spraying with two-part finishes, make sure the right catalyst is used in the correct proportions.

Spray finishing faults

It is often said that one of the skills of the finisher is the knack of remedying a fault without its showing. The ideal is, of course, not to make any mistakes – and prevention is always better than cure!

The more traditional finishes are often reversible, which means they can be removed fairly easily, without recourse to stripping or sanding back. Spray finishes are tougher, and are usually non-reversible. As a result, stripping may be the only cure for a major mistake. You therefore need to be aware of the preventive measures that can be taken to reduce the likelihood of faults.

Air leaks

SYMPTOM: Air hisses out of air holes in air cap.

POSSIBLE CAUSES: Foreign matter in valve; worn or damaged air valve; broken air-valve spring; valve stem needs lubrication; bent valve stem; packing nut too tight; gasket damaged or omitted.

CURE: Check and repair parts.

PREVENTION: Maintain and clean spray gun regularly.

Spray fog

SYMPTOM: Spray comes out of the gun as a mist.

POSSIBLE CAUSES: Material too thin; air pressure too high; gun held too far from surface.

PREVENTION: Add more base coat – or start again, using less thinner; reduce air pressure at regulator; hold gun closer to surface.

Pinholes

SYMPTOM: Tiny indentations or pinpricks are formed in the surface of the lacquer as it dries.

Pinholes

CAUSE: The lacquer is applied too heavily, which means that solvents are trapped underneath the surface and have to rise to the top to evaporate.

CURE: Sand back the surface and start again.

PREVENTION: Mix a thinner coat of lacquer; move the spray gun faster across the surface and increase the distance between gun and workpiece.

Overspray

SYMPTOM: The surface feels rough because the spray lies on the surface, forming small particles of dry paint or lacquer.

CAUSE: Insufficient care when using the spraygun.

CURE: Lightly sand the surface with fine sandpaper, and respray.

PREVENTION: Release the trigger after each stroke or pass. Use low air pressure.

Overspray

Fluttering spray

SYMPTOM: Air and material flow is hesitant or jerky.

POSSIBLE CAUSES: Insufficient material in container; cup tipped too far; fluid passage blocked; cracked fluid tube in cup; damaged tip or nozzle; material too heavy; clogged air vent in cup lid; damaged hose or dirty coupling nut; fault in trigger adjustment.

CURE: Check and mend part, or thin the material.

PREVENTION: Keep spray gun well maintained, and clean it thoroughly after use. Mix lacquer according to the manufacturer's instructions.

Fluid leaks

SYMPTOM: The finish leaks out through the nozzle of the gun.

POSSIBLE CAUSES: Dirty or worn fluid tip and nozzle; obstruction causing improper seating of needle; needle packing-nut too tight; broken fluid-needle spring; wrong needle.

CURE: Check, and adjust or replace part.

PREVENTION: Clean spray gun thoroughly, and lubricate moving parts.

Orange-peel effect

SYMPTOM: A slight ripple effect is left on the surface, like orange or lemon peel.

POSSIBLE CAUSES: Spraying too close to the surface; application too thick.

CURE: Sand the surface flat with progressively finer grits of sandpaper, then recoat. Try using lacquer retarder first, as that may reduce the orange-peel effect.

PREVENTION: Keep correct distance between gun and surface, about 8 inches, all the time; thin the lacquer, but without using too much thinner.

Orange-peel effect

Cratering

SYMPTOM: Small circular patches, resembling miniature volcanos.

CAUSE: Grease or silicone in the finish repels subsequent coats.

CURE: Deep sand and respray.

PREVENTION: Prepare surface thoroughly before beginning to spray.

Cratering

Blushing

SYMPTOM: A dull whiteness appears in the coat.

CAUSE: Damp workshop conditions.

CURE: Add lacquer retarder; or strip surface and start again.

PREVENTION: Keep minimum temperature above 65°F; insulate workshop to reduce humidity.

Runs

SYMPTOM: The finish runs down the surface.

POSSIBLE CAUSES: Holding the gun too close; applying too much material in one place; spraying over the same area twice.

CURE: Leave to dry, and then sand down with fine silicon-carbide paper before respraying.

PREVENTION: Hold gun further from surface; practice a consistent sweep over the piece, overlapping by no more than 50 percent on each sweep.

Aeration

SYMPTOM: Small bubbles appear, creating a milky effect.

POSSIBLE CAUSES: Too heavy a coat of lacquer (which traps air or solvent under the surface); or too much air pressure, which can dry the surface too quickly for solvent to evaporate or air to escape.

CURE: Spray on a wet-flow coat; or spray lacquer retarder and then respray.

PREVENTION: Keep spray gun moving, and make sure it is not too close to the surface.

Blistering

SYMPTOM: Small blisters on the surface.

CAUSE: Water or grease in the air line getting into the atomized material.

CURE: Sand surface and respray.

PREVENTION: Clean air line and drain air regulator.

Blistering

Blooming

SYMPTOM: Film of condensation on the surface.

CAUSE: Humidity in the workshop.

CURE: Cut back with lacquer retarder; or strip surface and start again.

PREVENTION: Use a dehumidifier in the workshop, and keep the area well ventilated.

Wrinkling or cracking

SYMPTOM: Unwanted cracks or wrinkles appear in the finish.

CAUSE: When a second coat of lacquer is applied before the first has dried properly, the two finishes dry at different rates.

CURE: Sand and respray; or strip and start again if the cracks are deep.

PREVENTION: Check the finish manufacturer's instructions for drying, thinning and curing. Make sure the first coat is dry before applying the second.

Flaking

SYMPTOM: Finish breaks up.

CAUSE: Too much oil in filler or stain.

CURE: Strip back, then brush out filler and start again.

PREVENTION: Make sure the filler or stain is compatible with the finish.

White in the grain

SYMPTOM: White flecks under the finish.

CAUSE: Filler has not dried thoroughly. Or the fault has been caused by incompatibility between the filler and the finish.

CURE: Strip and respray.

PREVENTION: Make sure excess filler is cleaned off, and that it is completely dry before spraying.

White in the grain

HEALTH AND SAFETY

Some of the materials used for finishing are dangerous – indeed, many of them are poisonous, flammable or corrosive – so always take care when using or handling them. Store materials safely, and make sure that waste is disposed of in the proper manner. Fire precautions must be taken at all times, and protective clothing worn in case of spillage.

One important safety rule is that finishes must never be stored in or decanted into a food container or anything that resembles one. Saucers and ice-cream cartons mean food to adults as well as children – and it may be too late when someone realizes that the contents are not what he or she expected.

Protective clothing and equipment

Hands are the most frequent victims of chemicals. so always wear heavy-duty elbow-length industrial gloves. Household gloves do not provide adequate protection.

Whenever working with chemicals or in a dusty environment, wear safety goggles to protect your eyes from splashes or irritation. Alternatively, you can use a visor-type face guard, which you mav find more comfortable than goggles and less likely to steam up.

Respirators filtrate the air. When working with solvent-based materials, use a respirator with a carbon filter. Unless you are embarking on a huge job a simple mask will suit most purposes.

Besides protecting your skin and clothes, overalls reduce the risk of dust, hairs and fibers being transferred from clothing onto the surface of the work during finishing. When spraying, an overall that has a hood is an advantage as it protects your hair from spray. A PVC apron must be worn when working with bleaches, strippers and other chemicals – a cloth apron can be burned by chemicals and, if that happens, the material may keep burning substances in close contact with your skin.

Noise can be injurious, too. Sanders and other power tools make a deafening whine. Hearing protection is therefore essential when working with them. The best kind of earmuffs are the ones that look like earphones, but it is not always easy to wear them with goggles and a respirator – in which case, earplugs are a serviceable, if less effective, substitute. To prevent hearing loss and ear infections, clean earplugs regularly and keep them in a sealed box when you are not using them.

Storing caustic materials

Caustic materials must be stored in a locked cabinet when not being used. Always keep the materials in the

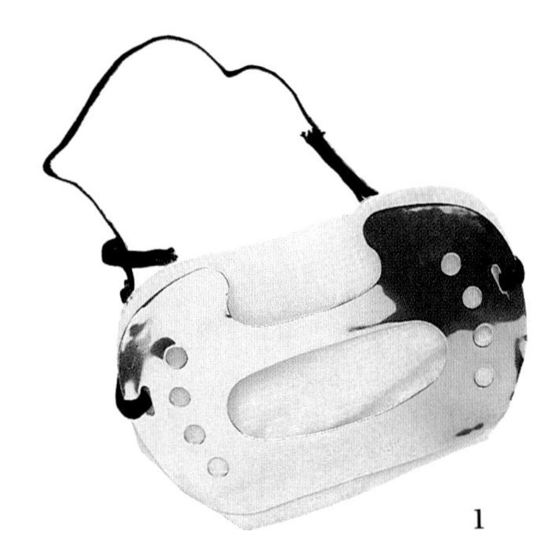

1

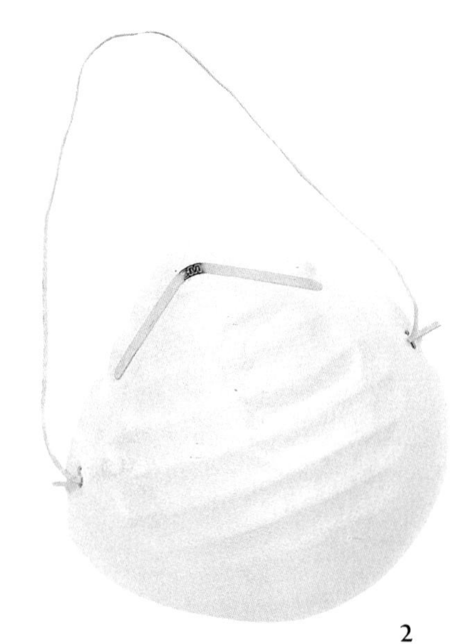

2

3

1 This type of mask has a filter made of gauze which can be thrown away after use.

2 Supplied in packs and useful when sanding, this mask has a nose clip which fastens over the nose to prevent dust from being inhaled.

3 A full-face respirator with changeable filter. Use while spraying or sanding to prevent dust and fumes from being inhaled.

container they were supplied in, and make sure the label does not become detached. If it is necessary to decant caustic material, pour it carefully into a non-corrosive container made of glass, plastic or earthenware. If any of the decanted material is left over, do not return it to its original container. Always wear gloves when handling caustic substances.

Labeling containers clearly is an essential safety precaution, but remember that children too young to read may be mobile and inquisitive and hungry or thirsty – so never use food containers, even if clearly labeled.

Waste disposal

Waste materials can and often do retain caustic characteristics. Correct disposal is therefore vital. Do not pour or throw chemicals or finishing materials down the drain – instead, find out from the appropriate authority where and how it is permissible to dispose of them.

Labeling

Do not remove manufacturers' labels from containers. They provide important information and warnings. It is worth dating finishes and other materials for future reference, as some have a finite shelf life and it is safest not to use materials that are past the specified date.

Dust and fumes

Most people realize that fumes are dangerous, but dust should not be underestimated as a health hazard – especially if you or your family suffer from hay fever, asthma or other respiratory diseases. Also, it has been established that wood dust can cause nasal cancer, though the incidence of the disease is primarily among people exposed to large quantities of wood dust. Many of the finishes and strippers that include hydrocarbon solvents can cause dizziness – which may lead to workshop accidents. It therefore makes sense to get into the habit of wearing a mask or respirator, when spraying and sanding.

Before buying a filter for a mask or a respirator, look at the recommended uses on the packet to make sure it will provide effective protection against fine dust and harmful fumes. Some filters are designed to catch coarse dust particles only, and are not adequate for constant use.

Fire precautions

Flammable materials must be stored in a fireproof metal cabinet or a fireproof bin with a lid on it. Storage bins and cabinets need to be kept locked and must display a notice warning that the contents are flammable.

Large quantities of chemicals and other combustible materials have to be stored in a brick building that has a retaining wall. A notice warning of the fire hazard must be prominently displayed on the exterior of the building. If you need more detailed information about regulations concerning flammable materials or about fire protection, contact the fire department, who will be glad to advise.

For effective fire prevention, position fire blankets, extinguishers, and fire buckets filled with sand (for dealing with spillages) around the workshop. A good-quality fire extinguisher that can cope with the relevant categories of fire is essential. Display a NO SMOKING sign and fit a smoke detector (or more than one in a large workshop). Fire exits must be clearly marked, easily accessible and unobstructed. If lacquer materials are likely to be used, spark-proof switches and double-sealed lighting must be installed.

Keep the workshop as clean as possible. Dust constitutes a fire hazard. In the event of an explosion in the workshop, fine dust is likely to be whipped out of nooks and crannies and blown around in clouds that can easily ignite. Secondary explosions caused by dust clouds can inflict greater damage and worse burns than the initial blast.

Common sense is good protection. Naked flames must never be permitted in the vicinity of flammable substances; and food or drink must never be consumed when there are poisonous materials around. But even seemingly harmless substances can be potentially dangerous. Linseed oil, for example, dries by oxidation, which can cause a piece of cloth to heat and spontaneously ignite. Never throw rolled-up cloths soaked in linseed into a waste bin – instead, put them in a bucket of water, then dispose of them safely. If they are not being used for the moment but may be needed for further work, unroll them and allow them to dry outdoors. Two-part finishes also present a fire hazard, since they heat up during the curing process, and should always be used with care.

GLOSSARY

Bars Metric measure of pressure.
Beveling Taking off sharp edges with a plane.
Blond polish Type of shellac-based polish used to produce natural finishes.
Building up The stage in *French polishing* when the polish is built up to give depth to the finish.
Buffing Using a soft cloth to produce a gloss finish.
Burnisher A tool used to produce a *burr* on a cabinet scraper by drawing the burnisher along the edge of the scraper at an angle of 5°.
Burnishing cream A fine abrasive cream, applied with a soft cloth, used to add sheen to a gloss finish.
Burr The fine hook of steel along the edge of a cabinet scraper, used for scraping fine shavings from the surface.
Button polish Golden brown polish made from denatured alcohol and *shellac* made in the shape of buttons.
Carnauba wax Hard wax with a high melting point used for floor polishes. A mixture of beeswax and carnauba wax is used in woodturning.
Catalyzed lacquers Two-pack modern finish, most often used as a spray finish. Supplied as flat or gloss, clear or colored.
Chemical stains Chemicals that are dissolved in water and, when applied to the surface, change the color of the wood by chemical reaction.
Chemical stripping Using chemicals to remove old finishes.
Clamping Using a clamp for pressure when gluing joints and repairing blisters.
Cleat A small nail or screw used to hold down a panel on the bench while the panel is being worked on.
Cobweb A spraying fault that occurs when sprayed *shellac* materials do not atomize properly and form a cobweb pattern on the surface.
Color mop Round-shaped brush made from soft bristles, supplied in sizes 6–10, used for applying color.
Creep The way stain is absorbed along the grain.
Cross grain Grain structure that runs at an angle to the main grain direction. Sanding across the grain is usually to be avoided.
Cut back Rubbing a finish with fine sandpaper until the finish is flat and smooth.
Danish oil An oil finish that cures by oxidation (reaction with oxygen). Particularly useful for oily woods such as teak.
Distressing Making a piece of furniture look old by bruising the surface and giving it a faded appearance.
Doping Application of dope, which is a mixture of *dye*, *pigment* and *French polish*, using a color *mop* or brush to make a semi-transparent color.
Dye A translucent color that is dissolved in a medium and used as a stain.
Ethyl acetate A solvent used with *cellulose thinners*.
Fad A pear-shaped piece of batting used to apply French polish to nooks and crannies and also as the core of a *polishing pad*.
Fadding Applying *French polish* with a *fad* before *building up*.
French polish *Shellac* and denatured alcohol mixed to produce a polish, which is also supplied as garnet, white, pale, button and blond polish.
French polishing General term referring to the application of *shellac* polish with a *polishing pad*.
Glazes A mixture of *mineral spirits*, *pigment*, gold size and oil. Similar to a varnish and used for special effects like graining and marbling.
Green coppera A *chemical stain* used to produce green to gray hues.
Grit grades Sizes of grit used on sandpapers. High numbers, such as 360, refer to fine grit while 80 is a coarse paper.
Heartwood The center of a log that has stopped growing, and is usually darker and harder than the outer layer of *sapwood*.
Key Abrading the surface of a finish to roughen it as a base for further coats of finish.
Medium density fiberboard (MDF) Fiberboard, similar to particleboard, but denser. Made from wood dust bonded by a resin.
Medullary rays Grain pattern in oak that runs across the grain, contrasting with the rest of the wood. The pattern is enhanced by quarter-sawing the wood.
Mineral spirits Hydrocarbon solvent used to thin oil stains, scumbles, gold size and *glazes*.
Neutralize To make chemically neutral (neither acidic nor alkaline).
Nigrosine water stain Traditional *water stain*, giving a black color for ebonizing.
Oil dyes; alcohol colors; alcohol analine dyes *Dyes* that are dissolved in either alcohol or denatured alcohol to produce translucent colors.
Oiling Process of applying oil to produce an oiled finish; for example, Danish or linseed oil applied to teak.
Oxalic acid crystals White crystals used as a mild bleach, when in

saturated solution, to clean off iron or blue stains.
Pigments Colors that do not dissolve, but are suspended in a medium to produce opaque colors. Mixed with paints, scumbles and glazes.
Pigment stain Semi-transparent stain made from finely ground colors that remain in suspension.
Polishing pad A *fad* wrapped in a white cotton cloth, used for *French polishing*.
Polyester resin Two-part resin finish, which cures by chemical reaction, with one part acting as a catalyst.
Polyurethane oil Synthetic oil finish.
Proprietary reviver Used for rejuvenating old finishes.
Pumice powder Fine abrasive powder for dulling. Used with a shoe brush.
Raising the grain Wetting wood to expand the cells of the wood before applying a finish.
Sanding sealer A sealer that incorporates a sanding agent to make sanding easier.
Sapwood Layer of wood surrounding the *heartwood* which carries the sap through the tree.
Saturated solution When no more solid material can be dissolved in a solution.
Scumbles A mixture of gold size, *pigments* and *mineral spirits* used in graining and decorative finishes
Sealing coat First coat of finish used to seal the surface of the wood before applying further coats.
Shellac resin A yellowish resin secreted by the lac beetle. When dissolved in solvent it is used in *French polish*.
Shellac sanding sealer Sealer with *shellac* base which includes a sanding agent to fill the pores of the grain.
Skein batting Fine batting covered in thin paper and used as the core of the *polishing pad*.
Stain Translucent *dye* dissolved in a medium, be it oil, water or alcohol.
Stripping Removing old finishes.
Table top or bar top finish Type of *French polish* which gives a tougher finish than other shellac polishes.
Thinner Solvent used to thin finishes.
Thixotropic agent Additive to paints that stops pigments settling and helps to reduce the chance of runs.
Tung oil Vegetable oil for oil finishes, also used in some paints and lacquers.
Urea formaldehyde glue Resin glue used in modern furniture and often supplied in powder form which is then mixed with water.
Varnish stains Varnish mixed with a *dye* and supplied in a range of colors.
Varnish Clear material that dries by oxidation, forming a thin protective coating.
Veneer Thin sheet of wood, sliced from the log, and fastened to the surface of a piece with glue.
Veneer punch Tool used to cut out faults in *veneer*, which can then be replaced with matching veneer.
Water stain *Stain* made from water-soluble dyes.
Wax stains Wax and *stain* combination available in a range of colors, producing a colored wax effect.
Waxing Applying a wax finish.
Wet and dry paper Sandpaper made from silicon carbide that uses water as a lubricant. Self-lubricating sandpapers incorporate a powder to take away the dust, which can scratch the surface.
White polish *French polish* using bleached *shellac* for natural or light finishes.

INDEX

Page numbers in *italics* indicate illustrations

E

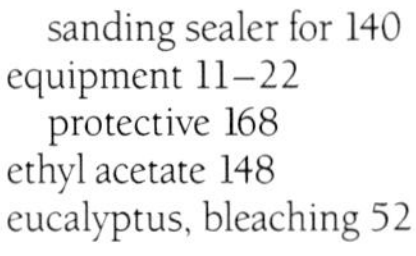

F

G

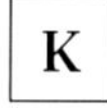

U

V

W

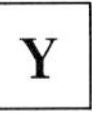
Y

USEFUL NAMES AND ADDRESSES

The following suppliers offer a mail-order service.

CONSTANTINE'S
2050 Eastchester Rd.
Bronx, NY 10461
(800) 223–8087

GARRETT WADE
161 Ave. of the Americas
New York, NY 10013
(800) 221–2942

LIBERON SUPPLIES
PO Box 86
Mendocino, CA 95460
(800) 245–5611

WOODWORKERS SUPPLY
5604 Alameda Pl. N.E.
Albuquerque, NM 87113
(800) 645–9292

JANOVIC PLAZA
30–35 Thomson Ave.
(Faux Finishing Supplies)
Long Island City
New York, NY 11101
(800) 772–4381